Sunset Western Garden Book
THE 20-MINUTE GARDENER

Projects, Plants, and Designs for Quick and Easy Gardening

Edited by Kathleen Norris Brenzel

Sunset

©2013 by Time Home Entertainment Inc.
135 West 50th Street, New York, NY 10020

ISBN-10: 0-376-03006-2
ISBN-13: 978-0-376-03006-1
Library of Congress Control Number: 2012945700
First Printing 2013
Printed in the United States of America.

OXMOOR HOUSE, INC.
Editorial Director: Leah McLaughlin
Creative Director: Felicity Keane
Brand Manager: Fonda Hitchcock
Managing Editor: Rebecca Benton

TIME HOME ENTERTAINMENT INC.
Publisher: Jim Childs
VP, Strategy & Business Development: Steven
    Sandonato
Executive Director, Marketing Services: Carol Pittard
Executive Director, Retail & Special Sales: Tom Misfud
Director, Bookazine Development and Marketing:
    Laura Adam
Executive Publishing Director: Joy Butts
Associate Publishing Director: Megan Pearlman
Finance Director: Glenn Buonocore
Associate General Counsel: Helen Wan

SUNSET PUBLISHING
President: Barb Newton
VP, Editor-in-Chief: Kitty Morgan
Creative Director: Mia Daminato

CONTRIBUTORS TO THIS BOOK
Editor: Kathleen Norris Brenzel
Art Director: Catherine Jacobes
Writers: Sharon Cohoon, Jim McCausland, Tom Wilhite
Managing Editor: Judith Dunham
Production Manager: Linda M. Bouchard
Copy Editor: Elissa Rabellino
Photo Editor: Linda Lamb Peters
Photo Coordinator: Danielle Johnson
Senior Imaging Specialist: Kimberley Navabpour
Project Editor: Sarah H. Doss
Proofreader: Denise Griffiths
Indexer: Mary Pelletier-Hunyadi

To order additional publications, call 1-800-765-6400
For more books to enrich your life,
    visit oxmoorhouse.com
Visit Sunset online at sunset.com
For the most comprehensive selection of
    Sunset books, visit sunsetbooks.com
For more exciting home and garden ideas,
    visit myhomeideas.com

SPECIAL THANKS
Julie Chai, Erika Ehmsen, Mark Hawkins, Charla Lawhon,
Laura Martin, Marisa Park, Marie Pence, Alan Phinney,
Johanna Silver, Margaret Sloan, Katie Tamony

Contents

No Time to Garden? Here Are Solutions

If you've picked up this book, chances are you already have a garden. You just want it to look its best, with a minimum of work on your part. Like most of us, you're probably already juggling career, family, and community obligations, plus activities like early-morning workouts, evening dinners with friends, and occasional weekend getaways. And if you manage to squeeze in an hour of gardening on the weekends, you consider yourself lucky.

Sure, you could hire crews to do the mow-and-blow for you, or throw in the trowel and roll out the AstroTurf. Or even ignore that outdoor space altogether.

But there's a better (and cheaper) approach: tend your garden a little bit at a time instead of a lot all at once. That's the premise of this book. On the following pages, we show you how to keep your garden looking good in as little as 20 minutes a day: Quick fixes using colorful outdoor fabrics, furnishings, and found objects. Easy projects that can make your garden look even better, like planting a water garden in a pot, or creating the look of water with a dry streambed, or building a border entirely with plants in containers. Simple techniques for clipping spent blooms and dividing perennials, with step-by-step guidelines. Top plants for easy-care gardens.

Where to start? Check out the guidelines and tips on the next few pages. Then browse through the rest of the book for more ideas and advice. Finally, plunge into your outdoor tasks as time allows (hint: just break down each chore into quick, easily manageable chunks). Once your garden looks more inviting than intimidating to you, you'll want to linger there often over summer meals with friends, or relax there with a glass of wine in the evenings. Who knows—you may find that you'd rather spend more time in your own backyard than anywhere else.

—Kathleen Brenzel

TIP To help define an outdoor room, use a hedge as pictured on the facing page (it's *Pittosporum tenuifolium* 'Silver Sheen'), or—even easier—put down an outdoor rug like the one above.

Start with an Easy-Care Design

An easy-care garden is filled with undemanding plants. Areas that need a bit more care, such as flower borders and veggie beds, are small enough that you can conveniently reach the plants in the center or back from all sides. Paths are never less than 4 feet wide, although spur paths can be 2 feet wide if you will never need to access them with rolling garden equipment. Paths and patios may be paved with loose materials such as gravel or decomposed granite, which drain well when it rains and allow irrigation water through to plant roots. Sharp-edged gravel and crushed rock pack firmly and give the path a natural look.

Breezy features Maintenance is minimal in this Portland, Oregon, front yard, thanks to a few key features. Most of the plants, including the dwarf *Ilex* in the foreground, are evergreen and look good all year. Aged steel edging defines the beds; it lasts much longer than wooden benderboard, so it doesn't need frequent replacing. Decorative gravel mulch just requires annual tidying. Containers, filled with annuals and perennials (including a bronze phormium), are grouped for easy access; flat stones around them function as steps. Design: Laura M. Crockett, Garden Diva Designs.

TIP Cluster containers of different heights together for easiest watering and tending.

Choose Easy-Care Plants

If you already have a garden, you have plants in place that you like. But when the time comes to add or replace plants, go for the toughest ones for your region. They may not be the hottest, trendiest varieties on the market; they're likely the ones you see over and over again in city median strips and older neighborhoods—the ones that never fail. They should suit your climate and garden, need little pruning or feeding, and get by on little water once their roots have established in the soil. Instead of lawn, use tough, ground-hugging plants to create waves of texture and subtle color. Dymondia, mounding green prostrate juniper, blue *Senecio mandraliscae,* and creeping thyme are examples.

Plant shade lovers in shade, sun lovers in sun. Give them the room they need to grow.

Vivid *(facing page)* If you need a colorful accent or two, mix in a few bright splashes using foliage or flowers that stand out from the surrounding greenery. Orange pincushion *(Leucospermum),* an evergreen shrub from South Africa, is pictured here. Other tough easy-care shrubs that stay low include *Callistemon* 'Little John', grevilleas, and some ceanothus and mahonias.

Water-wise *(right)* Featuring all-but-bulletproof plants, this display in Colorado requires little care and watering only every two weeks or so. 'Mersea Yellow' penstemon and 'Moonlight' yarrow sparkle against lavender-blue 'Six Hills Giant' catmint and purple 'Maynight' meadow sage. A granite bridge and dry streambed—along with 'Iseli White Bud' mugo pine—keep things looking good all year, and they suggest the presence of water without the maintenance.

TIP Embrace emptiness. Bare spaces are as important as filled-in areas for making a garden feel serene and uncrowded. They're easier to tend too. Leave the center of the garden open and avoid crowding plants.

Add Simple Accents

Like icing on the cake, the right accents can transform seemingly ordinary gardens into magical open-air rooms. An outdoor painting can turn a wall or fence into a gallery. Furnishings and fabrics can wake up mostly green spaces with splashes of vivid color. Even found objects such as pieces of log or fallen palm debris can add eye-catching finishing touches when displayed in the right place.

Natural *(top left)* The palm sheaf on this patio table is real (blown down in a storm); the "log" stool is resin. Both give a modern but natural look to this patio table in Venice, California.

Playful *(bottom left)* Diamond-patterned cushions and shapely orange chairs give a modern edge to this small city patio. The privacy screen behind is decidedly green; it's clumping (not running) bamboo, which thrives, and behaves itself, in narrow spaces.

Bold *(facing page)* Changes in materials help carve out distinct rooms in this Los Angeles garden. But it's the bold red metal Fermob table, red cushions, espresso brown stainless steel benches, striped cushions, and wrought-iron side chairs that are the stars of the outdoor dining room in the foreground. The simple "floor" is decomposed granite. Orange cannas and *Brugmansia* 'Charles Grimaldi' edge the lawn just beyond, which is small enough for easy mowing yet big enough for child's play. Design: Judy Kameon, Michael Kirchmann Jr., and Ivette Soler.

TIP Use furnishings and fabrics to add pops of color where plants won't work— in small gardens, especially.

Be Resourceful

Life is a game, or at least it could be in your own backyard. If you need a small patio or a short fence, think outside the box to get it. Consider giving recycled materials such as broken concrete, tumbled glass, or recycled barn wood new uses in your garden. Use flea market finds or travel treasures to add playful touches to bare patio walls.

Salvage finds *(facing page)* In this San Francisco backyard, gently curving paths link several stylish spaces. Many of the materials are recycled. The 16-foot-diameter patio is made of granite remnants—mostly dumpster finds—mixed with metal sewer caps and bricks. In its center, a 28-inch-diameter metal wok, turned into a wood-burning fire bowl, sits on a steel base made by the owner. The rescued shed behind would have been a teardown, but with new windows it's now a backyard getaway. Most of the plants need little in the way of care or even water. They include honey bush *(Melianthus major)* and a potted Monterey cypress *(Cupressus macrocarpa* 'Saligna Aurea'). Design: James Pettigrew and Sean Stout, Organic Mechanics.

Playful finds *(right)* A colorful daisy sculpture mounted to the wall brightens a narrow planting bed behind a set-in bench, and gives the illusion that it's growing atop the tall, grassy foliage. Design: Kathleen Shaeffer.

TIP Make garden chores pleasant. Clip spent roses as you check out the garden with your morning coffee in hand. Or run—don't walk—when pushing a reel mower to cut the grass. You'll burn more calories that way.

Setting Up Your Space

Garden chores go faster when everything you need is close at hand. Tuck a potting table into a garden corner, then stock it with the basic tools and supplies you'll need to tend the plants you grow.

Create a Workstation

Keep it simple, easily accessible, and well organized. Don't forget to add storage for tools and pots so everything is a reach away.

Potting Table and Storage

No need for anything fancy—use recycled furniture and scrap materials. Or purchase basic, easy-to-install shelving and cabinets that fit your space.

Instant table *(facing page)* Peruse flea markets and thrift stores for a sturdy table that is waist high. The one shown here is 3 to 4 feet long and about 2 feet wide. Attach shelving for pots and set out containers to hold tools.

Potting ladder *(right)* Dig out an old wooden ladder you no longer use or seek out one at a yard sale. To the rungs, screw slatted shelves made of scrap lumber. Add an old drawer for catching loose potting soil. If you like, finish the shelf ends by capping them with shelving brackets painted white.

Alternative shed *(below)* Make a space-saving tool-shed from storage units mounted on the side of your house or garage. The double doors have gate hinges, and each unit is topped with a galvanized steel roof.

POTTING SOIL

Keep soil mix in an old tub or other container. Tuck it under your potting table so it is always handy.

Gather Essential Tools

Here are 10 basics you don't want to be without. You'll find that tasks are quick and easy when you have the right tools.

ROUND-POINT SHOVEL Loosens soil, transfers soil to a pile or wheelbarrow, and digs planting holes.

GARDEN SPADE Prepares soil for planting and digs narrow, straight-sided trenches.

WEEDER Digs out deep-rooted weeds. A bent shaft or ball attachment provides the leverage needed to pop weeds out of the ground.

BOW RAKE Breaks up dirt clods, levels soil, tamps seedbeds, and works amendments into a planting bed.

LEAF RAKE Sweeps up leaves, collects grass clippings and other lightweight debris into easy-to-gather piles, and spreads mulch.

TROWEL Plants, cultivates, weeds, and scoops fertilizers and amendments from nursery bags.

A WORD ABOUT GLOVES

For light chores like deadheading, inexpensive cotton gloves —still the most comfortable—work fine. For tough jobs like digging or heavy pruning, opt for a sturdy glove with built-in padding such as the Landscape Gloves pictured.

HIDE TOOLS IN THE GARDEN

A trick for storing hand tools where you need them is to use an old mailbox. Locate the box in a bed near a path or just outside the back door. Secure it to a 4-by-4 redwood post with a 3-inch-long lag screw inserted through holes drilled in the top center of the post and the bottom center of the box. If you want to be able to move the box later, use sand to anchor the post in a 2-foot-deep hole. Other-wise, you can also set the post in concrete.

PRUNER Snips off dead flowers and shortens stems and small wooden branches—up to the size of your little finger.

HEDGE PRUNER Shapes hedges, shears flowering shrubs after bloom, and cuts back large perennials.

HOSE Delivers water to garden beds and planting containers. Connects to sprinklers or soaker hoses to irrigate large areas.

ALL-PURPOSE TRUG Transports raked leaves and pulled weeds, holds mulch and soil, and carries harvested produce.

SEED STORAGE

To keep seeds fresh, slip them, still in their envelopes, into a jar with a tight-fitting lid, then store in a cool, dry place.

Keep Plantings Accessible

Beds and borders are easier to tend when you can reach all plants—from every side. They can be curved, square, permanent, or portable.

A Free-Form Bed

Create a bed that wanders along a walkway, curves around an expanse of lawn, or rims the edge of a deck or terrace.

Size To prevent ornamental grasses and shrubs from looking crowded, keep the border at least 5 feet in width. Wind that thick ribbon through as much of your garden as you want. If you are planning a long bed, consider planting it in sections. Put in the most visible portion the first year and let it establish. Then repeat the same plants in adjoining sections the next year. The newcomers will catch up quickly.

Plants Splashes of silvery gray, green, and maroon foliage are interspersed with blooms in shades of pink. 'Palace Purple' heuchera, 'Eaton Canyon' fountain grass, and 'David's Choice' artemisia mingle with 'Mobile Pink' abutilon, 'Passionate Blush' gaura, 'Waverley' salvia, false heather, purple coneflower, zinnia, and hydrangea.

Why it works As the border curves through the backyard, it connects lawn, paths, and deck, and is visible from inside the house. The clusters of foliage and flowers soften and hide the edge of the deck, and the border is reachable from all sides for easy tending.

'Mobile Pink' abutilon

'Profusion Apricot' zinnia

'Alcosa' savoy cabbage

A Winter "Keyhole"

Shaped like its namesake, the bed is attractive to look at as well as convenient to maintain. When the seasons change, so can the plantings.

Size Start with a simple garden. This one is about 13 feet long and 8 feet across. The center path is 2 feet wide, and the bed is 3 feet wide. For easy harvesting, locate the border near the kitchen.

Plants For cool-season crops, choose leafy greens and cruciferous vegetables suited to close planting. This keyhole is planted with arugula, 'Marvel of Four Seasons' lettuce with bronze-tipped leaves, 'Bright Lights' Swiss chard, 'Green Wave' mustard, curly-leafed and lacinato kale, and broccoli raab. Round out the selection with 'Alcosa' savoy cabbage, 'Veronica' romanesco, and 'Cassius' cauliflower.

Why it works Because the keyhole pattern itself draws your attention, temporary bare spots between crops are hardly noticeable. The crossbar portion is a perfect place for a vertical grower such as snow peas or snap beans.

SUMMER SWITCH

When air and soil temperatures start to heat up, it's time to begin replacing cool-season crops with sun worshippers.

VEGETABLES Plant corn, cucumbers, tomatoes, green beans, squash, eggplant, sweet and chile peppers, okra, and melons. Leave room for the herbs that complement summer veggies so well, such as basil, dill, oregano, mint, and thyme.

FLOWERS Add ornamentals, like sunflowers, cosmos, marigold, and sweet alyssum, that lure the beneficial insects that prey on the bad guys. For fun, plant flowers that attract butterflies, such as coneflower and black-eyed Susan.

Square Beds

Accessible from all sides, square beds make gardening a breeze. To avoid having to step into the planted area—you don't want to pack down the soil—keep beds no larger than 4 feet square.

Stir-fry garden *(facing page)* Plant what you love to eat. Most of the produce from this Arizona garden, which is planted in a grid of 3-foot steel-rimmed squares, ends up sizzling in a wok. Partially sinking the beds, as was done here, helps cool the soil—a useful technique in a hot climate.

Western classic *(right)* Cedar planks painted barn red and lined with dry-stacked stone give the traditional four-square vegetable garden a regional spin. The stones also provide a handy ledge for garden tools and harvest baskets. Generous stone paths plus a wide border of mowed lawn make the whole space easy to navigate.

HOW MUCH CAN YOU GROW?

TOMATOES In a sunny 2-foot-square bed, tuck one plant of a prolific variety, such as 'Sun Gold' or 'Early Girl'.

BASIL In a 3-foot-square bed, grow a tomato plant plus three basils.

CHIVES AND CUCUMBERS In a 4-foot-square bed like this one, add a row of chives alongside the basil. Beyond the tomato, plant a cucumber vine, such as disease-resistant 'Diva'.

Round Beds

Circular beds are easy to fit into small gardens and look particularly pretty planted with leafy crops or herbs.

"Bubbles" *(left)* Fabric sacks packed with rice straw surround raised beds of Swiss chard and leaf lettuces. The flexible sacks can be arranged to make beds of any shape.

Bull's-eye *(facing page)* Concentric bands of flexible aluminum create a 6-foot raised bed holding eight herbs. Flat-leafed parsley, lemon thyme, and garden sages fill the lowest level. A trio of basils, 'African Blue', 'Greek Window Box', and purple, pack the middle tier. Chives crown the top.

Half-moon *(below)* A pea gravel path runs between two half-moon beds, each about 3 feet wide and 11 feet long. Beans, sunflowers, tomatoes, and other tall plants occupy the back, allowing sunlight to reach short growers such as herbs and flowers. A fieldstone edging gives the beds structure.

TIP If you change your mind a lot, you'll love the bull's-eye beds opposite. They break down in a flash for relocation or storage.

Instant Beds

Too busy to spade or build a bed? Buy a kit like the ones here or use a recycled container and go directly to the fun part—planting.

Raised garden *(left)* You provide recycled or new 2-by-6 lumber, soil, and plants. A kit from Scout Regalia supplies a set of heavy steel brackets and screws, along with instructions for building the bed, which supports soil 12 inches deep. Just take down the bed when the harvest is over, or move it to a sunnier spot. And you can pack it with you if you need to move.

Boxed in *(facing page)* Repurposing an old wooden container into a planter like the one here is a time-saving trick. Drill holes in the bottom for drainage, and construction is done. Wooden wine boxes or fruit crates have enough depth for shallow-rooted leafy crops or herbs. Root crops and sprawlers like tomatoes need more depth. Look for toy or other storage chests as well.

READY-MADE BEDS

INSTANT RAISED BED Four specially designed steel corner braces, called M Braces, hold 2-by-4s into a sturdy raised bed. You cut the lumber, or have it cut to size, and then slide into the braces. Beds can be as small as 2 feet square or as long as 12 feet per side.

BALCONY BOX Made of cedar, the MinifarmBox has a clever notch-and-pin design—hence no tools required for assembly. The slatted base comes with a soil screen. This patio version is 48 inches long by 16 inches wide by 18 inches high. Heavy-duty casters make it easy to move around.

PORTABLE PLOT The durable, lightweight Bacsquare 4 garden fits into any spot where you have a 2-foot-square space. A variety of vegetables and herbs can be grown in the four 16-inch-deep pockets. When empty, the fiber container folds for easy storage. Pots of other sizes are available.

Choose the Right Container

Consider color, shape, material, and size—not too large or too small to accommodate a plant's root growth. The options seem infinite.

CERAMIC The rolled-rim cylinder is the most elemental container. It is available in many sizes and colors.

PLASTIC Lightweight and inexpensive, plastic doesn't retain heat. It comes in lots of pretty shapes and colors.

METAL Handsome and durable, metal can be heavy. It retains heat and may rust, particularly in humid climates.

QUARRY POLYRESIN This material provides the appearance of stone without the weight. It is handsome and durable, but can be pricey.

BARGAIN POT Shop for good used pots at a fraction of their original prices at garage sales and flea markets. Or snatch up a new piece heavily discounted because of some tiny flaw.

MATCH THE POT TO THE PLANT

LEAFY CROPS don't need much root space, but they do need room to spread. Shallow rectangular containers, which allow you to pack more crops in less space, are ideal.

BIGGER VEGETABLES like eggplant and peppers grow mostly upright and need more room to develop the roots necessary to support their height. Deep, relatively narrow pots at least 16 inches in diameter suit them best.

TIP Select a container whose color picks up the hues of your plants. This container shows off *Agave attenuata* 'Ray of Light', surrounded by 'Silver Shadow' astelia, 'Black Adder' phormium, and *Plectranthus* 'Mike's Fuzzy Wuzzy'.

Quick Fixes

Even the smallest accents can transform a quiet garden into a magical outdoor room. You can paint a garden wall for a pop of color, tuck in some recycled pavers, or plant a "living sculpture." Your goal: Make the garden uniquely your own.

No lighting in your garden? No problem.
Just add a little glow to your outdoor
party by floating some votive candles
in a birdbath.

Accent with Color

Plants don't have to do all the work. Add a big pot in a vibrant hue, and then build on the theme.

Transformation through Turquoise

A hip-high ceramic pot in a glossy azure blue provided the inspiration for this garden. The homeowner converted the container into a focal-point fountain and repeated its color lavishly throughout the whole space.

Paint In their original wood tones, the picnic table and benches on the deck had little impact. Given a coat of turquoise paint, they're smile-inducing showstoppers (below). And, normally, who pays attention to a standard terra-cotta pot? Wainscot the bottom half a contrasting blue, though, and everyone notices.

Fabric A rusty but still serviceable wrought-iron sofa looks fresh again thanks to a coverlet made of striped sheets. No upholstery costs needed for this shabby-chic look. The area rug under the coffee table, which reinforces the outdoor room feel, is made of recycled plastics.

Metal An inexpensive candle lantern takes on a new personality when painted tangerine. The warm shade complements the cool blues in the ceramics and fabrics, and picks up the coppery succulents in the nearby pot.

Colorful Glass and Ceramic

Adding well-placed ceramic urns or glass globes is one of the simplest ways to put a little punch in a garden. The intensity of their colors and the glossiness of their surfaces focus attention where you want it.

Jazz up a pond *(facing page)* Glass balls floating in a small square pond add a dash of color and humor to this narrow, mostly green garden. Don't have a pond? Float glass balls in a large bowl of water. This will have the same effect.

Dress a patio *(right)* The grid of concrete pavers slashing diagonally across a lawn is this garden's strongest feature. A single blue ceramic pot at one end and more bright pots on the lanai draw your attention to the striking design.

Highlight a planting *(below)* A bright ceramic globe makes a modern statement in front of upright sculptural plants such as agaves, aloes, and flax. It leads the eye to a spot you want people to notice.

TIP Keep the backdrop simple enough to show off your colorful pieces. Ponds, patios, and low clusters of greenery work well.

Paint

Imagine a sky blue wall behind a row of yellow and orange nasturtiums and blue cornflowers. Or a mint green wall backing a cluster of metal cafe chairs painted the color of strawberry sherbet. Such arresting color schemes are at home in the West, especially in sunny climates and in gardens that surround Mediterranean, contemporary, or adobe-style houses. Choose vivid or subtle hues to accent your garden's best features, and then get out a brush.

Add a backdrop *(left)* A cool blue wall forms a tranquil backdrop for a pair of lounge chairs and also adds a pleasing contrast to the home's golden walls and cinnamon red cushions.

Set a mood *(facing page)* Dress your patio walls with paint, and you don't need much else to warm up the space. In this garden, luscious paint colors such as soft rose and sun-washed ochre create a romantic setting for intimate gatherings.

Create an illusion *(below)* Use paint to define a garden room. This rust red wall section edges a dining patio. During evening meals outdoors, votive candles glow on the narrow built-in shelf, washing the wall's surface with tiny pools of orange-reflected light.

TIP To avoid streaking latex paints, apply after morning dew and at least two hours before evening damp. Make sure that surfaces are free of dirt, grease, rust, and paint flakes.

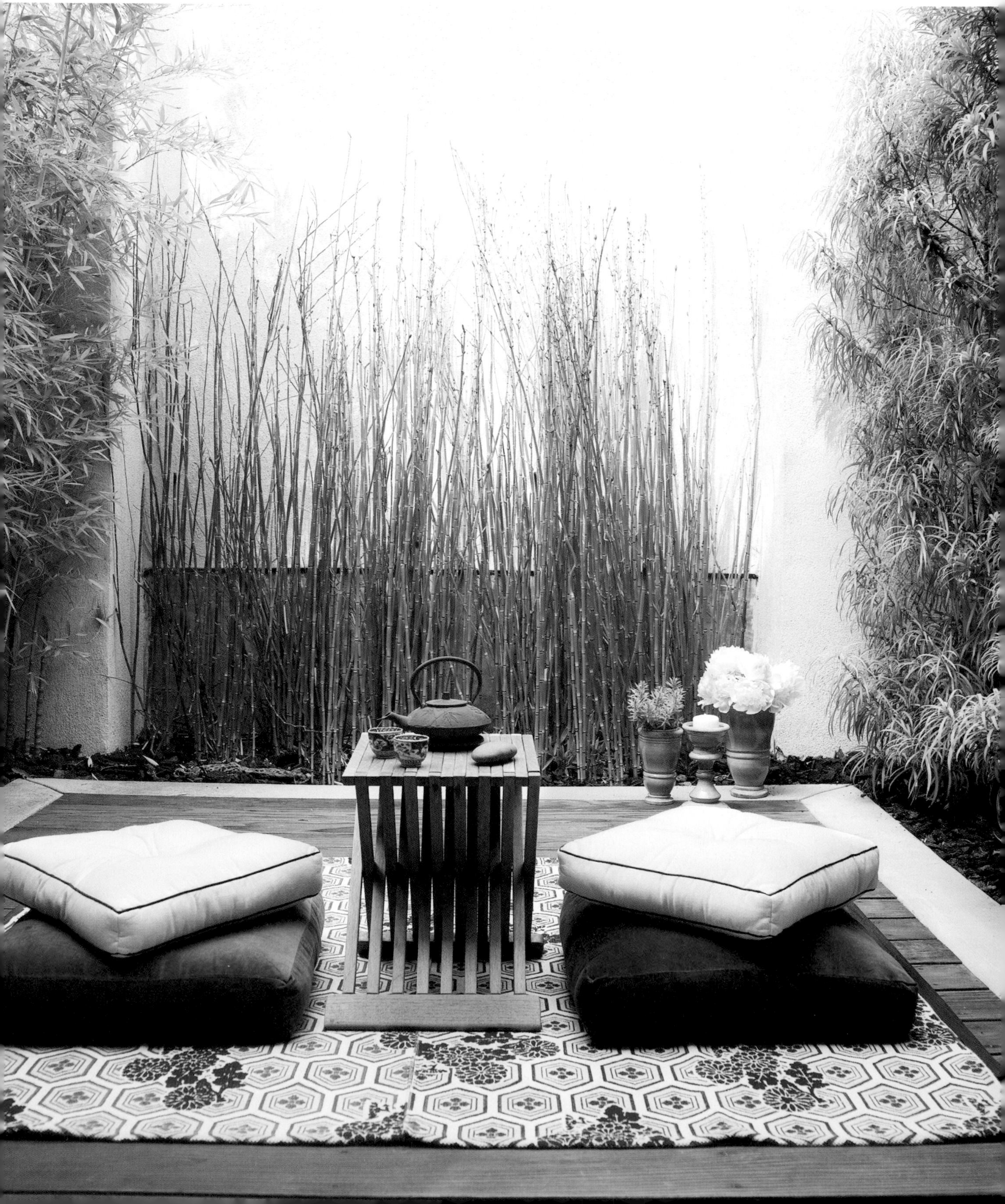

Fabric

Properly treated, fabric can survive considerable abuse and do hard work. Or use it as you would indoors —to soften a space and give it personality.

Accessorize with fabric

(facing page and below) A lightly cushioned mat printed with a Japanese motif, two pairs of coordinating seat cushions, and a low table—and you've got an outdoor tearoom like the one at left. Even easier: Plop a row of pillows in an assortment of fabrics on a built-in bench, and who could resist dropping in?

Build a modified cabana

(right) A white sailcloth roof over a simple square frame creates protection from overhead sun in this outdoor seating area. It also makes the space feel like a poolside resort. If you have multistory residences on either side of your home, as was the case here, a shade canopy adds privacy.

TIP The ideal fabrics for outdoor use are tough and stand up to sunlight. They come in many colors and patterns. Find them at outdoor fabric specialists such as Sunbrella.

Repurpose and Restyle

You don't need a fat wallet to have a great-looking garden. All that's required are sharp eyes for spotting bargains plus a little imagination.

High Style on a Low Budget

This sheltered patio feels as lush as a tropical resort, but it was created with a tiny budget. Its secret? Everything in it was either recycled or purchased at bargain prices.

Re-cover furniture The sofa at the back was bought at a swap meet; the second one was found abandoned in an alley. With new cushions, both pieces are back in business. The wicker coffee table was a sharply discounted floor sample. The few dings just give it character.

Use candle power To enjoy your garden after dark, you need lighting, but who says it has to come from electricity? Candles in hanging lanterns illuminate the space without the expense of wiring. And more romantically too.

Add passed-along plants Many of the plants, like the *Yucca gloriosa variegata* below, were rescued from a friend moving out of state. Others started as cuttings.

Save on accessories Purely decorative items, such as the loosely woven baskets hanging from the beams, are good places to economize. Shop for them at import stores, and scour garage sales and swap meets.

Bargain Beauties

Don't just look for things obviously designed for gardens. Imagine, as these homeowners did, how something could be repurposed in an unexpected way.

Fake a border *(left)* Group planted pots in various sizes together to create a similar effect. For interest, choose a variety of sizes and shapes. Here, all the pots are metal. If you use different materials, keep them in the same color range.

Plant a backdrop *(facing page)* No garden walls to train ivy on? Plant between the slats of salvaged shutters. Staple weed cloth together to form pockets for soil, and attach the pockets to the back of the shutters. Plant with easy-care succulents.

Create a living centerpiece *(facing page)* A tray planted with shallow-rooted succulents resting on the bottom shelf of an otherwise nondescript coffee table turns it into a showpiece.

Improvise a planter *(below)* A laundry tub is large enough to hold lots of plants and costs much less than a ceramic one of comparable size. A coat of bright paint hides its origins.

TIP Start by shopping your garage or basement. You might find just the right treasure to repurpose as a container.

Found Objects

Every piece of furniture, every paver, and most of the plants in this small backyard were either salvaged locally or found at a flea market. The bases for tables were picked up from a flea market and then topped with glass. The hundreds of succulents tucked into containers and flower beds are the descendants of a couple dozen rescued cuttings. Fresh ideas for using found materials are everywhere.

Pick a color scheme *(facing page)*
Accents of warm brown and red add pops of vivid color among the garden's serene greens. Cushions, tables, and a cocoa-colored stoneware-jar fountain trickling softly in the foreground repeat the palette.

Use containers as garden art *(right)*
A vintage stone trough, filled with blue-green echeverias, accents a planting of baby's tears.

Add blooming accents *(below)*
Flowers on a single cymbidium, displayed on the low wall beside the patio, repeat the hues of the cushions and furnishings.

continued

TIP Don't forget materials such as broken concrete and stone. Both make marvelous accents for groundcovers and shrubs.

Offer surprises *(left)* Vintage Chinese stone weights, with holes that once held ropes for hanging, add an artistic finish to a patch of baby's tears. Shiny-leafed *Acanthus mollis* grows behind.

Repurpose where possible *(facing page)* An old rain drum and a wooden industrial-machinery mold serve as table bases. Each is topped with a piece of glass, cut to fit. The retro road sign on the house wall glows during evenings outdoors. It's less expensive than built-in lighting and more fun.

Turn a slab into a bench *(below)* A granite slab, found on-site, adds extra seating to the patio. The owner dug it up and then wedged it into the low retaining wall separating the patio from the upper garden. Baby's tears grows below it; Mexican feather grass and rosemary in back.

TIP Grow a fence using black bamboo plants, each in a 15-gallon pot, to create a privacy screen along the back of a yard. They cost far less than a real fence.

Travel Treasures

Incorporate lots of well-weathered pieces brought back from places where you've traveled or purchased from import stores. Now your city garden becomes your backyard Bali.

Souvenir seating *(facing page)* Breaking up this urban space from a single into multiple levels and replacing the original concrete slab with limestone pavers did much to soften and add interest to this garden. But it is the eclectic collection of furnishings that provides a cosmopolitan flair. A pair of elephant doors from India disguise the blank wall at the back of the garden. In front of them, rustic teak slab benches from Indonesia nestle up to an iron cauldron from the Philippines that serves as a firepit. The futon-like daybed is not old—it is made of two lounge chairs pushed together and topped by cushions—but the pillows are covered with vintage fabrics.

Glass floats *(top right)* Philippine fishing floats and Mexican slag glass in nearly the same shade combined in a pot look almost as cool as running water. Plants nearby that are associated with damp areas, such as papyrus, contribute to the effect.

Temple accents *(bottom right)* A disk of carved white marble from India mounted on a pedestal is surrounded by papyrus and *Tecoma × alata* (orange bells). The sculpture's location creates the illusion that you might have just stumbled across it. The random scattering of old millstones adds to the illusion. The casualness of the *Aeonium* planting does as well.

Stage a Setting

Make your empty outdoor space party perfect. Combine bargain finds such as outdoor rugs and pillows with things you already own.

Deck It Out

Furnishing your deck in an unconventional way that requires less furniture will surprise your guests for sure. Doesn't that sound like a good way to start a party?

Forget chairs Provide lots of cushions on a soft rug instead. The change of perspective will amuse your guests and put them in a festive mood—after all, it's hard to be uptight when you're sitting on the floor.

Improvise a low table The one used here is actually the base of an ottoman. Its white cushion top is used on the rug for sitting. Or saw the legs off a garage sale find and give it a quick spray-painting.

Pick the right rug Since it will be the first thing your guests notice, its pattern should be strong and striking. A simple graphic design, like this blue, yellow, and white stripe, is ideal. The sunny yellow pot below echoes the similar color in the rug.

Provide portable shade Umbrellas cost a lot less than permanent structures and are more flexible. Take them down at night to gaze at the stars, or move them away completely for dance space.

Dress Your Patio

Two designers looked at the same small strip of patio and came up with totally different solutions for making it an inviting spot in which to relax. The patio at right was decked out in a crisp, contemporary motif, while the one at left went for a tropical island vibe. The looks are quite different, but the techniques used turn out to be much the same.

Use big pieces It may sound counterintuitive, but petite furniture makes a small space seem tinier. A few oversize pieces, especially chairs, on the other hand, make it feel more generous than it actually is. Ditto containers. A few large pots create a lot of drama; a dozen small ones go unnoticed.

Keep the color range narrow Select one primary color—say, orange—and use variations of it for variety. Or go with analogous colors—ones next to each other on the color wheel, such as yellow and yellow-green. Too many competing hues in a tight space are jarring.

Take advantage of vertical space Line up a row of imposing tall, narrow pots along a bare wall, as pictured at right. Or hide it with a row of clumping bamboo, as shown at left. Then stick a bouquet of Balinese umbrellas in a pot to show off against the green background.

Reinforce your theme The patio at right used just a few plants with strong textures—the restios in orange pots along the fence, for instance—to accent in streamlined style. The island patio, appropriately, went for something lusher—giant leaves (elephant's ear), bright plants (croton), and glamorous tropical flowers (orchids, bromeliads, ginger).

TIP You can do anything you like with small spaces—just not all at once. Start by choosing your theme, and then stick to it.

Easy Accessories

This inviting backyard feels mature, but the plantings are actually quite young. Clever camouflaging and colorful distractions simply create the illusion that it is well established.

Pop in plants Set in potted plants straight from the nursery to hide bare spots in the garden. The ferns in the foreground, for instance, are all new arrivals.

Set a green table Make the garden feel lusher by bringing in other shades of green in furniture and accessories, as was done here with the bistro chairs, chartreuse tablecloth, and emerald minibar.

Steal from the indoors Use your good china, glasses, and flatware. Fill some vases. Maybe even borrow an indoor rug for the evening. Make the table—and by extension the guests—the focal point.

Add footlights Candles in clear vessels clustered in corners serve dual purposes. They make the space safer—no one tumbling over hedges or stumbling on stairs. But they also make it look more theatrical, and your guests will feel like stars.

TIP Vines a long way from covering that dull wooden fence? Disguise it with art. Look for pieces made specifically for the outdoors, such as the metal panels used here. Pick up something inexpensive and expendable at a garage sale. Or bring out a piece of indoor art just for the evening.

Punctuate with Plants

The difference between a so-so garden and a great one can be the addition of the right plant, or several plants, for the desired effect.

Finishing Touches

The right plant can work magic in your garden. Try one of these techniques.

Add contrast *(facing page)* A single burgundy-leafed plant (*Cordyline* 'Festival Grass' in this case) makes an otherwise green garden come alive. Its tall cobalt blue container adds to the drama.

Change scale *(right)* This border is mostly green. The gardener introduced *Gunnera*, a plant with almost comically large leaves. This whopper perennial grows 8 feet tall and wide with leaves up to 8 feet across. Any question where the focus of the garden is now?

Repeat shape and color *(below)* Unrelieved hardscape alone can feel harsh. The band of well-spaced pheasant's-tail grass (*Anemanthele lessoniana*) is the perfect solution. Simple and low growing, it helps soften the terrace as well as frame the view. The grass changes with the seasons: it starts out green in the spring, turns bronzy with feathery purple flowers in summer, and deepens to copper in fall.

TIP Choose plants that are big, bold, and sculptural. Or try small ones and use multiples. These finishing touches are your garden's focal point—you can't miss them.

Living Sculpture

Plants with muscular stems and foliage or with clean, crisp outlines make striking centerpieces in the garden. Wherever you plant them is where your eye will travel. Select a single plant or a handful of big ones with strong shapes, and choose a spot where they have a chance to show off. Easy, immediate, permanent interest—just like that.

Dress an entry *(left)* A single *Agave* 'Mediopicta Alba' in a charcoal-colored stone bowl holds its own in a front entry. The *Agave* leaves mimic the warm and cool tones of the building materials: the yellow stripes echo the honeyed shades of the stucco and teak, and the blue-green picks up the coolness of the steel.

Go vertical *(facing page)* A trio of tree aloes *(Aloe thraskii)* is almost all this backyard needs. They require little root room, and their topknots create striking patterns against the walls behind them.

Anchor a path *(below)* A fountain of flax is the focal point of the borders on either side of this path. Vibrant 'Maori Queen' phormium reigns in front, surrounded by blue *Senecio mandraliscae*.

TIP Once you decide on your sculptural plants, choose their companions. They should be lower growing, softer in shape, and less vivid in color.

Accents Underfoot

Breaking up an expanse of hardscape with plants makes the living areas feel gentler and more welcoming. These intrusions can be streamlined and geometrical, if that's your style. Or for a wilder, more casual look, place them more randomly. No plant will stand up to foot traffic as well as brick or stone, but some are tougher than others. *Dymondia,* blue star creeper, and woolly thyme are examples.

Plant a carpet *(facing page)* The blue-green stripes of *Dymondia margaretae* create the look of a mod rug on this poolside patio. Like arrows, they point to the cozy fireside corner and to a big Brazilian pepper tree.

Put down eye candy *(top right)* Insert tiny pocket gardens here and there. This arrangement of *Echeveria* rosettes and *Senecio mandraliscae* is a good example of what to aim for. Several plants, several foliage colors, several shapes. Everything you'd do in a regular garden but in miniature. How can you not pause to admire the composition?

Tuck in surprises *(bottom right)* Plants grown between pavers don't have to be low growing. You can squeeze in something taller, such as this young *Euphorbia rigida* protected with a handful of river rocks, to deliberately slow down foot traffic. Small grasses, small bulbs, or annuals with a wildflower look would do the same thing. Avoid planting in patterns. You want it to look as if nature did the work.

TIP To plant between pavers, dig out the soil between them to a depth of 3 or 4 inches. Replace it with rich planting mix, poured onto the paving, then swept into the cracks with a broom. Sprinkle the mix with water to settle it, let it dry slightly, and plant. Fill in around plants with soil, almost to paver level.

Inspired Ideas, Easy Projects

Maybe you have a forgotten corner covered with bare dirt that could use a spray of flowers, or a path that needs a fringe of green. Perhaps that new container you bought calls for a few striking plants to complete the picture. Here are fresh ways to tackle your garden's problem spots.

If you want the feel of grass underfoot without the hassles of a big lawn, plant a living footstool. Simply fill a container with soil, add a piece of sod, and water.

Plant Beds, Bare Spaces

Fill them with flowers, herbs, edibles, or foliage that pops in the moonlight. Or plant a mini-garden of succulents.

Pollinator Garden

With a few easy-care flowers, you can turn a forgotten corner of the garden into a pollinator bar for all kinds of winged creatures. Bees, butterflies, and hummingbirds will eagerly, if unknowingly, take on the task of transferring pollen from one flower to another as they forage for nectar or pollen, ensuring better crops for your fruit and vegetable plants. Flitting among the brightly colored summer flowers such as the yellow yarrow *(Achillea)* and pink cone-flower *(Fchinacea)* pictured opposite, they'll also bring beauty and motion to your garden. Six other pollinator favorites are listed below.

A / Borage *(Borago officinalis)* Star-shaped flowers appear in summer. Annual; sun or part shade.

B / Sunflower Bright and bold, they're beacons for honeybees. Be sure to choose pollen-bearing varieties. Annual; full sun.

C / Butterfly weed *(Asclepias tuberosa)* Small starlike blooms cluster at branch tips. Perennial; full sun.

D / Bee balm *(Monarda)* Clusters of long-tubed flowers in summer also attract hummingbirds. Perennial; sun, or light shade in hottest climates.

E / Fennel Airy umbrellas of yellow florets in summer attract bees. Annual or perennial; full sun.

F / Lantana Tiny flowers in tight clusters all year in mild climates. Evergreen shrub (annual in colder climate); full sun.

Cutting Garden

Want to pick flowers for bouquets month after month? For a striking look in both garden and vase, choose plants with contrasting hues. The bed pictured opposite emphasizes sunny yellows, oranges, and reds. Splashes of chocolate, deep purples, and burgundies temper the fiery tones. Plant tall growers in the center or toward the rear, and position trailers, such as calibrachoa, to soften the bed's edges.

Cut flowers early in the morning or just after sunset. Bring along a bucket of tepid water, and plunge the cut stems in the water. When arranging the blooms, recut each stem underwater. Then pull off any foliage or flowers that will be below the water level in the vase.

A / 'Oranges and Lemons' gaillardia Daisylike blooms in bright orange and yellow grow on plants 1½ feet high or more.

B / Calibrachoa Flowers, available in many colors, resemble dainty petunias. Trailers reach 6 to 10 inches.

C / 'Mystic Desire' dahlia Bright scarlet flowers with chocolate centers rise 2 feet above blackish brown foliage.

D / *Salpiglossis* 'Chocolate Royale' Velvety trumpets in rich browns grow on 1-foot-high plants.

E / 'Benary's Giant Lime' zinnia Plants 2½ to 3½ feet high bear cool lime-colored flowers.

F / 'Sonata White' cosmos White blooms up to 3 inches across grow on plants 1½ to 2 feet high.

Moon Garden

Come nightfall, most garden plants disappear into darkness. Those with white flowers and silvery foliage stand out dramatically from the shadows, especially when illuminated by moonlight.

Arrange the garden around a patio, or add a bench for cozy nighttime viewing. The plants in the garden here are excellent choices for summer-bloomers. Consider adding a few plants that flower in spring and fall to prolong the effect. Or include a plant or two with fragrant blossoms. Angel's trumpet (*Brugmansia*) and angelwing jasmine have perfumed white or light-colored flowers. Solar lights can supplement the moonlight.

A / Cosmos Fluttery snow-white blooms, about 3 inches across, have crinkled petals.

B / Gaura Delicate white blossoms, tinged with pink, resemble butterflies perched on wiry, arching spikes.

C / *Nemesia caerulea* 'Compact Innocence' Tiny blooms cover low mounds of foliage.

D / Lamb's ears Velvety, silvery white leaves form a low, spreading groundcover. Flowers, borne on stems about 1½ feet high, bloom in late spring and summer.

E / *Artemisia* 'Powis Castle' Silvery foliage creates a lacy mound up to 3 feet high. The leaves have an alluring fruity fragrance.

F / *Atriplex lentiformis breweri* Shrub with silvery gray leaves grows 5 to 7 feet tall and 6 to 8 feet wide. Can be sheared into a hedge.

Unthirsty Herb Garden

An herb garden has many pluses. It is both aromatic and attractive. It is water-wise. And it provides fresh seasonings just steps away from the kitchen. The garden here hosts old favorites like parsley as well as newer introductions, such as conehead thyme (similar in flavor to winter savory) and Italian oregano thyme (a thyme with oregano overtones). All are perennials, with the exception of parsley, which can be planted each fall or early spring, as climate dictates.

A / Italian oregano thyme Leaves of this 1-foot-high herb have a zesty thyme flavor that enhances tomato-based dishes.

B / English thyme The spreading plant, up to 1 foot high, has small roundish leaves used to season meats, stews, and tomato-based sauces.

C / Lemon thyme Leaves have a pleasing lemon fragrance and subtle citrus flavor. The spreading plant grows up to 1 foot high.

D / Garden sage Shrubby perennial, 1 to 3 feet high, has velvety leaves and bears lavender-blue flowers from late spring into summer. Add to stews.

E / 'Berggarten' sage This compact grower reaching about 16 inches high has soft grayish green leaves and fewer flowers than other culinary sages. Delicious in stuffings and gravies.

F / Conehead thyme Leaves from the 3-foot-high mounding plant taste like thyme with the heat turned up. The spicy purple blooms are used for garnish.

G / Flat-leafed parsley Fresh sprigs and minced leaves are classic garnishes. Height ranges from 6 to 12 inches.

H / Greek oregano Fuzzy gray-green leaves have a spicy flavor. They are at their strongest if harvested when the plant is in bud but before it flowers.

Graptosedum

A Succulent Pocket

A grouping of succulents can tuck into any small space—the tableau is handsome from the moment you finish it. Seek out succulents that have cool hues and fleshy leaves. They will always appear fresh and have a seasonless look. Use fast-draining soil. Dress the planting with pea gravel.

Paver pocket *(facing page)* Plants from 4-inch and 6-inch nursery pots fill an area the size of a large paver. Clusters of *Graptosedum* are mixed in with three varieties of *Echeveria*: 'Afterglow' echeveria, *Echeveria × imbricata*, and 'Ruffles' echeveria (*E. gibbiflora*).

Deck mates *(right)* A trio of *Aeonium*—ebony 'Zwartkop', blond-edged 'Sunburst', and solid green *A. urbicum*—softens the corner of a raised deck. A row of ice blue *Echeveria* below the steps continues the rosette theme and introduces another color.

TIP Succulents don't need much root space. They can be content in a pocket as small as a foot square and a few inches deep. Shop for dwarf varieties. Besides being small to begin with, they grow slowly.

Plant a Low-Water Lawn

The look? Definitely meadow. The secret: Grasses that live on rainfall alone. The follow-up: You mow just once or twice a year to keep things tidy.

Instead of a conventional lawn, consider planting an unthirsty, no-mow "meadow" like the one pictured opposite, in coastal California; it resembles ones that grow naturally in the same region. Native Pacific hair grass (*Deschampsia cespitosa holciformis*) makes it work. Planted with custom-grown plugs, it took 18 months to fill in. Though native grasses can live on rainfall alone, this garden's subsurface drip irrigation waters it for five minutes twice weekly, so the turf stays greener. Annual or biannual mowing keeps it tidy.

Because each plug is a clump of grass with its own mature root system, it takes hold and fills in more quickly than seeds and doesn't demand as much initial watering. Use a good hand trowel or bulb planter to speed the planting process.

1 **Prep the soil.** Till in a 3-inch layer of clean, weed-free topsoil or compost; then rake in corn gluten (a natural preemergent herbicide). Or prep the soil two weeks ahead, water well to germinate weeds, and hoe them off before planting.

2 **Purchase plugs.** A flat of 70 plugs is enough to cover 31 square feet.

3 **Plant.** Remove the plugs from their sleeves; water well. Plant the plugs about 8 inches apart.

BEST GRASSES BY REGION

DESERT Fine fescue, buffalo grass, or blue grama.

NORTHERN CALIFORNIA AND THE NORTHWEST Fine fescue and hair grass (*Deschampsia*).

ROCKY MOUNTAINS Buffalo grass or blue grama below 6,500 feet; fine fescue above.

SOUTHERN CALIFORNIA Fine fescue, 'UC Verde' buffalo grass (along coast).

TIP Evergreen groundcover sedges such as *Carex pansa* also make softly mounding mini-meadows. To add spots of color, mix in low-growing flowers such as coreopsis and blanket flower.

Plant Seasonal Containers

Try low-care plants in light, breezy colors for summer and in deep, rich hues for autumn.

Color Burst

Arching, silvery astelia leaves and variegated ivory and pale green euphorbia create a lush, stunning backdrop that sets off bright tangerine blooms. The combination is soft and vibrant at the same time.

The Plants

Kalanchoe calandiva **'Goldengirl Yellow'** **Fluffy clusters of tiny blooms in a bright citrusy shade rise above fleshy, deep green leaves.**

Astelia **'Silver Shadow'** **This perennial has shimmering, strappy foliage in a clump that reaches 3 feet high and wide.**

Euphorbia characias **'Silver Swan'** **Mint-and-cream leaves topped with nearly white blooms grow about 2½ feet high and wide.**

Easy Being Green

A mix of textures makes this monochromatic trio pop. Though the plants' colors are all variations on chartreuse, their forms provide variety. Rigid, spiky phormium plays off the succulent, needle-like strands of 'Angelina' sedum and a giant aeonium rosette. They all take low water for a combo that looks good with little care.

The Plants

Phormium 'Apricot Queen' **Its spear-like leaves are pale yellow and green, with a touch of blush in cool weather. It's a perfect anchor for the rear of a grouping.**

Sedum rupestre 'Angelina' **This fast-growing ground-cover fills out quickly during the growing season and will spill softly out of containers.**

Aeonium decorum 'Sunburst' **Leaves of pale green edged in cream with hints of pink are perfect against solid greens and an ivory pot.**

Fire and Ice

Tie a grouping of plants together by choosing a palette common to all of them. Here, a wine-colored heucherella anchors the other two plants: an olive and deep pink spiky phormium and a low-growing blue-and-burgundy succulent.

The Plants

Phormium 'Sundowner' Upright, strappy leaves start out olive green with stripes of vibrant reddish pink that age to cream near the edges.

Echeveria nodulosa **This succulent has icy blue-green leaves with swirls of maroon markings.**

Heucherella **'Sweet Tea'** Ruffled, maplelike foliage on low mounds looks good year-round.

Cocoa Blast

For a dramatic look, choose large pots in a single shade, and fill each one with a plant in a similar color. This trio of large chocolate pots, in graduated sizes, shows off bronzy, round-leafed smoke tree, spiky phormium, and mounding heuchera.

The Plants

Heuchera 'Sugar Plum' **Dark burgundy leaves brushed with silvery green keep their rich color year-round. Their mounding form contrasts with that of the upright plants.**

Cotinus coggygria 'Royal Purple' **Deep plum leaves remain into autumn, then turn reddish before dropping in winter. This shrub reaches 12 to 15 feet tall and wide, perfect for an oversize container.**

Phormium 'Platt's Black' **One of the darkest varieties, reaching 2 to 3 feet high, has an upright form that livens up this single-toned scheme.**

Plant a Pool in a Pot

Even a small water feature on a deck or in a garden creates a serene, relaxed mood. It is also an oasis that invites birds to drink and bathe.

For height and drama, combine tall plants with those that have strappy leaves and low growers that spill over the edge.

Find out how deep to submerge each plant. For some, the soil line needs to be at the water's surface. For others, the soil should be entirely underwater. Aquatic plants from a nursery are already potted in appropriate soil. Free-floating varieties are packed in water.

1 Find a spot. Place a watertight container in a sunny spot protected from the wind. Once you add water, the pot may be too heavy to pick up and move.

2 Make a foundation. Fill the bottom of the pot with gravel and stones to create a level base. Sprinkle a layer of gravel in each nursery pot to keep the soil from floating out.

3 Arrange the plants. Position marginal plants with their soil line just below the water surface. Use bricks, small pavers, or overturned pots to elevate them. Deep-water plants can be set as much as 12 inches below the surface, either on the stone base or on a paver or overturned pot.

4 Add water. Fill the container with water up to ½ inch below the rim. Add a mosquito dunk or mosquito bits to kill larvae (harmless to wildlife). Once a year, empty the container and clean it with a solution of 1 part bleach to 4 parts water. Rinse thoroughly, then refill.

The Plants

Black taro (*Colocasia esculenta* 'Fontanesii') Bewitching blackish purple stems hold aloft deep green heart-shaped foliage.

Golden sweet flag (*Acorus gramineus* 'Ogon') Clumping grasslike foliage in striped green with bright yellow releases a pleasant aroma when crushed.

Indian rhubarb (*Darmera peltata* 'Umbrella Plant') Stalks 2 to 6 feet tall support shield-shaped leaves. Pink blooms appear in spring before the foliage emerges. In fall, the leaves take on brilliant color.

Little giant papyrus (*Cyperus papyrus* 'Dwarf Form') Stems 2 to 3 feet high are topped with soft round bursts of bright green filament-like foliage. Adds drama and height to a container.

Parrot's feather (*Myriophyllum brasiliense*) Soft feather foliage floats and sprawls on the water's surface.

Star grass (*Dichromena colorata*) Snowy white seed bracts on this grasslike sedge resemble twinkling stars.

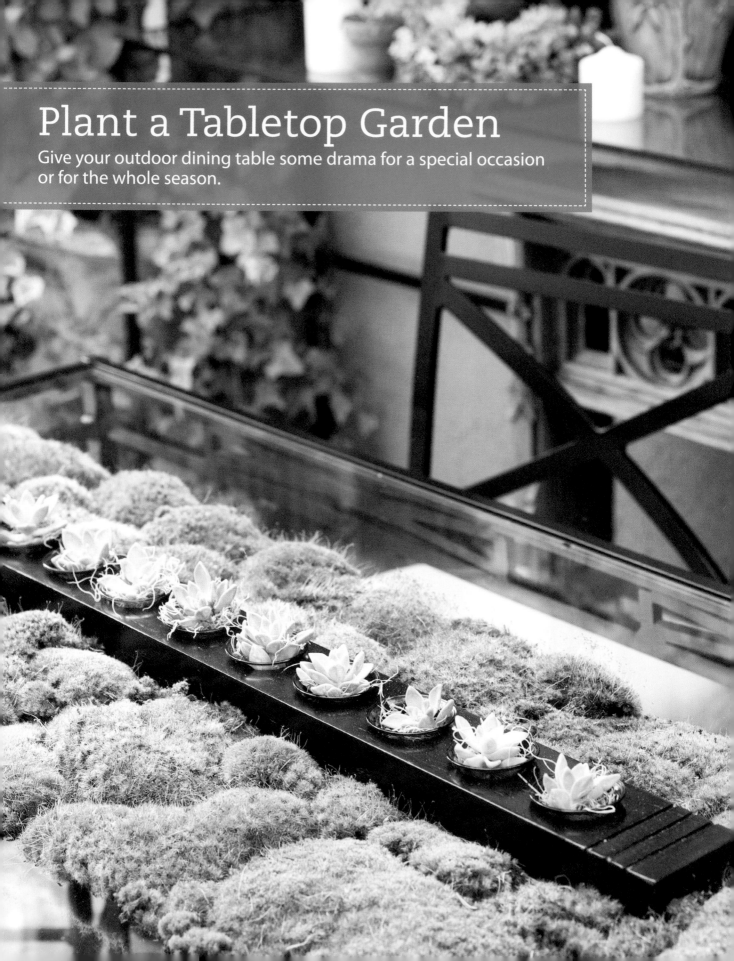

Plant a Tabletop Garden

Give your outdoor dining table some drama for a special occasion or for the whole season.

Living Centerpieces

A row of potted plants marching down the center of the table always looks charming. But these two ideas are more of a surprise and almost as fast to execute.

Votive tray *(facing page)* Pop a tiny plant into each receptacle of a votive candleholder. Don't bother adding soil, since the plants will only be there a short time—you can transfer them to the garden after the party. Small succulents are ideal. *Graptopetalum* were the choice here. But you could also use compact perennials such as violas or sea thrift, or plugs of creeping thyme or Scotch moss. Cuttings work great, and they're even easier. If you prefer a small started plant, brush off some or all of the soil in the rootball. The plant will survive temporarily. For a longer-lasting arrangement, use *Tillandsia*; air plants never need soil. If you want to get a little fancier, add a border of floral moss around the votive holder as was done here.

Table runner *(right)* Insert a box with drainage holes into an old table. Fill your new planter with easy-care succulents. Now you have a centerpiece that will last the entire outdoor dining season. Don't have an old table to sacrifice to the project? Build one out of shipping pallets. Use the pallets for the top and the sunken planter, and add legs—the more worn, the better. Coat the table with some natural wax stain for a bit of weather protection.

Frame Succulents

A frame filled with succulents is a living composition that resembles a colorful, textural tapestry.

A miniature succulent garden has an irresistible appeal. It's easy to assemble and care for. As a bonus, it can be moved from place to place. Ready-made succulent frames in various materials are available online from Succulent Gardens (*sgplants. com*) and other sources.

1 **Gather cuttings.** Break small "pups" from succulents that you already grow. The stems should be at least ¼ inch long. Set the cuttings aside in a cool area for a few days to allow the stem ends to dry and form calluses. The 6-by-12-inch frame shown here uses 60 cuttings.

2 **Add soil.** Set the frame, mesh side up, on a flat surface. Fill with moist cactus mix, working the mix through the mesh with your fingers.

3 **Plant.** Push the stem ends through the mesh and into the soil. Let the frame lie flat in a cool, bright location for 7 to 10 days until the plants take root; then begin watering. When the plants are securely rooted—after 4 to 12 weeks —display the frame upright in an area with morning or filtered sun. Water every 7 to 10 days.

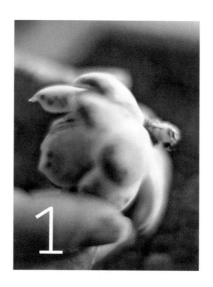

DESIGN TIPS

For striking effects in a framed succulent picture, try these ideas.

MAKE A SUBTLE BACKDROP
Group succulents with similar sizes and shapes, and slightly contrasting colors.

ADD BRILLIANT ACCENTS
Insert a small mass of succulents in a vivid color. It's like a stroke of bright pigment from a painter's brush.

Build a Border

Start with a few eye-catching plants or pick a color theme, and then fill in the composition.

Variations on a Color

A mixture of plum, purple, and light violet adds depth to this garden in Eugene, Oregon. Rich burgundy smoke tree *(Cotinus coggygria)*, royal purple iris, and Spanish lavender flowers play off the blue-green, silver, and chartreuse foliage plants, listed at right, to create continuity along the border.

The Filler Plants

'Karl Foerster' feather reed grass (*Calamagrostis × acutiflora*) Graceful clumps make a 3-to-4-foot fountain of green. Purplish, 6-foot flowers appear in late spring, turn gold in summer.

Hellebore (*Helleborus × sternii*) Evergreen foliage and winter flowers earn this a place in the front of any mixed perennial border. To 12 inches tall and wide.

'Variegatus' Japanese silver grass (*Miscanthus sinensis*) Among the most elegant of the grasses, this grows 5 to 6 feet tall, with flowers rising 7 to 9 feet. The low wall helps support it.

'Papoose' Sitka spruce (*Picea sitchensis* 'Tenas') This dwarf native grows just 2 inches per year, starting out round, but gradually becoming conical. Color is blue-green.

Hot-to-Cool Contrasts

Fiery shades look even more dramatic when paired with pale tones. Here, plum-and-red coleus (*Solenostemon*), along with lipstick red dahlias and yellow French marigolds striped with red, add pops of vivid color among softer silvers, greens, and rose of plants listed at right. Purple fountain grass rises behind.

The Filler Plants

'Vancouver Centennial' geranium *(Pelargonium hortorum)*
Many gardeners grow this for its leaves, whose wine-colored centers have light green edges and veins. To 1 foot high and 18 inches wide.

'Matrona' sedum
Plants are 2 feet high and wide, with rose-edged, gray-green leaves that give rise to mauve-pink flowers on red stems. Blooms turn chocolate brown in winter.

Silver spreader *(Artemisia caucasica, A. lanata)*
This is among the best of a few groundcover artemisias, growing 3 to 12 inches high, 18 to 24 inches wide. Foliage is silvery green.

A Warm Bed
in the Shade

A flaming *Acer palmatum* 'Bloodgood'
arches over this border on Bainbridge Island,
Washington. Beneath its canopy, *Heuchera*
'Blackout' repeats the tree's red highlights and
adds punch beside a pale green sedum and
coppery *Carex flagellifera*. The filler plants, listed
at right, add contrasts of color, texture, and scale.

The Filler Plants

**Hair grass
(*Deschampsia
flexuosa*) Fine-
textured grass
sports airy clouds
of pale yellow-green
flowers in summer.
It grows 1 to 2 feet
high and wide.**

**Japanese sweet flag
(*Acorus gramineus*
'Ogon') Small,
grasslike perennial,
1 foot high, has
golden yellow,
narrow leaves.**

**Spirea (*S. japonica*
'Goldflame') Foliage
on this upright
deciduous shrub
starts out bronze
but matures to
yellowish green,
turning reddish
orange in fall. It
grows to 2½ feet
high and wide.**

A Cool Spot in the Sun

The two stars of this small garden, in Southern California, are a muscular icy blue *Agave attenuata* 'Nova', which grows 5 feet wide, and a towering New Zealand flax (*Phormium* 'Sundowner'), which grows to about 6 feet tall and wide. The filler plants, listed at right, set off these bold beauties.

The Filler Plants

Dymondia margaretae **Short (2 to 3 inches high), dense groundcover has narrow gray-green leaves rolled at the edges to show cottony white undersides. Drought-tolerant once established.**

Echeveria **'Afterglow' The small succulent grows in a loose rosette shape. This variety sports a particularly striking color—lavender-pink leaves with a powdery finish.**

Golden bamboo (*Phyllostachys aurea***) Large grass with woody stems is dense and upright. Growing 6 to 10 feet tall, it makes a good screen. Foliage is a soft neutral green.**

Mediterranean Border

A border only 11 feet long by 5 feet deep holds Mediterranean perennials with mostly blue flowers that begin blooming in early spring. Catmint and penstemon start off the show. The dark orange whorls of lion's tail emerge mid- to late summer, changing the monochromatic color scheme to a complementary one. Planted toward the front of the border, Santa Barbara daisy continues to flower nearly all year.

The Filler Plants

Bog sage *(Salvia uliginosa)* **Upright perennial, 4 to 6 feet tall, bears sky blue flowers that bloom from late spring through fall.**

Catmint *(Nepeta × faassenii)* **A 1-foot-high mound of soft gray-green leaves produces an abundance of lavender-blue flowers.**

Lavandin *(Lavandula × intermedia)* **This group of sterile hybrids is a cross of English and spike lavenders. Plants reach 2 feet high.**

Lion's tail *(Leonotis leonurus)* **Perennial 4 to 6 feet tall and wide delivers whorls of downy orange flowers.**

Santa Barbara daisy *(Erigeron karvinskianus)* **Trailing plant, 10 to 20 inches high, has plentiful dainty white flowers.**

Penstemon *(P. × gloxinioides)* **Upright perennial with narrow green leaves and bell-shaped blooms reaches 2 to 4 feet tall. 'Midnight' has dark bluish purple flowers.**

Desert Border

The plants around this deeply recessed patio bear the sun's full brunt. So they have to be tough. Wispy grasses, *Pennisetum orientale* and *Stipa tenuissima,* grow around the rock at left, while a feathery cassia *(Senna artemisioides)* forms an airy green screen at right. Cactus and blooming perennials (listed at right) grow between.

The Filler Plants

Blanket flower (*Gaillardia × grandiflora*) Daisylike flowers are held aloft on stems with gray-green leaves. 'Arizona Sun' is about 10 inches high and bears vibrant blooms with orange-red petals tipped with yellow.

Blue Cleveland sage (*Salvia clevelandii*) Highly fragrant gray leaves and equally fragrant violet-blue flowers grace this evergreen shrub that grows 3 to 5 feet tall and 5 to 8 feet wide.

Golden barrel cactus (*Echinocactus grusonii*) This cylindrical cactus has prominent ribs and showy yellow spines. A slow grower, it can reach 4 feet tall.

Red lantana (*L. montevidensis*) The mounding evergreen shrub blooms much of the year. Average height is 2 to 3 feet, but larger varieties are available, as are other colors.

Create a Curved Path

A graceful path is easy to design. After it's in place, fringe it with handsome ornamentals—or devote the beds to edibles.

There is something about a curve that makes you want to follow it, especially when it ends in an inviting place to sit. Big drifts of chartreuse-flowered euphorbia brighten both sides of the path *(facing page)*, and blue and white flowers and silvery foliage add contrast. Aromatic herbs release their scent along the way, inviting you to linger.

TIP Every path needs a destination. Add a beckoning birdbath, piece of art, or chair and table.

1 **Outline the path.** Use lengths of rope or garden hose, adjusting them to get the shape you want.

2 **Add the edging.** Dig a 3-inch-deep path channel and edge it with benderboard. Fill with ⅜-inch crushed gravel.

Dress Your Driveway

These narrow and oh-so-visible strips of pavement can be more than parking lots. Make better use of yours with one of these ideas.

New Life for Unused Spaces

With today's small gardens, the amount of space devoted to driveways seems like a waste of real estate. How much better to make the area look like a continuation of the garden or use it to expand your outdoor living quarters.

Cover the driveway *(facing page)* Blanket the concrete with a thick layer of river rock—you don't even need to go to the expense of breaking up the slab and hauling it away. Then set down a winding path of thick flat stones atop the rock bed, and line the perimeters with evergreen plants in good-size pots. The final touch: Offset screens that obscure the end of the rustic walkway. Who has to know that it only leads to the garage?

Create a patio *(right)* If you still want to park off the street, consider stealing just the back half of the driveway, as these home-owners did. Convert the garage to a home office or studio, encourage vines to crawl up the front to disguise those big doors, and add a row of pots in front. Then use the borrowed space for outdoor dining, a barbe-cue, a cocktail lounge, or a game room.

Carve out planting space *(left)* Don't want to lose the use of your garage? Create a planter down the center of the driveway, and place in it creeping thyme, sedums, star creeper—anything short enough that cars can pass over it will work. Immediately the whole area looks softer. Now squeeze in some taller plants along both sides. If you're really short on space, espalier—train plants to grow sideways. You're greening up verti-cally as well as horizontally.

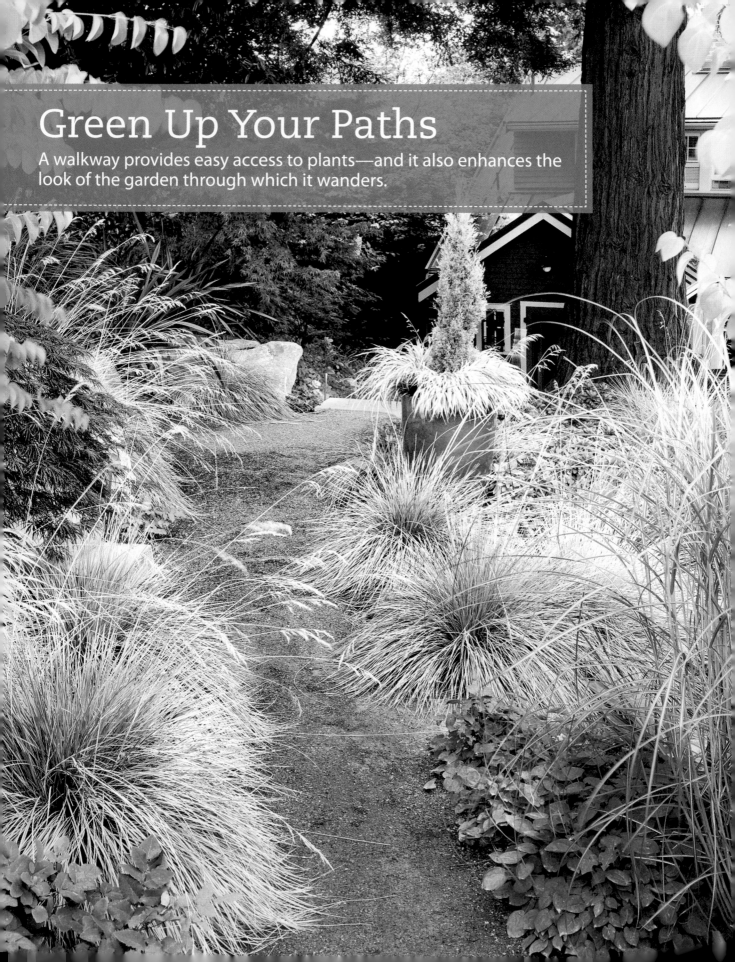

Green Up Your Paths

A walkway provides easy access to plants—and it also enhances the look of the garden through which it wanders.

Two Ways to Approach a Path

Are you more at home in a setting that reminds you of the wild, or do you like more creature comforts? Construct a walkway that matches your personality.

Soften the sides *(facing page)* This path looks as if it had been created by nature rather than the gardener. The material is much of the reason. Crushed basalt was used here, but decomposed granite and wood mulch would work too. The wildness of the plants also contributes to the illusion. Blue oat grass *(Helictotrichon sempervirens)* and creeping woodland plants such as *Epimedium* sprawl along the edges.

Add ribbons of green *(right)* The strong geometry of this path clearly demonstrates that it was designed. Concrete pavers separated by bands of groundcover snake through the garden like a striped ribbon. The look is polished but softer than solid poured concrete. The green strips also help the garden to absorb more rainfall. Setting plants back from the path highlights it even more.

TIP Three good plants for placing between pavers or steppingstones are Scotch moss *(Sagina subulata)*, Corsican mint, and creeping thyme. The first two provide a greener look; the thyme has grayer foliage, a natural for a Mediterranean garden. The mint and thyme release fragrance when stepped on—a nice plus.

Build a Streambed

A dry streambed does double-duty in garden design, bringing the sense of water into a landscape and, after a cloudburst, carrying water away.

A realistic dry creek works like one you might find in nature—always sinuous, broadening as it goes, and bedded with boulders and gravel. Two people can make one like this 17-foot-long watercourse in about four hours.

1 **Lay out the course.** Use a garden hose to mark out the course of your dry creek. Like an artist working with perspective, make it generally narrow at the source and broader at the other end, with some parts wide, others narrow.

2 **Excavate a shallow bed.** Make the creekbed broad and shallow. This one is 1 to 5 feet wide and 3 inches deep. Scoop out hollows where you want large, round rocks to go, mounding excavated soil on either side of the creek.

3 **Line the bed.** Lay landscape fabric over the streambed to keep weeds down. Fold and pleat the cloth to fit curves, narrows, and wider stretches.

4 **Add rocks and pebbles.** Place large rocks first, setting them on fabric nested over the hollows prepared in step 2. Then place smaller river-washed pebbles and gravel.

TIP Crowd the edges of your creekbed with plants that look as if they belong, such as heucheras, true geraniums, and sedges (*Carex*).

Techniques

Every garden, even one designed for low maintenance, needs good soil to thrive, along with occasional watering, feeding, and pruning—depending on the types of plants you grow. Here are simple techniques for keeping your plants healthy.

Give new transplants a thorough soaking with a hose after planting, even if a drip system will eventually take over the watering chores. That way, the roots will get off to the best possible start.

Fix Your Soil

Good soil is key to successful gardening. Make sure that yours is fast draining yet moisture retentive, neither too dense nor too loose.

Check Soil Texture

All soils contain minerals and varying amounts of organic material, air, and water. Texture describes the size of a soil's mineral particles. These include large, coarse sand particles; small silt particles; and tiny particles of clay. Soil texture affects watering and fertilizing schedules, and in some cases it determines the kinds of plants you will be able to grow. Here's how you can figure out which soil type you have.

Water the soil Thoroughly wet a patch of soil in your garden, and then let it dry out for a day.

Feel the soil Pick up a handful and squeeze it firmly. If it forms a tight ball and feels slippery, it is predominantly clay. If it feels gritty and crumbles when you open your hand, it is sandy. If it is slightly crumbly but still holds a loose ball, it is loam.

A / SANDY (LIGHT) SOILS are made up of large mineral particles that allow water and nutrients to drain away freely. Plants growing in them need water and feeding more often.

B / LOAM contains mineral particles of various sizes, organic matter, and enough air for healthy root growth. It drains well but doesn't dry out—or lose nutrients —too fast.

C / CLAY (HEAVY) SOILS have tiny, tightly packed particles, helping them to hold the greatest volume of nutrients in soluble form. But they're sticky when wet, hard when dry, and slow to drain.

Amend the Soil

Here's the best way to add the amendments listed here to your soil.

Dampen the soil Water the soil thoroughly and let dry for a few days.

Dig the soil Go to a depth of about 10 inches. Break up dirt clods, and remove any stones or debris.

Add the amendment Spread it over the soil. Add fertilizer according to package directions, if desired. Mix with a spading fork, incorporating the amendment evenly into the soil. Level the bed with a rake, breaking up any remaining clods of earth.

Water well Let the improved soil settle for a few days after watering.

SOIL AMENDMENTS

Compost is easy to make (see page 107). The other amendments are sold in large bags at nurseries. Your nursery can help you select the best type for your soil.

COMPOST Garden trimmings and other organic material are allowed to decompose into a valuable soil conditioner.

MANURE Aged or composted manures should be applied sparingly. Add about 1 pound of dry steer manure per 1 square foot of soil surface, or 1 pound of dry poultry manure per 5 square feet. Work into the soil a month before planting.

WOOD PRODUCTS Ground bark improves clay soil but can rob it of nitrogen. Add nitrogen along with the bark, or look for nitrogen-fortified products such as redwood soil conditioner.

SPHAGNUM PEAT MOSS It helps lighten and acidify soil, but there are concerns over the damage that may result from the over-mining of peat bogs. Coir fiber, a by-product of the coconut fiber industry, is similar in texture but won't acidify the soil the way peat does. It comes in bales, bricks, and discs that expand when soaked in water to make 5 to 10 quarts of fluffy material.

Make Compost

Composting is a natural process that converts raw organic materials into valuable soil conditioner. A pile of leaves, branches, and other garden trimmings will eventually decompose. You can speed up the process by creating optimum conditions for the organisms responsible for decay.

You will need "browns" (such as dry leaves, twigs, sawdust, wood chips, or shredded newspaper) and "greens" (like fresh grass clippings, fruit and vegetable scraps, coffee grounds, tea bags, crushed eggshells, or aged steer or chicken manure). Shred or chop all materials into small pieces. You can make a freestanding pile like the one shown at right, or use the option shown below. Go to *sunset.com/compost* for more advice, including a list of composting dos and don'ts.

EASY COMPOSTER

Bend a length of wire to 4 feet in diameter. It should be 3 or 4 feet tall. Support it with stakes. To turn the pile, lift and move the cylinder to one side, and then fork the materials back into it.

HOW TO MAKE A FREESTANDING PILE

A pile like the one here is easy to tend and creates the right mixture of air, water, and nitrogen-rich nutrients for the materials to decompose.

1. PICK A SPOT. It should be 4 or 5 feet square; part shade is best. Go over the soil with a spading fork. Then start spreading layers. The first layer (4 to 6 inches thick) is brown, the second (2 to 3 inches thick) is green, and the third is brown. Two or three times during the layering process, throw on a shovelful of finished compost, if available.

2. MOISTEN THE LAYERS. Water each layer so that the finished pile is as damp as a wrung-out sponge. Add a fourth layer of bagged chicken or steer manure. Cover the pile with a 6-inch cap of straw to hold in nitrogen and shed rain.

3. TEND THE PILE. Let it heat up for 10 to 14 days until the temperature inside reaches 140°F to 150°F. Then pull off the straw cap and turn the pile by pushing it over and dividing it. Reassemble it (but not in layers) and put the straw cap back on. When the temperature climbs to 130°F to 140°F, turn the pile again.

4. CHECK THE COMPOST. After turning the pile three times in 4 to 6 months (adding water if it starts to dry out), examine the finished compost. It should have an earthy smell and lots of worms and pill bugs. Nothing that went into it should be recognizable.

Plant

Once your soil is prepared, it's time to get your plants growing. Sow seeds or plant nursery starts according to these easy steps.

HOW TO START SEEDS INDOORS

For most annual flowers and vegetables, sow seeds indoors four to eight weeks before it's time to transplant the seedlings outdoors.

FILL, SOW, AND LABEL Use small pots or cell-packs, and fill to just below the rim with a light, porous seed-starting mix. Moisten the mix; let drain. Follow the guidelines on the seed packet, and cover seeds with the recommended amount of mix. Moisten lightly, and label your containers, since many seedlings look alike.

CARE When the soil surface feels dry, spray with a fine mist. Once seeds germinate, move the container to a warm area with bright light. As the seedlings grow, thin out the weakest ones. About 10 days before planting out, harden off the seedlings by setting them outdoors for a few hours each day to get them acclimated.

DAYS TO HARVEST

Whether you're growing vegetables from seeds or transplants, you'll encounter days-to-harvest information on seed packets or labels. Unfortunately, the term is not standardized: some companies mean "days from sowing to harvest," while others mean "days from transplant to harvest." In both cases, the seller assumes perfect growing conditions. In mild-summer climates, tomatoes or melons might take 50 percent longer to mature than days-to-harvest notes predict. When you shop, find out how the grower made the calculations printed in the catalog or on the tag. Then you'll know what to expect in garden performance.

HOW TO SOW SEEDS IN THE GARDEN

Some annuals and vegetables grow best if the seeds are sowed where the plants will be grown in the garden.

SOW SEEDS IN ROWS Use a trowel or the corner of a hoe to dig a furrow to the correct depth (check seed packets for depth and spacing recommendations). Sow the seeds evenly, and pat the soil gently over them. To make straight rows, stretch a string between two stakes, and plant beneath it. Or lay a board on the soil's surface and then plant along its edge.

MAKE A MOUND Group plants in a cluster on a low mound of soil, rather than in rows. This is a traditional way to grow sprawling plants such as squash and melons. Sow five or six seeds in a circle, and pat soil over them.

BROADCAST SEEDS Sowing wide bands of vegetables across a bed is more space efficient than row-planting for smaller crops such as lettuce, carrots, radishes, or mesclun. Scatter the seeds evenly over the soil. Cover by scattering soil over the seeds or by raking gently, first in one direction and then again at right angles. Pat the soil to firm it.

KEEP WEEDS AT BAY

One of the easiest ways to control weeds is to lay down landscape fabric, which prevents weed seeds from reaching soil and deprives any existing weeds of light. Unlike black plastic, it is porous and allows air and water to reach plant roots. Landscape fabric is best used around permanent plants that don't need changing often.

UNROLL THE FABRIC OVER PREPARED SOIL Stake the corners in place, or secure by burying them with soil. Using scissors or a utility knife, cut Xs in the fabric where you'll set plants; fold back the fabric.

DIG A HOLE FOR EACH ROOTBALL Insert the rootball through an X into the soil, press to firm the plant in place, and then smooth down the fabric and cover it with a 2-inch layer of mulch such as fine ground bark.

HOW TO PLANT SEEDLINGS

Water each seedling before removing it from the container. The hole for each plant should be the same depth as the container and 1 to 2 inches wider.

LOOSEN THE ROOTS With your fingers, lightly separate the roots so that they can grow out into the soil. If the bottom of the rootball has a pad of coiled roots, pull it off.

PLANT Place each plant in its hole so that the top of the rootball is even with the soil surface. Firm the soil around the roots.

WATER Irrigate deeply with a gentle flow that won't disturb the soil or roots.

HOW TO PLANT FROM NURSERY CONTAINERS

If the shrub, tree, or perennial is in a 1-gallon container or larger, tap the bottom and sides sharply to loosen the rootball and allow the plant to slide out.

DIG A PLANTING HOLE It should be at least twice as wide as the rootball and a little deeper, leaving a central plateau of soil 1 to 2 inches high on which to set the root system. This prevents the plant from settling too much. Roughen the sides of the hole to help the roots penetrate the soil.

SET THE PLANT IN THE HOLE Spread the roots over the plateau of soil. The top of the rootball should be 1 to 2 inches above the surrounding soil. Backfill with the soil you dug from the hole (along with a little compost or commercial planting mix if your soil is poor). Firm the soil around the roots with your hands.

MAKE A WATERING BASIN Create a mound of soil around the plant. Gently pour water into the basin, and add more soil if needed.

SPREAD MULCH Arrange the mulch around the plant, keeping it several inches away from the stem or trunk.

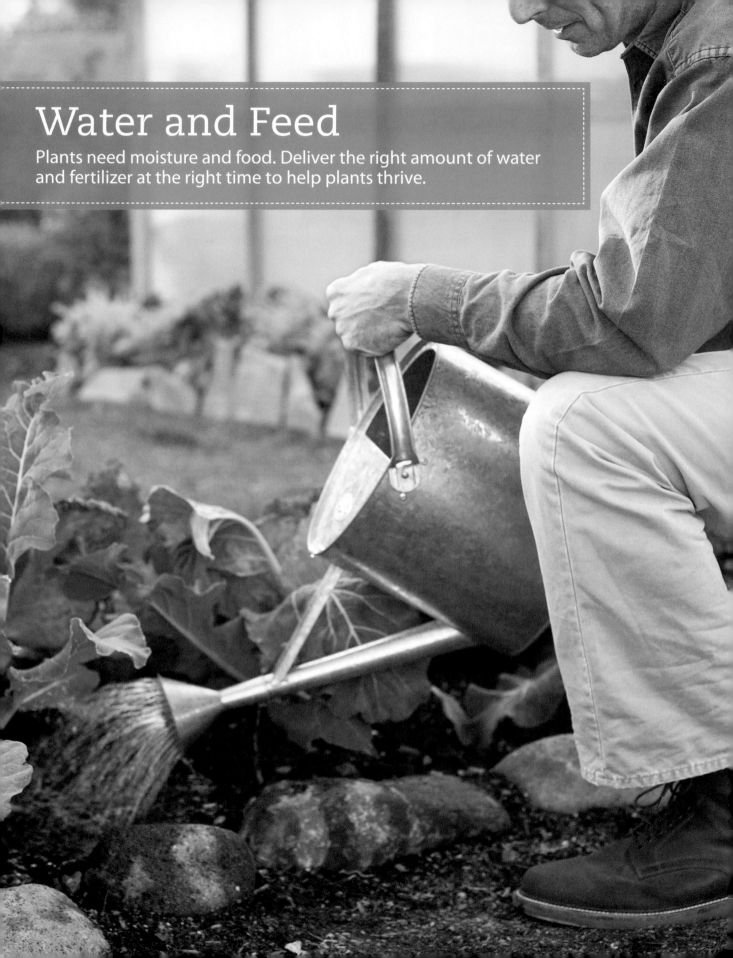

Water and Feed

Plants need moisture and food. Deliver the right amount of water and fertilizer at the right time to help plants thrive.

Water

The method you choose will depend on the size of your garden, how often you need to water, and how much equipment you want to acquire.

Flood the soil Applying water in basins or furrows (dug into the soil when you set out plants or sow seeds) is an effective way to irrigate large plants. Basins, circular depressions surrounding the plants, need to be expanded as the plants grow. Furrows, or shallow ditches, dug near plants in rows work well on level ground and are especially popular in vegetable beds. Dig broad, shallow furrows rather than narrow, deep ones, since water moves primarily downward rather than sideways.

Lay soaker hoses These long tubes made of perforated or porous plastic or rubber with hose fittings at one end are useful for slow, steady delivery of water. They are ideal for watering rows of vegetables; to water beds, snake the soaker around the plants. For trees and shrubs, coil the soaker around the outer edges of the root zone.

Water wisely Water young seedlings and transplants as often as two or three times a day in hot, windy weather, keeping the soil moist but not soggy. As plants grow and their roots reach deeper, you can water less frequently. Mature trees, shrubs, and vines generally can go longer between soakings than annuals and perennials. Plants in containers need more frequent watering than those in the ground.

Reach the roots Once plants are established, water them deeply to moisten the entire root zone. This encourages roots to grow down farther. Deeper roots have access to more moisture, which allows the plants to go longer between waterings.

Fertilize

All plants benefit from feeding at planting time. After that, most trees, shrubs, and vines thrive with a yearly application of organic compost in early spring. Annual vegetables and flowers, perennials, lawns, and fruit trees may need supplemental feeding during the growing season. (Check individual plant listings.) Fertilizers may be organic (made from the remains or by-products of living organisms) or inorganic (made from synthetic substances). The two forms are dry and liquid. Always follow package directions.

Dry fertilizers Powders, granules, or pellets can be spread on the ground or dug into the soil. Controlled-release types may be beadlike granules, spikes, or tablets. Dig granules into soil at planting time, or scratch them into the soil surface. Use a mallet to pound spikes into the ground; dig holes for tablets.

Liquid fertilizers These are sold as crystals, granules, or liquid concentrates that you mix with water and apply with a hose or spray bottle. Follow label directions.

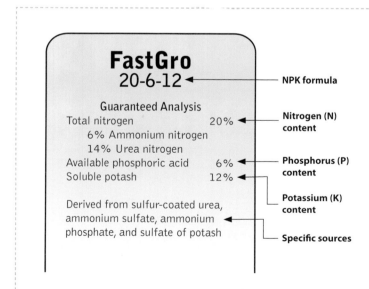

READ THE LABEL

The label will list the percentage by weight of the three macronutrients, abbreviated as NPK. Almost any complete fertilizer (one containing nitrogen, phosphorus, and potassium) will do. Specialized blends—ones for acid-loving plants, flowers, lawns, citrus, roses, tomatoes, and vegetables—may be a little better for their intended plant groups than general-purpose fertilizers, but the difference isn't critical. See "Regional Gardening Calendars" (beginning on page 268) for recommendations.

Work with Nature

A healthy garden hosts abundant insect life, including beneficials that keep pests in check. Use prevention first.

Lady beetle

A Natural Approach

Deal with garden pests by following the tenets of integrated pest management (IPM), a philosophy whose primary aim is prevention. IPM uses biological, cultural, and physical controls to help avoid serious insect, disease, and other pest problems and to reduce pests' effects to tolerable levels. Chemical controls using pesticides are employed only as a last resort.

IPM begins with good cultural practices. Choose plants that are adapted to your climate and garden conditions. Buy varieties that are resistant to diseases or unpalatable to pests. Water and fertilize appropriately to promote health, and check plants frequently to spot problems before they get out of hand.

PHYSICAL CONTROLS

Handpick pests Snails, caterpillars, insect egg masses, and other pests can be easily plucked off and destroyed.

Prune infested plant parts Branches, canes, and leaves that show evidence of actively developing pest infestations should be clipped off and put in the trash, not the compost heap.

Blast pests with water To dislodge or kill small insects such as aphids, thrips, and spider mites, simply spray them with a strong jet of water from the hose.

BIOLOGICAL CONTROLS

Every garden has a homegrown army of pest controls. Among the most beneficial insects are assassin bugs, damsel bugs, lacewings, and lady beetles, all of which feed on a variety of pests such as aphids, leafhoppers, and mites. Parasitic wasps and tachinid flies lay eggs onto or inside of pests; as the larvae develop, they kill their host. Parasitic nematodes introduce a fatal bacterium into pests; other nematodes control pests like root weevils and cutworms that dwell in the soil.

Lacewing

NATURAL PESTICIDES

These are products whose active ingredients come from a plant, animal, or mineral, or whose action results from a biological process. They should be used as a last resort, since most can harm people, pets, or plants if used incorrectly. Most will kill beneficial insects too. Check labels for a list of target pests, and always follow directions carefully.

BACILLUS THURINGIENSIS (BT) A naturally occurring bacterium whose several strains each target a different kind of insect.

NEEM OIL Particularly effective botanical oil that controls a variety of pests and diseases.

FOOD-GRADE OILS AND EXTRACTS Commercial versions of homemade repellents and pesticides such as citrus peel, garlic, and hot pepper.

HORTICULTURAL OILS Typically, highly refined petroleum or botanical oils that act on contact by smothering pests.

INSECTICIDAL SOAP Made from potassium salts of fatty acids from plants and animals. Hard water inactivates the soap, so mix the concentrate with distilled water or rainwater.

Tend

Perform simple tasks regularly to keep your lawn, ornamentals, and container plants looking good and growing well.

Mow and Feed Lawns

The key to having a great-looking lawn? Perform some simple tasks regularly rather than wait for time-consuming problems to show up.

If you have an established lawn, irrigate it as deeply and infrequently as possible. This encourages deep rooting and also conserves water. In mild climates, once or twice a week should be adequate during warm weather; in hotter regions, you'll need to water more often. Contact your local water department or cooperative extension office for specific lawn watering guidelines for your area.

Irrigate in cycles Many sprinklers apply water faster than the soil can absorb it. To prevent runoff, water in cycles. Sprinkle until just before runoff or puddling occurs (typically 10 to 15 minutes); then repeat the cycle in an hour. To improve water penetration and reduce runoff, aerate and dethatch your lawn once a year.

Feed regularly Most lawns are heavy feeders, requiring regular applications of high-nitrogen fertilizer. In the desert, iron may also be beneficial. Give cool-season lawns two applications of fertilizer—one in spring and another in fall. Fertilize warm-season lawns several times from late spring into late summer (Bermuda grass only lightly in summer) and lightly in fall. Apply dry fertilizers using a spreader; overlap the spreader's wheel marks so that swaths just touch as you pass over. Check the fertilizer package for recommended application rates. If you cut back on watering because of drought, hold back on fertilizer as well.

Mow Cut the grass at least weekly. In general, never take more than a third of the leaf blade off each time. If you do, the loss of food-producing leaf blade temporarily checks root growth. See the mowing heights below. Use a sharp mower blade. A dull blade leaves the grass ragged and brown on the tips. A sharp blade cuts fast and clean, leaving the grass healthy.

Patch To keep the lawn looking good, give it a tune-up once a year, in fall. Patch dead or damaged spots with the same type of grass as the existing lawn. In Arizona and California, overseed winter-dormant grasses such as Bermuda with ryegrass.

HOW TO MAINTAIN A LAWN

For bluegrass and fescue, mow when the grass is 3 to 4 inches high; set your mower at 2 to 3 inches. Cut Bermuda grass when it's not quite 2 inches high; set your mower at 1 inch. Then follow these steps to keep lawns looking neat.

AFTER MOWING A ROW, slightly overlap that row when starting the next one (so that the grass beneath the mower wheel gets cut).

TO GIVE THE LAWN A TIDY EDGE near gravel paths and adjacent flower beds, use a half-moon edger. Plunge the tool into the lawn's edge as shown to cut off errant shoots.

INSPECT YOUR IRRIGATION SYSTEM OCCASIONALLY while it's running. Repair broken heads promptly, and adjust sprinklers so that they don't overshoot onto paving.

Groom Plants

Many flowering annuals and perennials will bloom longer and more profusely if you periodically remove the spent flowers. While you're at it, pick off any dead or discolored leaves, and pinch back any new growth that can spoil the plant's shape.

Deadhead rhododendrons *(left)* After rhododendrons bloom and flowers fall off, the spiky base of each truss remains. Snap off each of these just above the emerging leaf buds, as shown here. This makes the shrub look better and allows the plant to channel its energy into new growth instead of seed production.

Clip roses *(facing page)* Most roses benefit from moderate pruning at the end of the dormant season, but while they're in bloom, you can consider cutting flowers as a form of ongoing pruning. Be sure to use sharp pruners. Cut off enough stem to support the flower in a vase, but don't deprive the plant of too much foliage. Always leave a stem with at least two sets of five-leaflet leaves.

Prune pines *(below)* The best time to shape pines is in spring, when new growth emerges in showy "candles." To fatten up a rangy pine or to keep a young one chunky, cut the candles in half before they open into needles in the spring. You can also remove entire unwanted limbs to accent a pine's branching pattern, but before you cut, remember that a new limb won't sprout to take its place.

THIN APPLES

In late spring or early summer, apple trees spontaneously abort unpollinated fruit (a process called June drop). That's a good time to thin the remaining apples to keep trees from producing too much small fruit. Thin triple clusters to doubles, and double clusters to singles. However, don't thin at all if your tree is bearing lightly for the year.

Before

After

Divide Perennials

To reinvigorate clump-forming perennials—and to get more plants for free—simply split their rootballs into sections and replant them.

To divide overcrowded plants in the ground or in containers, follow these simple steps. In mild-winter climates, it's best to divide spring- and summer-blooming plants in fall. Where winters are cold, divide plants earlier.

1 Lift the plant. Gently dig up the overcrowded plant, or ease it out of its container.

2 Divide the roots. Use your fingers to tease some soil from the rootball and loosen it slightly. Look for natural dividing points between clumps of stems where you can easily pull it apart. Or, as shown here, use a sharp tool to slice the plant into roughly equal sections, each with plenty of healthy-looking roots.

3 Replant the divisions. Plant each section in its own container or find a new spot for it in the garden. Water well.

PLANTS TO DIVIDE THIS WAY

Agapanthus	**Gaillardia**	**Nepeta**
Agastache	**Geranium**	**Rudbeckia**
Aster	**Helenium**	**Salvia**
Astilbe	**Heuchera**	**Scabiosa**
Bergenia	**Iberis**	**Sedum**
Brunnera	**Leucanthemum**	**Verbena**
Clivia	**Limonium**	

3

Refresh Crowded Plants

If a plant is crowded in its container, or if roots are creeping out the bottom, it's ready for roomier quarters.

Repotting can also help a plant that is growing poorly but has no sign of pests or disease. The best time to do this job is in early summer.

1 Use fresh potting soil. Select a new container that's an inch or two larger in width and depth than the current one. If the container has been used previously, clean it with a stiff brush and a solution of 1 part bleach mixed with 10 parts water. Rinse the container thoroughly. Fill about one-third of it with commercial potting mix.

2 Remove the plant from its old pot. If you can manage it, turn the container almost upside down and support the top of the soil with one hand. Shake slowly to dislodge the plant. If the rootball is stuck, try working a narrow trowel around the perimeter to dislodge it.

3 Loosen the roots. Examine the rootball. If you notice lots of thick roots circling around the rootball, cut them back by one-third. Gently tease the remaining roots out of the rootball and form into a loose bundle. If any roots are black or smelly, cut or pull them out.

4 Transfer to the new pot. Make sure you place the plant in the new container at its original depth. Fill in with the new soil mix and press gently. Give your plant a thorough, gentle watering to help roots settle in, and add a bit more mix if you see low spots.

Easy-Care Plants

If you are a busy gardener, easy-care plants are your best friends. Many thrive with little water once established, need minimal pruning to stay shapely, and don't drop lots of litter. They can get by with little fussing on your part. On the following pages are some outstanding choices.

Agapanthus

LILY-OF-THE-NILE
Agapanthus family (*Agapanthaceae*)
PERENNIALS FROM FLESHY RHIZOMES

✎ **ZONES 6–9, 12–24, H1, H2 FOR EVERGREEN KINDS; ZONES 4–9, 12–21 FOR DECIDUOUS KINDS**

☼ ◑ **FULL SUN; AFTERNOON SHADE IN HOTTEST AREAS**

◊ ◖ ◖ **LITTLE TO REGULAR WATER**

⚕ **TUBERS ARE TOXIC TO LIVESTOCK**

These South African natives are so trouble-free that they practically take care of themselves. They form fountain-like clumps of strap-shaped leaves that can be evergreen or deciduous. In summer, they send up spherical clusters of blue or white funnel-shaped flowers.

Species. The most common include the evergreen *A. africanus*, whose blue flowers rise 18 in., with 20 to 50 blooms per cluster; the deciduous *A. inapertus pendulus* 'Graskop', which forms 2-ft. clumps of leaves and sends up 3-ft. stems of gracefully drooping, violet-blue blossoms; and evergreen *A. praecox orientalis*, whose big clumps of broad, arching leaves produce 4-to-5-ft.-tall stems, each with up to 100 blue flowers. There are also white ('Albus'), double ('Flore Pleno'), and some with striped leaves. *A. p.* 'Variegatus' is variegated.

A. selections and hybrids. Look for 'Baby Pete' (6–9 in., blue), 'Peter Pan' (18-in. blue flowers on a 1-ft. clump), 'Tinkerbell' (18-in. blue flowers with white-edged leaves), and 'Rancho White' (18-in. white flowers). 'Blue Storm' and cold-tolerant 'Black Pantha' have especially deep blue flowers on 2½-ft. stalks. 'Midnight Blue' and 'Storm Cloud' also have extremely deep blue flowers; they grow 4 ft. tall. 'Ellamae', also deep blue, reaches 5 ft.

TIP In garden beds, mix agapanthus with other easy-care summer perennials, including pink-flowered *Amaryllis belladonna* and *Phlox paniculata*, and orange red-hot poker (*Kniphofia uvaria*).

Agapanthus africanus 'Queen Anne'

HOW TO GROW IT

Soil Best in loamy soil but will grow in heavy soils.

Planting Set it out from containers, spacing plants 1–1½ ft. apart, depending on variety size.

Water These plants flourish with regular water, but established plants can thrive without irrigation during prolonged dry periods in most areas. In the low desert, give them supplemental water.

Care notes Evergreen kinds need winter mulch in Zone 6. Bait for snails and slugs. Divide plants every 6 years or so.

Agastache

Mint family (*Lamiaceae*)
PERENNIALS

ZONES VARY BY SPECIES

FULL SUN OR PART SHADE

MODERATE WATER

Some gardeners grow these as much for the aroma of their foliage as for their tubular summer flowers, which hummingbirds love. Most kinds grow 2–3 ft. high and have upright stems packed with whorls of pink, purple, blue, red, or orange flowers that work easily into the garden and do well in containers.

A. aurantiaca. ORANGE HUMMINGBIRD MINT. Zones 3–24. From northern Mexico. Reaches 2½ ft. high and 2 ft. wide, with pink flowers fading to orange. 'Coronado' has yellow blooms suffused with orange. 'Apricot Sprite' grows 18 in. high.

A. cana. TEXAS HUMMINGBIRD MINT. Zones 2–24. From Texas, New Mexico. To 2–3 ft. high and 1½ ft. across. Blooms heavily, bearing reddish pink flowers that smell like bubble gum. 'Purple Pygmy' grows just 16 in. high.

A. hybrids. Zones 4–24. The most popular include 'Blue Fortune', to 3 ft. high and 1½ ft. wide, with powder blue flowers; 'Firebird', to 3 ft. high and 2 ft. wide, in coppery orange, coral pink, and red; the Nectar series (Apricot Nectar, Grape Nectar, Grapefruit Nectar, Orange Nectar, Raspberry Nectar), to 18 in. high and 15 in. wide; 'Purple Haze', to 3 ft. high and 2 ft. wide, with smoky purple flowers; 'Raspberry Summer', to 2½ ft. high and 2 ft. wide, with large spikes of dark pink flowers; and 'Summer Love', to 3 ft. high and 2 ft. wide, with large rose-purple flowers.

A. rugosa. KOREAN HUMMINGBIRD MINT. Zones 4–24. From Korea. Grows to 5 ft. tall and 2 ft. wide. Licorice-scented foliage is glossy green with a purple tinge; flowers are purplish blue. Tolerates wet winters. 'Golden Jubilee' grows 2–3 ft. high and 2 ft. wide, with yellow-green new growth.

A. rupestris. LICORICE MINT, SUNSET HYSSOP. Zones 1–24. From southern Arizona, northern Mexico. Grows to 2½ ft. high and 1½ ft. wide, and has narrow, fragrant gray-green leaves and spikes of orange flowers with lavender calyxes. 'Apache Sunset' has orange flowers, rose-purple buds.

Agastache **'Raspberry Summer'**

HOW TO GROW IT

Soil Loamy garden soil; good drainage essential for American species.

Planting Plant from containers as available in mild-winter areas, or plant in spring and summer where winters are cold.

Fertilizer Apply complete fertilizer at the beginning of the growing season.

Care notes Plants rebloom if deadheaded.

Aquilegia

COLUMBINE
Buttercup family *(Ranunculaceae)*
PERENNIALS

⬛ **ZONES VARY BY SPECIES**

☼ ◑ **FULL SUN OR PART SHADE**

💧 **REGULAR WATER**

Classic woodland flowers, columbines have foliage reminiscent of maidenhair fern *(Adiantum)* and delicate flowers in pastels, clear colors, and white. Upright plants range from 5 in. to 4 ft. tall, with slender, branching stems and erect or nodding flowers to 3 in. across, often with sepals and petals in contrasting colors; blooms usually have nectar-bearing spurs. Double-flowered types lack the delicacy of singles, but they make a bolder color mass. Blooms appear in spring and early summer.

A. chrysantha. GOLDEN COLUMBINE. Zones 1–24. Native to Arizona, New Mexico, and adjacent Mexico, this grows to 4 ft. tall and 2 ft. wide. Upright, soft yellow, 1½-to-3-in. flowers have slender, hooked spurs 2–2½ in. long. 'Yellow Queen' has golden yellow blooms.

A. coerulea (A. caerulea). ROCKY MOUNTAIN COLUMBINE. Zones A1–A3; 1–11, 14–24. This Rocky Mountain native (and state flower of Colorado) grows 1½–3 ft. high and 2 ft. wide. Blue-and-white flowers are erect, 2–3 in. across, with straight or spreading spurs to 2 in. long.

A. flabellata. Zones A2, A3; 1–9, 14–24. Japan. Grows 8–18 in. high and 1 ft. wide, with 1½-in.-long, nodding, two-toned flowers in lilac-blue and creamy white. The Cameo series is 4–8 in. high and has white flowers with blue, pink, or rose. 'Nana' grows 5 in. high.

A. hybrids. Zones A2, A3; 1–10, 14–24. These include graceful, long-spurred McKana hybrids (to 3 ft. high and 2 ft. wide); long-spurred red-and-white 'Crimson Star' (2 ft. high and wide); Biedermeier (1 ft. high and wide); Origami (16–18 in. high); and Winky (12–15 in. high).

Most need to be replaced every 3 or 4 years.

Aquilegia flabellata

HOW TO GROW IT

Soil Plants are not fussy about soil as long as it is well drained.

Planting Start these from nursery containers, or scatter seeds under tall trees in autumn.

Fertilizer Give hybrid kinds complete fertilizer as growth starts in spring.

Care notes Deadhead for repeat bloom, or let spent flowers form seed capsules and self-sow.

Asparagus, ornamental

Asparagus family *(Asparagaceae)*
PERENNIALS, SHRUBS, OR VINES

ZONES 12–24; H1, H2; EXCEPT AS NOTED

FULL SUN OR PART SHADE

REGULAR WATER

These ornamentals are grown mostly for their foliage, but some produce small, fragrant flowers and colorful berries. The green foliage sprays are made up of short branches that are needlelike in some types, broader in others. The true leaves are inconspicuous.

The plants thrive in sun in cool-summer climates and look greenest in part shade; they turn yellow in dense shade. All survive light frost. If tops are frosted, plants may regrow from roots.

A. densiflorus. The species is most commonly known through the following forms, both good in containers.

'Myers' *(A. meyeri, A. myersii).* MYERS ASPARAGUS, FOXTAIL FERN. Many stiffly upright stems reach 2 ft. or more, densely clothed with needlelike deep green "leaves" reminiscent of foxtails. Slowly forms a 3-to-4-ft.-wide clump.

'Sprengeri' *(A. sprengeri).* SPRENGER ASPARAGUS. Arching or drooping stems 3–6 ft. long are loosely clothed in shiny, bright green, needlelike "leaves." Berries are bright red. Popular for hanging baskets. Can climb a trellis by means of small hooked prickles. Tolerates poor soil and is slightly hardier than 'Myers'. A form sold as 'Sprengeri Compacta' or *A. sarmentosus* 'Compacta' is denser, with shorter stems.

A. retrofractus (A. macowanii). Zones 12–24. This erect, shrubby, slightly climbing plant is very tender. Slender, silvery gray stems grow slowly to 8–10 ft. tall. Fluffy, rich green tufts; clusters of small white flowers. Handsome in containers.

A. setaceus (A. plumosus). ASPARAGUS FERN. This branching woody vine climbs by wiry, spiny stems to 10–20 ft. Tiny threadlike branches form feathery dark green sprays that resemble fern fronds. Tiny white flowers; purple-black berries. Useful as a screen against walls and fences. Dwarf 'Nanus' is good in containers. 'Pyramidalis' has an upswept, windblown look and is less vigorous than the species.

Asparagus densiflorus **'Myers'**

HOW TO GROW IT

Soil Plant in well-drained soil amended with peat moss or ground bark.

Planting Plant from containers in spring after danger of frost has passed.

Fertilizer Apply complete fertilizer in spring.

Water Fleshy roots sustain plants for some time without water, but they grow better when watered regularly.

Care notes Trim out old shoots to make room for new growth.

Aster

Sunflower family *(Asteraceae)*
PERENNIALS

⚡ ZONES 1–24, EXCEPT AS NOTED

☼ FULL SUN, EXCEPT AS NOTED

⚫ REGULAR WATER, EXCEPT AS NOTED

Standouts in the summer-to-fall garden, asters come in trademark blue, white, red, pink, lavender, and purple, mostly with yellow centers. They are invaluable in large borders, among shrubs, and in containers.

A word about aster names. Don't confuse the perennial asters on this list with China aster *(Callistephus chinensis)*, which is a distantly related annual. Also, the nomenclature of asters is disputed and somewhat confused; you might find many of these varieties sold under different botanical names (such as *Symphyotrichum*). Finally, "Michaelmas daisy" loosely refers to any fall-flowering aster but more properly applies only to *A. novi-belgii*. The name derives from the English feast day of St. Michael the archangel, which comes on September 29, when many asters are at peak bloom.

A. dumosus 'Sapphire'. This selection of a species from the eastern United States grows 1–1½ ft. high and 1½–2 ft. wide. A compact, dense plant that blooms profusely in late summer and autumn; flowers are lilac-blue. Good in containers.

A. ericoides prostratus 'Snow Flurry'. Large white daisies rise above an 18-in., compact mound of foliage in fall. Doesn't require staking and needs only moderate water.

A. × frikartii 'Mönch'. Zones 2b–24. This hybrid forms loose mounds 2 ft. high and wide, with dark green, hairy leaves and abundant lavender-blue, 2½-in. single flowers; excellent cut. Blooms early summer to fall—nearly all year in mild climates if deadheaded. This variety is good for cutting. It is named for its Swiss breeder, Frikart, and an alpine peak.

A. laevis. SMOOTH ASTER. Zones 1–10, 14–21. Native to central and eastern North America. Grows 3½ ft. high, 1½ ft. wide, with smooth, mildew-free foliage and clustered deep purplish blue, 1-in. flower heads. 'Bluebird' is one of the best; at 4 ft. tall, it belongs at the back of the perennial border.

A. lateriflorus. Zones 1–10, 14–21. This North American species grows to 4 ft. tall and wide. Most selections are in the 2-ft. range, with profuse branching, tiny leaves, and a haze of small purplish pink flowers.

Aster novae-angliae 'Alma Potschke'

Autumn foliage is coppery purplish red. 'Lady in Black' and 'Prince' have blackish purple stems and leaves; blooms are white with a red center. Part shade.

A. novae-angliae. NEW ENGLAND ASTER. Native east of the Rockies. To 3–5 ft. tall and nearly as wide, with hairy leaves to 5 in. long. Violet-blue flowers are 2 in. wide, with selections in white, pink, near-red, and deep purple. 'Alma Potschke' bears salmon-pink single blooms on 2-to-4-ft. stems in late summer, early fall. 'Purple Dome' is mildew-resistant, to 1½ ft. high. Full sun or part shade.

A. novi-belgii. NEW YORK ASTER, MICHAELMAS DAISY. Native to eastern North America. Grows to 4 ft. tall and 3 ft. wide, with full clusters of bright blue-violet flowers and smooth leaves to 5 in. long. Selections vary from less than a foot high to over 4 ft., with flowers in

Aster × frikartii

The Versatility of Asters

Like many American natives, asters got their breeding in Europe, and then came back to grace our gardens. Here are three strategies for getting the most out of these versatile perennials.

STRETCH THEM. Asters make wonderful extended borders that recall their roadside heritage—long strips along curving walkways, for example. Use a single color for this, and choose an aster variety that doesn't have to be staked.

MASS THEM. Try planting several colors of the same species and similar size together in a bed or planting block. Shades of pink, white, blue, and purple are beautiful together.

MIX THEM. Large clumps of blue or purple asters make striking companions for tall ornamental grasses, such as *Miscanthus sinensis* 'Morning Light', and gray-leafed plants, like *Artemisia* 'Powis Castle'. They also serve as useful temporary fillers in newly planted shrub beds. As the shrubs grow, just remove the asters.

white, cream, blue, lavender, purple, rose, and pink. Two good ones are 'Professor Anton Kippenberg' (lavender-blue, semidouble, 15 in. high) and 'Winston S. Churchill' (dark red, double, 2 ft. high). This species is good for cutting.

A. **'Triumph'.** This compact summer-flowering hybrid grows about 1 ft. high, 15 in. wide, with abundant blue-purple flowers. Its size makes it perfect for containers.

A. **'Wood's Blue', 'Wood's Pink', 'Wood's Purple'.** Each of the plants in this mildew-resistant, hybrid series grows about 15 in. high and wide. All are well suited, alone or in combination, for containers.

HOW TO GROW IT

Soil Asters adapt to most soils, but growth is most luxuriant in fertile soil; add organic matter at planting time.

Planting Plant from nursery containers as early as you can get them in spring or summer.

Fertilizer Apply complete controlled-release fertilizer at planting time.

Care notes Taller kinds may be cut back by half in late spring to encourage bushiness; very tall asters may need staking.

TIP If you've never grown asters, start with A. × *frikartii* 'Mönch', a very old hybrid. Many think it is the best aster available.

Astilbe × arendsii

FALSE SPIREA
Saxifrage family *(Saxifragaceae)*
PERENNIALS

✎ **ZONES A2, A3; 1–7, 14–17; SHORT-LIVED IN ZONES 8, 9, 18–24**

☀ ☽ **FULL SUN IN COOLER CLIMATES ONLY**

💧 **REGULAR WATER**

Astilbes are perfect for shady perennial borders, woodland path edges, and containers. Their flowers, which bloom from late spring through summer, are light and airy. The small white, pink, or red blooms are carried in graceful, branching, feathery clusters on wiry stems from 1 to 5 ft. tall. Most plants grow 2–3 ft. high and wide. Leaves are typically divided into several leaflets, for a soft, textural look.

In cool-summer climates, plants can withstand full sun with regular water. Survival in coldest areas (Zones 1a, 1b, 2a) depends on snow cover or winter mulch.

Most astilbes sold belong to the *A.* × *arendsii* hybrid group or are sold as such. The plants differ chiefly in technical details. The following are some of the best.

'Bressingham Beauty'. Midseason. Pink plumes, 3 ft.

'Bridal Veil'. Midseason to late. Full white plumes, 3 ft. high.

Color Flash series. Midseason. Pink flowers and colorful foliage; about 2 ft. high. Leaves gradually turn from green to burgundy. 'Color Flash Lime' has light green foliage that picks up bright yellow tones.

'Fanal'. Early. Blood red flowers, bronzy foliage, 1½–2½ ft. high.

'Peach Blossom'. Midseason. Light salmon-pink, 2 ft. high.

'Rheinland'. Early. Deep pink, 2–2½ ft. high.

'Younique'. Midseason. White, 20 in. high.

Among excellent species, the Chinese *A. chinensis* resembles *A.* × *arendsii* hybrids but generally blooms in late summer, grows taller, and tolerates dryness a little better. Examples include 'Finale', with pink blooms, to 20 in. high, and the Visions series, in lavender-purple, pink, and reddish purple, to 15 in. high. *A. c. pumila* has low mats of leaves topped by 1-ft.-high, lilac-pink flower clusters. *A. c. taquetii* 'Superba' has bright pinkish purple flowers in spikelike clusters 4–5 ft. tall.

Astilbe × *arendsii* **'Fanal'**

HOW TO GROW IT

Soil Astilbes need moist (but not boggy), rich soil containing ample humus.

Planting Set out from nursery containers as early as you can get the plants.

Fertilizer Apply controlled-release fertilizer in spring, and top dress with a mulch of finished compost. Apply liquid fertilizer to containerized astilbes every 2 weeks during the growing season.

Care notes Cut off faded flowering stems, and divide clumps every 4 or 5 years.

Bergenia

Saxifrage family *(Saxifragaceae)*
PERENNIALS

✎ **ZONES A1–A3; 1–9, 12–24; EXCEPT AS NOTED**

☀ ◐ ● **FULL SUN IN MILD-SUMMER CLIMATES; OTHERWISE, PART OR FULL SHADE**

💧 **MODERATE WATER**

Early bloom and big evergreen (except in the coldest climates) leaves make bergenia a staple of the spring garden. Foliage clumps usually reach 12–18 in. high, with nodding clusters of pink, white, purple, or red flowers on thick stalks that rise above the leaves.

Try bergenias in borders or as groundcovers.

B. ciliata (B. ligulata). FRILLY BERGENIA. Zones 5–9, 14–24. A choice plant, but this one is more tender than others: foliage and flowers are damaged in hard frosts, but it will survive 0°F (–18°C). Lustrous light green, nearly round leaves to 1 ft. across, smooth edged but fringed with soft hairs; bronzy when new. White, rose, or purplish flowers.

B. cordifolia. HEARTLEAF BERGENIA. Glossy, roundish leaves are heart-shaped at base, with wavy, toothed edges. Bears rose or lilac flowers in pendulous clusters. 'Tubby Andrews' has leaves splashed with golden yellow; flowers are pink. 'Winterglut' ('Winter Glow') has bright red flowers and leathery green leaves that turn reddish bronze in fall and winter.

B. crassifolia. WINTER-BLOOMING BERGENIA. Dark green, 8-in.-wide leaves have wavy, sparsely toothed edges. Rose, lilac, or purple flowers form dense clusters on erect stems. Blooms midwinter to early spring, depending on climate.

B. hybrids. Some of the best are of English or German origin.

'Abendglut' ('Evening Glow'). Dark red flowers and dark reddish leaves with crimped edges.

'Bressingham Ruby'. Rose-red blooms rise over green leaves that turn bronzy purple in winter.

'Bressingham White'. White flowers.

'Dragonfly'. Small (10 in. high), narrow-leafed plant with pink blooms, purple-tinged winter leaves.

'Herbstblute' ('Autumn Glory'). Leaves turn purplish in fall, when it may rebloom.

'Morning Red' ('Morgenrote'). Bronzy leaves, dark red flowers.

'Silberlicht' ('Silver Light'). Large, slightly toothed leaves and white blossoms.

Bergenia 'Abendglut'

HOW TO GROW IT

Soil Bergenias tolerate poor soil but do better in good soil.

Planting Plant 1½ ft. apart from nursery containers or divisions.

Fertilizer Apply regular fertilizer after bloom.

Water Tolerant of some drought, these do better with moderate watering.

Care notes Divide crowded clumps in late winter or early spring.

Brunnera macrophylla

BUGLOSS
Borage family *(Boraginaceae)*
PERENNIAL

🌱 **ZONES 1–24**

☀ ◑ **FULL SUN IN COOLER CLIMATES ONLY**

💧 **REGULAR WATER**

Probably grown more for foliage than for flowers, these big-leafed woodland plants thrive in the rich organic soil under tall trees and shrubs. They grow in clumps 1½ ft. high and 2 ft. wide; leaves are heart-shaped and dark green. Airy clusters of tiny, yellow-centered, clear blue flowers look like related forget-me-nots *(Myosotis)*. Variegated kinds are subject to leaf scorching in hot sun.

Brunnera clumps expand slowly from ever-extending roots (but not aggressively enough to be a problem). Where soil is moist, summers cool, and the climate mild, plants may self-sow and naturalize.

Besides the green species, look for the following, which are more widely sold.

'Diane's Gold'. A beautiful golden green that seems to glow in shade.

'Jack Frost'. Perhaps the most widely sold, has silvery leaves veined and bordered in green.

'Langtrees'. Has a necklace of white marks penciled around the inside of each leaf. Doesn't revert to all green, as do some other variegated forms.

'Looking Glass'. Leaves are nearly white.

Brunnera works well with heucheras, hostas, and similar woodland plants, freely self-sowing once established.

TIP When brunnera is grown in shade, spring blooms keep coming into summer.

Brunnera macrophylla **'Jack Frost'**

HOW TO GROW IT

Soil Needs well-drained, moisture-retentive soil.

Planting Though this is most commonly planted from nursery containers, it is also relatively easy from seeds. Just put the seeds in the freezer for a month before sowing to increase germination.

Fertilizer Fertilize once at the beginning of the season, and again after bloom.

Water Brunnera performs best if roots are never allowed to dry out completely.

Care notes Increase by dividing clumps in fall.

Clivia miniata

Amaryllis family (*Amaryllidaceae*)
PERENNIAL FROM TUBEROUS RHIZOMES

✎ **ZONES 12–17, 19–24 (SEE BELOW); H1, H2; OR INDOORS**

◑ ● **PART TO FULL SHADE; BRIGHT INDIRECT LIGHT**

💧 **REGULAR WATER**

Clivia miniata

Brilliant clusters of funnel-shaped orange flowers on 2-ft. stalks rise from these impressive, dense clumps of dark green, strap-shaped evergreen leaves. Excellent shade plants, they thrive in garden borders, beds, or (especially) containers. The flowering period ranges from early winter to midspring, but most are spring-bloomers. Ornamental berries follow flowers; they are orange in orange-flowered plants, yellow in yellow-flowered selections.

French and Belgian hybrids have very wide leaves and yellow to deep red-orange blooms on thick, rigid stalks. 'Flame' is an exceptionally hot orange-red. Solomone hybrids come in yellow, cream, red, and pastel shades. There are also varieties with variegated leaves. 'San Marcos Yellow' has clear yellow blooms.

Clivias grow best in relatively frost-free areas or well-protected parts of garden; mix them with azaleas, ferns, other shade plants. Temperatures lower than 30°F to 25°F (–1°C to –4°C) will damage them. In areas too cold for year-round outdoor culture, grow clivias in pots; then move them to sheltered locations or bring them indoors (and water sparingly) in winter. Plants bloom best with restricted roots and suffer from repotting, so don't repot unless top growth and bloom are declining.

HOW TO GROW IT

Soil In garden beds, amend soil with organic matter before planting. In containers, use potting mix with good drainage.

Planting Set the rhizomes 1½–2 ft. apart, then let the clumps grow undisturbed for years.

Fertilizer Plants grow well in the ground with just occasional fertilizing. Container plants bloom best with weekly feedings of liquid fertilizer from first appearance of flower buds to the end of bloom.

Water Supply regular irrigation when new growth appears, but back off after flowering and on through summer and winter.

Care notes Bait for slugs and snails.

TIP Clivia flowers have variable fragrance: give them the sniff test before you buy.

Erysimum hybrids

WALLFLOWER
Cabbage family (*Brassicaceae*)
PERENNIALS

✎ ZONES 4–9, 14–24, EXCEPT AS NOTED

☼ ◐ FULL SUN OR LIGHT SHADE

◌ MODERATE WATER

These delightful spring-bloomers all have the typical clustered four-petaled flowers that give the crucifers (meaning "cross-shaped") their name, but their habits and uses differ widely. Some are scented; most make good cut flowers. Many excellent choices are available.

'Apricot Twist'. Purple buds give way to fragrant, yellow-orange to deep orange flowers. To 2 ft. high and wide.

'Bowles Mauve'. Grows to 3 ft. high and 4 ft. wide, with narrow gray-green leaves held on erect stems, each topped by a 1½-ft.-long, narrow, spikelike cluster of mauve flowers. In areas with cool summers and mild winters, bloom is practically continual; elsewhere, plants bloom from winter through spring. Often short-lived.

'Fragrant Star'. Variegated leaves and fragrant yellow flowers arise from chocolate purple buds. Sterile flowers guarantee extra-long bloom. Compact growth 1½ ft. high, 2 ft. wide.

'Fragrant Sunshine'. Like 'Fragrant Star', but with all-green foliage.

'Glow Orange'. Grows to 12 in. high, 15 in. wide, with honey-scented orange flowers in early spring.

'Pastel Patchwork'. Grows 16 in. high, 14 in. wide, with fragrant flowers in pastel shades of lilac, yellow, and orange. Blooms spring and fall, nearly all year in mild climates.

'Rysi Bronze'. Grows 18 in. high and wide, with fragrant yellow flowers flushed with orange. Blooms spring into summer.

'Rysi Gold'. Like 'Rysi Bronze', but with clear golden yellow flowers.

'Wenlock Beauty'. To 2 ft. high and wide, with springtime flowers varying from buff to purple in a single spike.

There are also a few excellent varieties selected from species. One of the most popular is *E. linifolium* 'Variegatum' (Zones 4–6, 14–24), with shrubby growth to 2 ft. high, 2–3 ft. wide. It is prized for its narrow, 3½-in.-long leaves, which are gray-green and edged in creamy white. Mauve flowers about ½ in. wide bloom from spring to fall.

Erysimum **'Fragrant Star'**

HOW TO GROW IT

Soil These tolerate lean soil as long as drainage is good.

Planting Usually sold in full bloom; plant as soon as available.

Water After the first year's irrigation, plants develop some drought tolerance.

Care notes Deadheading encourages continued bloom.

Euphorbia characias

Spurge family *(Euphorbiaceae)*
PERENNIAL

🖊 **ZONES 4–24, EXCEPT AS NOTED**

☼ **FULL SUN, EXCEPT AS NOTED**

💧 **MODERATE WATER**

◊ **SAP IS IRRITATING OR POISONOUS**

For gardens, this Mediterranean native is the most popular among 2,000 species. Upright stems crowded with narrow blue-green leaves form a dome-shaped bush 4 ft. tall and wide. Chartreuse or lime green flowers in dense, round to cylindrical clusters appear in late winter, early spring. Color holds with only slight fading until seeds ripen. Among most euphorbias, what looks like a flower is technically a cyathium, a structure (unique to this genus) that consists of fused bracts that form a cup around the very small true flowers.

Euphorbias have milky white sap that is irritating on skin contact and toxic if ingested (degree of irritation or toxicity varies, depending on species). Wear gloves when pruning or working near these plants, and be careful not to get the sap in your eyes. Before using cut flowers in arrangements, dip stems in boiling water or hold in a flame for a few seconds to prevent sap bleed.

All of the following are fairly drought-resistant.

'Black Pearl'. Has large inflorescences; cyathia have darkest red, nearly black nectar glands.

'Humpty Dumpty'. A short (to 2½ ft. high), vigorous selection.

'Portuguese Velvet'. Has blue-gray, lightly hairy leaves and large bronzy golden inflorescences.

'Tasmanian Tiger'. Grows 3 ft. high and wide, with leaves and flower bracts edged in white.

E. c. wulfenii (E. wulfenii), the most commonly grown form, has broader clusters of yellow flowers. 'Lambrook Gold' is choice, with glowing yellow blooms.

E. × martini (Zones 3–24) is a hybrid with *E. amygdaloides*. Usually misspelled as *E. × martinii*. Grows 2–3 ft. high and wide, with dense clusters of brown-centered chartreuse flowers in late winter, spring. Evergreen leaves are often tinged purple when young. Stems are red in winter. 'Red Martin' has leaves held nearly upright, showing off red color of stems and new foliage. Full sun or light shade. Fairly drought-resistant.

Euphorbia characias wulfenii

HOW TO GROW IT

Planting Plant in spring. Goes well with red tulips that flower at the same time.

Care notes When stalks turn yellow after seeds ripen, they should be cut out at the base, since new shoots have already made growth for next year's flowers.

Gaillardia × grandiflora

BLANKET FLOWER
Sunflower family (*Asteraceae*)
PERENNIAL

🌿 **ZONES 1–24; H1, H2**

☼ **FULL SUN**

💧 **MODERATE WATER**

Beloved for their warm, often two-toned flowers and exceptionally long period of bloom, these are hybrids between *G. aristata* (a perennial) and *G. pulchella* (an annual). Plants grow 2–4 ft. tall, 1½ ft. wide, with gray-green foliage and single or double daisylike flowers 3–4 in. across that appear in summer and fall. Flower color range includes various shades of red and yellow, with orange or maroon bands.

Plants thrive in heat and attract butterflies. Following are some of the best.

'Arizona Sun', about 10 in. high, has orange-red petals with yellow tips. 'Goblin' grows 1 ft. high, with large deep red flowers bordered in yellow. 'Goblin Yellow' is similar but has yellow blooms. 'Mesa Yellow' is compact and uniform at 1½ ft. high, with solid yellow flowers that bloom 2–3 weeks earlier than the others listed here. Also about 1½ ft. high are 'Fanfare', with a burgundy center and trumpet-shaped orange petals tipped in yellow, and 'Oranges and Lemons', with orange centers and yellow-tipped orange petals. In the 2-ft.-high range are 'Dazzler', with bright red petals tipped in yellow; 'Frenzy', with rich red, yellow-tipped tubular petals; 'Mandarin', with mahogany centers and flame orange, yellow-tipped petals; and 'Tizzy', with trumpet-shaped petals of pinkish orange. Among 2½-ft.-high varieties are 'Amber Wheels', with frilled, golden yellow, red-centered flowers; deep red 'Burgunder'; and pure orange 'Tokajer'.

TIP Where native soil is poor-draining, heavy clay, grow these in raised beds, on mounds of lighter topsoil, or in containers.

Gaillardia × *grandiflora* 'Frenzy'

HOW TO GROW IT

Soil Plants need soil that drains well and is not too rich.

Planting Set out plants anytime, or start seeds in spring for summer-to-fall bloom.

Care notes These thrive in heat. In mild climates, grow them against south-facing walls.

Geranium

CRANESBILL
Geranium family (*Geraniaceae*)
PERENNIALS

◪ **ZONES VARY BY TYPE**

☼ ◖ **AFTERNOON SHADE IN HOTTEST CLIMATES**

⬤ **REGULAR WATER**

Easy and deer-proof, true geraniums aren't to be confused with bright-flowered, fleshy-leafed *Pelargonium*, also called geranium. True geraniums can take more cold. They grow in mounded or trailing forms, with flowers in blue, purple, magenta, pink, and white. Beaklike fruit accounts for the common name, "cranesbill." The leaves are roundish or kidney-shaped, lobed or deeply cut. Cool- and mild-summer regions are best.

Among hundreds of species and hybrids, here are some excellent choices.

'Brookside'. Zones 2b–9, 14–24. To 2½ ft. high and as wide, with deeply serrated, 3-in.-wide leaves. Plant is covered from late spring into summer with bowl-shaped flowers to 2 in. across. Long-lasting blooms are rich, deep blue with pale centers and pink veins. 'Orion' has larger, bluer flowers. Cut back both after flowering for repeat bloom.

'Johnson's Blue'. Zones A2, A3; 2–9, 14–24. Mounds 1½–2 ft. wide and spreads by rhizomes; excellent summer groundcover. Roundish veined leaves have deeply divided lobes. Abundant 2-in., blue-violet flowers in loose clusters from spring to fall.

'Patricia'. Zones 2–9, 14–24. Durable plants reach 2½ ft. high and 3 ft. wide, with deeply lobed and veined leaves. Flowers, to 1½ in. wide, are warm reddish magenta with deep burgundy veins and centers. Blooms spring to late summer. Cut back after first flush of bloom for fresh growth and flowers.

'Rozanne'. Zones 2–11, 14–24. Plants mound 1½–2 ft. high and spread a little wider, with deeply lobed, dark green leaves; foliage flushes red in fall. Stunning flowers, to 2½ in. wide, are rich violet-blue with a large white eye. Blooms all summer and into autumn, doing especially well in warm, sunny spots. For freshest spring growth, cut back plants in late fall.

'Tiny Monster'. Zones A3; 2–9, 14–21. This spreading groundcover grows 10 in. high, to 24 in. wide, producing sterile pink flowers with red veins from late spring through late summer. Red to bronzy purple fall color.

Geranium **'Johnson's Blue'**

HOW TO GROW IT

Planting Plant with each variety's mature width in mind. Many will self-sow.

Care notes When crowded clumps decline after many years, divide in early spring.

Gunnera tinctoria

Gunnera family *(Gunneraceae)*
PERENNIAL

ZONES 4–6, 14–17, 20–24

PART SHADE

AMPLE WATER

It's easy to imagine this huge-leafed Chilean native growing among the dinosaurs. Big, bold, awe-inspiring clumps grow 8 ft. tall and as wide or wider. Leaves are cupped, flaring, and conspicuously veined, with lobed, toothed, somewhat frilled margins. And they're huge— 4–8 ft. wide, rising on 4-to-6-ft.-long, hair-covered stalks. New sets of leaves grow each spring. In mild-winter areas, old leaves remain green for more than a year; elsewhere, leaves die back completely in winter. Flower clusters to 1½ ft. long resemble corncobs clustered at the plant's base. Tiny fruits are red.

Gunneras grow best where water is abundant and constant.

A closely related species, *G. manicata*, is native to Brazil and Colombia. It takes the same growing conditions as *G. tinctoria* and varies only in the details. Leaves carried fairly horizontally. Spinelike hairs on leafstalks and leaf ribs are red. Leaf lobes are flatter than those of *G. tinctoria* and do not have frilled margins.

HOW TO GROW IT

Soil The plant needs soil rich in nutrients and organic material.

Fertilizer Feed three times a year, beginning when new growth starts, to keep leaves maximum size.

Water Gunneras must have abundant water to support their huge leaves. Even when that is supplied, give plants overhead sprinkling when humidity is low or drying winds occur.

Gunnera tinctoria

TIP Use plants where they can be the focal point in summer—beside a pool or dominating a bed of low, finely textured groundcover.

Helenium

SNEEZEWEED
Sunflower family (*Asteraceae*)
PERENNIALS

⚡ **ZONES 1–24, EXCEPT AS NOTED**

☀ **FULL SUN**

💧 **REGULAR WATER**

These coarse-looking, late-summer-to-fall daisies are especially effective in wild gardens. They make good companions for ornamental grasses, for example. Numerous leafy stems hold daisylike, typically brown-centered blossoms with yellow, orange, red, or coppery rays. All are good cut flowers.

Most heleniums are hybrids, including most of those sold under the name *H. autumnale*. The true native species grows to 5 ft. tall and 1½ ft. wide, with yellow, 2-in.-wide flowers. The hybrids have 2-to-3-in. flowers in shades of yellow, orange, red, rust, copper, and blends of these colors.

Tall types (4–5 ft. tall, 2 ft. wide) include 'Baudirektor Linne', brownish red with a brown center; 'Butterpat', light yellow with a deeper yellow center; 'Mardi Gras', yellow splashed with red and orange, and a brown center; and 'Waldtraut', with coppery brown rays around a dark central disk. Compact varieties (about 3 ft. high, 1½ ft. wide) include 'Coppelia', copper-orange with a brown disk; 'Crimson Beauty', dusky deep red with a brown disk; 'Double Trouble', fully double, bright yellow blooms; 'Moerheim Beauty', coppery red with a brown center; 'Rubinzwerg', rusty red with a yellow-and-brown center; and 'Wyndley', butter yellow with a yellow-brown central disk.

Some nurseries also offer a West Coast native called *H. bigelovii* (Zones 1–10, 14–24). From California and Oregon, it grows 2–3 ft. high, 1 ft. wide. Yellow blossoms to 2½ in. across have reflexed, or swept back, rays. Compact, free-flowering forms include 'The Bishop' and 'Tip Top'.

Helenium **'Double Trouble'**

HOW TO GROW IT

Planting These do best in warm parts of the garden—especially in mild-summer areas.

Care notes Trim off faded blossoms to encourage long bloom. Taller kinds require staking and are best in the back of borders; to avoid staking, cut plants back in midsummer to promote shorter, bushier growth. All need division and replanting every few years.

Helleborus

HELLEBORE
Buttercup family *(Ranunculaceae)*
PERENNIALS

✎ ZONES VARY BY TYPE

◐ ● PART OR FULL SHADE

◖ REGULAR WATER, EXCEPT AS NOTED

◊ ALL PARTS ARE POISONOUS IF INGESTED

Evergreen leaves, a low profile, and extended winter-to-spring bloom give hellebores a unique niche in the garden. Flowers can be single or double, open or cup-shaped, outward facing or drooping; they consist of a ring of petal-like sepals ranging from white and green through pink and red to deep purple (rarely yellow). Float flowers in water; or, to use in arrangements, first seal cut stem ends in a flame or by briefly dipping in boiling water.

Mass hellebores in light shade or use as a groundcover. Deer-proof.

H. × ballardiae. Zones 3–7, 14–24. Grows 1–1½ ft. high and 2 ft. wide, with 2½-in.-wide, outward-facing blooms on deep red stems. 'Cinnamon Snow' has dark green leaves and white flowers with warm rose and cinnamon tones. 'Pink Frost' has gray-green leaves with silvery veins; its flowers combine pale pink and rose.

H. × hybridus. Zones 2b–10, 14–24. Leaves have no obvious stems. Basal leaves have sharply toothed leaflets, branched flowering stems to 1 ft. high. Flowers are 2–4 in. wide. Some are sold under the breeder's name, such as Ballard's Group, which has flowers in several colors. Others are sold as color strains, such as Sunshine selections (white, pink, yellow, or red flowers), Royal Heritage strain (pink, purple, maroon, or white blooms), and Winter Queen mix (white, pink, maroon, or spotted flowers). Others, such as the double-flowered Party Dress group, are grouped by form. Moderate to regular water.

H. 'Ivory Prince'. Zones 2–9, 14–17. Grows 1 ft. high, 1½–2 ft. wide; stemless, dark green leaves are divided into several lobes with a few large teeth. Red buds open into ivory-white flowers that take on rose and chartreuse tones as they age.

Helleborus **Party Dress**

HOW TO GROW IT

Soil Plant in well-drained soil amended with plenty of organic matter. Plants prefer somewhat alkaline soil but also grow well in neutral to slightly acid conditions.

Planting Set out plants in autumn. Be gentle; hellebore roots don't like being disturbed. May self-sow; transplant seedlings in early spring.

Fertilizer Feed once or twice a year.

Care notes Shear off tattered old leaves in autumn.

Heuchera

CORAL BELLS, ALUM ROOT
Saxifrage family *(Saxifragaceae)*
PERENNIALS

✎ **ZONES 1–9, 14–24**

☀ ◑ **FULL SUN IN COOLER CLIMATES ONLY**

◐ ● **MODERATE TO REGULAR WATER**

Heucheras come in an array of sizes, foliage, and flower colors that work as well among other perennials as in containers, where they excel as fillers. Form is compact and mounding, with roundish, lobed, or scalloped evergreen leaves. Slender, wiry, 1-to-3-ft. stems bear loose clusters of tiny, nodding, bell-shaped flowers that last long in cut arrangements. Floral color range includes white, green, and red to pink shades. Bloom time varies from early spring to late summer, even into autumn.

The following varieties have been selected for their marvelously colored and sometimes ruffled foliage. All form mounds about 1½ ft. high and not quite as wide. Tiny summer flowers are held on thin stalks to 2–3 ft. high and are white to cream unless noted.

'Amethyst Myst'. Deep burgundy leaves age to silver with dark purple veins. Often short-lived in warm-summer areas.

'Caramel'. Leaves emerge dusky red and mature through apricot tones to golden yellow.

'Citronelle'. Leaves are chartreuse to bright lemon yellow.

'Crimson Curls'. Deep red, ruffled leaves, fading to gray-green in summer.

'Georgia Peach'. Leaves emerge peachy orange and age through red tones to rosy purple; dark veins and a silvery sheen.

'Green Spice'. Silver-gray leaves with dark green or purple veins.

'Marmalade'. Ruffled leaves emerge bright red and age to shades of orange and rich reddish brown; deep red flowers.

'Miracle'. Leaves emerge chartreuse with central splotches of burgundy and mature to brick red thinly edged in gold. Pale pink flowers.

'Obsidian'. Foliage deepest burgundy, nearly black, with glossy sheen.

'Peach Flambé'. Bright leaves of apricot to peach take on purple tones in winter.

'Plum Pudding'. Plum purple leaves with a silvery variegation and dark purple veins.

Heuchera **'Georgia Peach'**

'Silver Scrolls'. Silvery leaves with dark purple veins.

'Southern Comfort'. Very large (9 in.) leaves are peachy orange when new, taking on copper and amber tones as they age.

'Stormy Seas'. Leaves have tones of silver, lavender, and pewter, with red undersides on curly edges.

HOW TO GROW IT

Soil All do best in humus-rich soil; need good drainage.

Fertilizer Apply complete fertilizer in spring to encourage long flowering.

Care notes Divide clumps every 3 to 4 years in spring (fall in mild-winter climates).

Iberis sempervirens

EVERGREEN CANDYTUFT
Cabbage family (*Brassicaceae*)
PERENNIAL

✔ **ZONES 1–24**

☼ ☽ **FULL SUN OR PART SHADE**

💧 **REGULAR WATER**

Those sheets of pure white blossoms that light up gardens from early spring to summer are nearly always evergreen candytuft. Growing 12 in. (sometimes 18 in.) high, these spread about as wide. Narrow, shiny dark green leaves are attractive all year. Native to southern and western Europe, they thrive in containers and borders and have stems long enough for cutting. They also make fine edgings and small-scale groundcovers.

Lower, more compact varieties include 'Alexander's White', a 6-in.-high plant with fine-textured foliage; 'Little Gem', 4–6 in. high; and 'Purity', 6–12 in. high and wide spreading. 'Snowflake', 4–12 in. high and 1½–3 ft. wide, has broader, more leathery leaves than the species; it also has larger flowers in larger clusters on shorter stems. It is extremely showy in spring, with sporadic bloom through summer and fall. 'Snow White' grows into a 1-by-2-ft. mound. Early-flowering, upright 'Tahoe' grows to 1 ft. high and wide.

A pair of foot-high, spreading hybrids bring color into the mix: 'Absolutely Amethyst' is pinkish purple; 'Masterpiece' has 3-in. white flowers with pink centers.

HOW TO GROW IT

Planting Set these out in spring or fall.

Care notes Fastidious gardeners shear these lightly after bloom to stimulate new growth.

Iberis sempervirens

TIP Use candytuft to cool off the brilliant colors of neighboring aubrieta, basket of gold, *Lithodora diffusa*, and spring-flowering bulbs.

Leucanthemum × superbum

SHASTA DAISY
Sunflower family (*Asteraceae*)
PERENNIAL

☀ **ZONES A1–A3; 1–24; H1**

☀ ☽ **FULL SUN OR LIGHT SHADE**

💧 **MODERATE WATER**

Originally bred by Luther Burbank, and formerly sold as *Chrysanthemum maximum,* this is one of the most successful perennials ever. Plants grow 2–4 ft. tall, 2–3 ft. wide, with abundant white daisies in summer. Burbank's original hybrid, with coarse, leathery leaves and gold-centered, 2-to-4-in.-wide white flowers, has been largely superseded by longer-blooming varieties with larger, better-formed flowers. All bloom in summer; some start in late spring and continue into fall. All are splendid in borders and as cut flowers.

Among those that produce standard, single white flowers, try 'Alaska', 'Becky', or 'Brightside'; 'Amelia', harder to find, has huge, 4-to-5-in. blooms.

Good yellows include 'Banana Cream' and 'Broadway Lights', whose flowers open yellow and mature to white.

There are also many doubles, most of which hold up better in very light shade. 'Esther Reed' is an old, fully double Shasta; 'Aglaia' has frilled, white, semidouble flowers; 'Crazy Daisy' is a frilly white double with shredded-looking petals.

Among dwarfs, try 'Snowcap' (to 15 in. high) and 'Snow Lady' (to 12 in.); both have single white flowers.

TIP Shasta daisies flower heaviest with plenty of light: that's full sun in mild-summer areas and very light shade (from high-branching trees) where summers are hot.

Leucanthemum × superbum **'Brightside'**

HOW TO GROW IT

Soil Give these moist, well-drained, fairly rich soil.

Planting Set out container-grown plants at any time, divisions in autumn or early spring (divide established clumps every 2 to 3 years). These are also easy from spring-sown seed.

Fertilizer Feed plants before and during bloom to encourage large flowers.

Care notes Control slugs and snails. In coldest regions, mulch around plants without smothering foliage.

Limonium perezii

STATICE, SEA LAVENDER
Plumbago family (*Plumbaginaceae*)
PERENNIAL

🖋 **ZONES 13, 15–17, 20–24**

☼ **FULL SUN**

💧 **MODERATE WATER**

The Canary Islands native is familiar to almost anyone who has visited Southern California beaches, where *L. perezii* has widely naturalized. Its large (to 1 ft.), leathery green basal leaves contrast with airy flower clusters on nearly leafless, many-branched stems. Clumps are about 1½ ft. high, with flower clusters rising to 3 ft. and spreading nearly as wide. Each flower's papery outer calyx is rich purple and surrounds a white corolla. Long spring and summer bloom. Plants often self-sow.

This is a first-rate beach plant. Plants tolerate heat but are damaged by frost at 25°F (–4°C). Needs afternoon shade in Zone 13.

HOW TO GROW IT

Soil Provide sandy loam. Perfect drainage is essential for this one; it won't tolerate cold wet soil.

Water Irrigate during active growth, but then back off. During winter, plants can survive on rainfall alone (except in desert).

Care notes Cut back old foliage when new leaves appear.

Limonium perezii

TIP Flowers hold their colors when dried; just hang clusters upside down and out of bright light.

Nepeta

CATMINT
Mint family (*Lamiaceae*)
PERENNIALS

✎ **ZONES 1–24**

☀ ◑ **FULL SUN OR PART SHADE**

💧 **MODERATE WATER**

Aromatic foliage, long-lasting flowers, and easy care make this as attractive to gardeners as to cats, which sometimes roll in it. Spikes of two-lipped blue or blue-violet (or sometimes pink, white, or yellow) flowers appear in late spring and early summer, and rebloom if you shear plants lightly after first flowering. Plants make attractive, informal low hedges or edgings, especially when underplanted with alliums. They are resistant to deer and rabbits.

N. × *faassenii* grows into a silvery gray green, spreading mound to 1 ft. high, 1½–2 ft. wide. Leaves are scallop edged and heart-shaped. Loose, lax spikes of ½-in. lavender-blue flowers appear in late spring, early summer. Set plants 1–1½ ft. apart for groundcover. 'Blue Wonder', to 15 in. high, has medium blue flowers and darker sepals; 'Kit Kat' has tiny leaves and flowers on a standard-size plant. 'Select Blue' has darker flowers than the species and is sterile, so it won't reseed; 'Limelight' has lime green leaves and blue flowers.

The most widely sold catmint is 'Walker's Low', which is often incorrectly labeled as a variety of N. × *faassenii*. Growing up to 3 ft. high and wide, it has vivid lavender-blue flowers. Its name is derived not from its height but from the British garden in which it was found. This variety is less enticing to cats than many others.

In cold-winter climates, nepetas are occasionally used as a substitute for lavender (*Lavandula*) in borders and edgings. Most species don't do well in heat combined with high humidity. In Zones 12 and 13, most are best treated as winter annuals. They tolerate regular moisture if soil is well drained.

TIP Blue-flowered forms of catmint make a great cool border for beds of roses, since blue flowers complement almost all rose colors.

Nepeta 'Walker's Low'

HOW TO GROW IT

Planting Plant at any time.

Water After the first year, plants can take considerable drought, but less water limits mature size.

Care notes As soon as blossoms fade, shear plants back by half or cut faded flower stems to the ground to encourage rebloom. Cut to the ground again in winter to make room for the next season's growth.

Osteospermum hybrids

AFRICAN DAISY
Sunflower family (*Asteraceae*)
PERENNIALS

✎ **ZONES 8, 9, 12–24; ANYWHERE AS ANNUALS**

☼ **FULL SUN**

◖ ◗ **MODERATE TO REGULAR WATER**

Osteospermum hybrids are mounded or trailing in habit and bear a profusion of daisylike flowers over a long season. Narrowish oval leaves have smooth edges or a few large teeth. Flowers of most kinds open only in sunlight, but many have a second color on the backs of rays that shows on half-open flowers during overcast weather. Some flowers even have spoon-shaped petals (but these often revert to normal petals in cool weather).

Plants tolerate drought and neglect but look better with good garden soil and irrigation. Mass along driveways or paths, or use in borders. These are classic fillers for mixed-flower containers.

Osteospermum hybrids come in an amazing array of colors (single and bicolor) and flower shapes, with daisylike or spoon-shaped petals. Other characteristics include heat tolerance (as in the Summertime series), extra-large flowers (the Crescendo series), striking color combinations (the Zion series), and the ability to stay open on overcast days and at night (the Side series, as in Brightside, Seaside, and Wildside). Most top out at a foot high, but some grow much larger. Purple-flowering 'Nairobi Purple' ('African Queen') and 'Burgundy', for example, can reach 20 in. high.

Find colors you like; then read the plant labels to see whether the growth habit and other characteristics are what you want.

TIP Grow these perennials as summer annuals in areas beyond hardiness range and as winter annuals in hot desert regions.

***Osteospermum* Seaside**

HOW TO GROW IT

Soil Good garden soil markedly improves performance.

Fertilizer Apply controlled-release fertilizer at planting.

Water Regular irrigation improves performance.

Care notes Tip-pinch young plants to induce bushiness. Deadheading produces more blooms. Cut back old, sprawling branches to young side growth anytime from late summer to midautumn.

Penstemon

BORDER PENSTEMON, GARDEN PENSTEMON
Plantain family *(Plantaginaceae)*
PERENNIALS

✎ **ZONES 6–9, 14–24, EXCEPT AS NOTED**

☼ ◑ **PART SHADE IN HOTTEST CLIMATES**

◓ ● **MODERATE TO REGULAR WATER**

Though the West is filled with a remarkable array of wild penstemons, the hybrids work best in most gardens. (Wild kinds may die quickly if given too-rich soil and too much water, but they are useful in cold zones and the desert.) Most penstemons have narrow, pointed leaves; those in the basal foliage clump are larger, those on flower stems smaller. Narrowly bell-shaped, lipped flowers to 2 in. long come in shades of pink, red, wine, purple, blue, and white.

Plants live only 3 or 4 years, but they're deer-resistant and attract hummingbirds. The hybrids listed here can be grown as summer annuals in cold Zones 1–3 and as winter annuals in desert Zones 12–13. All are compact, bushy, upright plants to 2–4 ft. tall and to 3 ft. wide. Large summer flowers appear in loose spikes at stem ends. Mass these plants in borders or group with other summer-flowering plants.

'Alice Hindley'. Shiny foliage and pale lilac blooms with white throats.

'Apple Blossom'. Pink flowers with white throats.

'Blackbird'. Dark maroon blooms held on deep red stems.

'Dark Towers'. Zones 1–11, 14–24. Hybrid of complex parentage. Sturdy, upright grower to 2½ ft. high and 3 ft. wide, with glossy, deep burgundy leaves that retain their color all season. Soft pink blooms are held high in summer. Tolerates heat, cold, and high humidity.

'Delft Blue Riding Hood'. Two-toned flowers that really do have that blue-and-white Delft blue look.

'Elizabeth Cozzens'. Grows about 2½ ft. high and wide, with porcelain buds opening into lilac-pink flowers with magenta streaking in the throat. Bloom lasts from June to October.

'Firebird' ('Schoenholzeri'). Scarlet flowers on a vigorous, heavy-blooming plant.

'Garnet'. Fine-leafed plant with wine blooms. Long-lived and floriferous.

'Hidcote Pink'. Heavy producer of coral pink flowers with a white, maroon-streaked throat.

***Penstemon* 'Midnight'**

'Holly's White'. White with blush.

'Hot Pink Riding Hood'. Rose-pink flowers with white throat markings.

Kissed series (such as 'Violet Kissed', 'Wine Kissed'). These large-flowered selections have white-throated blooms with lips in bright colors.

P. Mexicali hybrids. Zones 1–3, 10. Bushy growth to 1½ ft. high and wide, with profuse narrow, shiny green leaves. Blossoms of 'Pike's Peak Purple' are violet, those of 'Red Rocks' bright rose. Burgundy and pink forms are also available. Highly recommended for Rocky Mountain and Great Plains states; they rival the border penstemons for showiness of leaf and flower, yet are much hardier to cold. Bloom all summer. Do well with moderate water but tolerate regular moisture. ❯❯

'Midnight'. Vigorous, bushy plant with deep green leaves and dark bluish purple blooms.

Phoenix series. Grows 2–3 ft. high and wide and comes in a variety of colors: 'Phoenix Appleblossom', 'Phoenix Magenta', 'Phoenix Pink', 'Phoenix Red', and 'Phoenix Violet'. In every case, the flower is the labeled color with a white throat.

'Red Riding Hood'. Bright red flowers.

'Sour Grapes'. The true variety has flowers in a combination of violet and metallic blue, but some plants sold under this name may have bright red-violet blooms.

HOW TO GROW IT

Soil Hybrids need fast-draining soil with plenty of organic amendment.

Planting Where they are grown as perennials, set out nursery transplants in fall for bloom in late spring and early summer. Where grown as annuals, set out in spring (or autumn in desert), or as soon as flowering penstemons are available.

Fertilizer Mix a light dose of complete, controlled-release fertilizer into the soil once at planting.

Water Though this group of penstemons prefers regular water, it is subject to root rot in wet, heavy soils.

Care notes After the flowers fade, cut back to side growth for another round of bloom in late summer, early fall.

TIP Penstemons can last up to 10 days as cut flowers. Water plants the night before you intend to cut, then snip flowers in the morning and immediately put them in water.

Penstemon 'Dark Towers'

Penstemons and Friends

Like asters, penstemons got much of their best, earliest breeding in Europe, then came back to America. They gained stylishness and a taste for better soil and more water, losing some of their hardiness along the way. In general, larger flowers mean less frost tolerance.

Like their wild relations, hybrid penstemons show especially well on hills and interplanted among landscape rocks. Use larger penstemons with larger rocks or boulders, and smaller ones in or against a rockery.

For pot culture, penstemons can be the whole show, or they can be used as focal-point plants, with smaller plants tucked in around the edges (white or purple sweet alyssum is good for this, depending on the color of the penstemon). Purple-leafed plants go especially well with red penstemons. Try one of the dark-leafed sweet potato vines for this.

Rudbeckia hirta

GLORIOSA DAISY, BLACK-EYED SUSAN
Sunflower family *(Asteraceae)*
PERENNIAL OR BIENNIAL

⬥ ZONES 1–11, 14–24, EXCEPT AS NOTED

☼ FULL SUN

◖◗ MODERATE TO REGULAR WATER

Tough and easy, these big, warm-colored daisies are stalwarts of the summer and autumn garden. Selected from Midwestern natives, they grow 3–4 ft. tall, 1½ ft. wide, with upright, branching habit. Stems and lance-shaped leaves to 4 in. long are rough and hairy. Daisylike, 2-to-4-in.-wide flowers have orange-yellow rays and a prominent purplish black cone. Good cut flowers.

Though the plants put on a great show, they are biennials or short-lived perennials. They are also grown as annuals because they bloom the first summer from seed. They are winter annuals in desert Zones 12, 13.

Here are some of the best. 'Indian Summer' produces 6-to-9-in. single to semidouble flowers in golden yellow. 'Irish Eyes' has 2-to-3-in. golden yellow flowers with a light green central cone that ages to brown. 'Prairie Sun' produces 5-in. golden yellow blooms with pale yellow tips and a light green central cone. For the front of the border, try lower-growing selections 'Goldilocks' (double flowers) and 'Toto', both 8–10 in. high; Becky Mix (12–15 in.); 'Tiger Eye' (16–24 in. high and wide, with unusually profuse bloom); 'Denver Daisy' (2 ft. high, 18 in. wide); 'Cherokee Sunset' (2–2½ ft. high, with large double or semidouble blooms); and 'Chim Chiminee' (to 30 in. high, 2 ft. wide, with quilled mahogany, yellow, bronze, and gold flowers).

The best-selling black-eyed Susan is *R. fulgida sullivantii* 'Goldsturm' (Zones 1–24); it bears 3-in., black-eyed yellow flowers on 2-to-2½-ft. stems from midsummer into fall. Closely related 'Early Bird Gold' has an especially long bloom season, running spring to fall. Both spread by rhizomes to form larger clumps.

Rudbeckia hirta **'Denver Daisy'**

HOW TO GROW IT

Soil Must be moisture retentive and fast draining (organic amendment does the trick).

Fertilizer The plants are heavy feeders. Apply controlled-release fertilizer at planting; then apply complete fertilizer in late summer.

Water Though *Rudbeckias* have no problem with heat, they need steady moisture.

Care notes Cutting encourages rebloom late in the season. Divide perennials when they become crowded, usually every few years.

Salvia

SAGE
Mint family *(Lamiaceae)*
PERENNIALS

◪ ZONES VARY BY SPECIES

☼ FULL SUN, EXCEPT AS NOTED

◗ ◖ MODERATE TO REGULAR WATER

The following perennial salvias are favorites in the 20-minute garden; they're easy to grow and care for, and they attract hummingbirds. All have square stems and whorls of two-lipped flowers. None have the drought tolerance of native Western sages, but they add much to the garden. Most of those that follow have fragrant leaves.

S. guaranitica (S. ambigens). ANISE-SCENTED SAGE. Perennial in Zones 8, 9, 14–24, and possibly in Zones 4–7; annual in colder climates. This fine, shrub-size, long-flowering sage has striking flowers and tolerates part shade, especially in hottest climates. It is upright and branching, to 5 ft. tall and nearly as wide. Spreads by short underground runners; roots form tubers resembling small sausages. Narrowly heart-shaped, sparsely hairy, mint green leaves can grow 5 in. long. Most common form bears 2-in. cobalt blue blossoms, carried several to each footlong stem; calyxes are bright green, turning purplish on sunny side. Flowers keep coming from early summer to frost.

This makes an elegant container plant in a large pot, but it needs support. Where it grows as a perennial, it gets woody by season's end—although that wood dies during winter and must be cut back to ground. The plant can be demolished by Mexican giant whitefly.

'Argentine Skies'. Has light blue flowers.

'Black and Blue'. By far the most widely sold of the group, this one bears blossoms that are deep blue with dark purplish blue calyxes. It's a little bigger than the species.

'Omaha Gold'. Violet-blue flowers and leaves margined in greenish gold.

S. nemorosa. WOODLAND SAGE. Zones 2–10, 14–24. This floriferous plant has spawned many excellent selections and hybrid offspring (most listed as S. × sylvestris, next page). These selections generally grow 1½–3 ft. high, spreading 2–3 ft. wide by rhizomes. Each forms a tight foliage rosette from which erect, branching flower stems arise. Wrinkled, dull green, finely toothed leaves are oval or lance-shaped. Lower leaves

Salvia × *sylvestris* **'Snow Hill'**

are stalked, to 4 in. long; upper ones are smaller, virtually stalkless, clasping the flower stem. Stems 3–6 in. long hold ¼-to-½-in. flowers in violet, purple, pink, or white, with persistent violet, purple, or green bracts. These bloom summer through fall if spent stems are removed. They tend to sprawl if not supported.

'Caradonna'. Bears violet blossoms.

'Marcus'. Has intensely violet flowers on plants 12 in. high and 18 in. wide.

New Dimension series. Both New Dimension Blue and New Dimension Rose grow about 10 in. high and wide.

'Ostfriesland' ('East Friesland'). Intensely violet-blue flowers.

Sensation series. Grows 12 in. high and 18 in. wide. Sensation Rose is among the most popular, with pink

Salvia guaranitica **'Black and Blue'**

Salvias for Containers

Salvias come in all sizes (many large). But a few are just the right size for growing in containers, and all respond well to the good drainage that containers provide. Start by packing a wide, not-too-deep terra-cotta container with three or four colors of Sensation salvias. To extend the color range, move beyond the hybrid salvias and try scarlet sage (*S. splendens*), whose vivid red blooms can spice up a young cape plumbago's cool blue ones. Try a potted dwarf pineapple sage (*S. elegans* 'Golden Delicious'), whose lime-colored leaves and red flowers make an eye-catching accent in a sunny herb garden. Or create a hummingbird garden by mixing purple *S. leucantha*, dark blue *S. guaranitica*, and deep-red-flowered *S. greggii* with red 'Firebird' penstemon and *Phygelius capensis* 'Scarlet' in a ceramic container at least 23 in. across. This last combination works well for a couple of years, but when plants outgrow the container, move them into the garden.

flowers. Also look for Sensation Deep Blue, Sensation Deep Rose, Sensation Deep Rose Improved, Sensation Sky Blue, and Sensation White.

S. × superba. This is a hybrid that probably has *S.* × *sylvestris* as one parent and possibly *S. amplexicaulis* as the other. It grows about 3 ft. high, but the following named varieties are smaller. Both flower from midspring through midautumn with regular water and deadheading. All make good cottage-garden plants.

'Adora'. Zones 2–10, 14–24. The foliage mound grows to 15 in. high and wide, with blue flower spikes rising to 30 in.

Merleau series. Zones 3–8, 14–24. Develops into a compact mound to 15 in. high and slightly less wide. 'Merleau' itself is purple-blue. 'Merleau Rose' has rose-pink flowers.

S. × sylvestris. Zones 2–10, 14–24. This is a hybrid between *S. nemorosa* and *S. pratensis*. It most resembles *S. nemorosa* but is more compact, with stems that are less leafy. Oblong to lance-shaped, medium green, scalloped leaves are wrinkled, softly hairy. Typically unbranched or few-branched flowering stems grow to 6–8 in. long, set with pinkish violet, ½-in. blossoms. Blooms summer through fall if faded flowers are removed.

'Blue Hill' ('Blauhügel'). To 2 ft.; has medium blue flowers.

'Blue Queen' ('Blaukönigin'). Grows 18 in. high and wide, has purple-blue flowers.

'Mainacht' ('May Night'). Grows 2–2½ ft., bears ¾-in. indigo flowers with green bracts (purplish at base); begins blooming in midspring.

'Snow Hill' ('Schneehügel'). Bears pure white blossoms with green bracts on a 2-ft. plant.

'Viola Klose'. Grows 18 in. high and wide; has lavender-blue flowers.

HOW TO GROW IT

Soil Choose fast-draining soil that contains enough organic matter to retain moisture.

Fertilizer Feed when plants start putting on new growth, and again after flowering.

Water Regular irrigation.

Care notes Cutting encourages rebloom late in the season.

Scabiosa columbaria

PINCUSHION FLOWER
Honeysuckle family *(Caprifoliaceae)*
PERENNIAL

ZONES 2–11, 14–24

FULL SUN TO PART SHADE

MODERATE TO REGULAR WATER

Named for stamens that reach out well beyond the domed flower heads, pincushion flower is a wonderful old-fashioned cottage-garden plant that is favored by beneficial insects but usually ignored by deer. Soft-looking 2-to-3-in. blossoms come in shades of blue, pink, and white, rising above 1-to-2-ft. mounds of finely cut, gray-green leaves. Bloom begins in midsummer and continues until frost if flowers are deadheaded or cut regularly. These make excellent cut flowers.

Native to Europe, Africa, and Asia, these do best and have longest bloom where summers are mild. In desert Zones 12 and 13, grow them as winter annuals. Good in mixed or mass plantings and also in containers.

Here are some of the best selections.

'Blue Note'. Blue flowers borne on a dwarf plant, 8–10 in. high.

'Harlequin Blue'. Long-stemmed, light blue flowers to 18 in. above a 12-to-14-in. mound of foliage.

'Mariposa Blue'. Blue flowers.

'Mariposa Violet'. Dark purple-blue flowers.

Several excellent hybrids are often incorrectly sold as *S. columbaria* selections, including the following.

'Butterfly Blue'. Plants can reach 2 ft., with a profusion of lavender-blue flowers over a long season.

'Pink Mist'. Very pretty bright pink flowers rise from a plant that grows to 18 in.

'Vivid Violet'. Plants grow to 11 in. high, 18 in. wide, with violet-pink flowers.

TIP Though pincushion flower produces ball blooms, its habit and color make it blend well in containers with similar-size plants, like *Agastache* and cape fuchsia.

Scabiosa columbaria **'Mariposa Violet'**

HOW TO GROW IT

Soil Fast-draining garden soil.

Plant Set out plants as soon as they are available in spring.

Fertilizer Apply a complete, controlled-release fertilizer at planting time.

Care notes This plant benefits greatly from deadheading.

Sedum Autumn Joy

STONECROP
Orpine family *(Crassulaceae)*
SUCCULENT PERENNIALS

⚡ **ZONES 1–10, 14–24**

☼ **FULL SUN**

◊ 💧 **LITTLE TO MODERATE WATER**

Unlike the myriad groundcover sedums that fill specialty nurseries and gardens, sedums in the Autumn Joy group grow 1–2 ft. high and about 2 ft. wide, so they fit well into mixed-perennials borders. All are hybrids of *S. telephium* and *S. spectabile*, which are both primarily Asian species.

For succulents, these take a remarkable amount of cold. Fleshy leaves are somewhat variable in size, shape, and color. Big, puffy flower heads appear in fall, usually in shades that run from light pink to raspberry. They are good in containers and make excellent cut flowers. Tops die down in winter.

'Autumn Joy' ('Herbstfreude'). The best known of the series, this one has spoon-shaped green leaves to 3 in. long and half as wide with toothed edges. Rounded clusters of blossoms are pink when they open in late summer or autumn, later age to coppery pink and finally to rust.

'Autumn Charm' ('Lajos'). White-edged leaves on 16-in. plants, light pink flowers.

'Autumn Delight' ('Beka'). Golden green leaves with darker edges on 18-to-24-in. plants, dusty pink flowers.

'Autumn Fire'. Green leaves and dusty pink flowers on 18-to-24-in. plants.

'Elsie's Gold'. Golden green leaves with cream edges, shell pink flowers.

'Mini Joy'. Similar to 'Autumn Joy' but a few inches shorter, with salmon-pink flowers.

TIP Sedums are easy to propagate by stem cuttings; even detached leaves will root and form new plants.

Sedum **'Autumn Joy'**

HOW TO GROW IT

Soil Best in soil that's not too rich, which keeps plants more compact and sturdy, and less likely to flop.

Planting Set out plants in spring in area with full sun.

Water These tolerate drought but do better with regular water.

Care notes Cut tops down to the crown in late fall or winter.

Verbena 'Homestead Purple'

GARDEN VERBENA
Verbena family (*Verbenaceae*)
PERENNIAL

 ZONES 2–24

 FULL SUN

 REGULAR WATER

This disease-resistant hybrid bears 3-in. clusters of small, tubular, five-petaled purple flowers. Bloom is nonstop from summer through frost. The well-branched plant grows fairly quickly to 2 ft. high and 3 ft. wide, possibly much wider in the Pacific Northwest. Use it in parking strips, along driveways, on dry banks; also attractive in wall crevices or as a trailer in big pots and hanging baskets.

A hybrid involving the North American species *V. canadensis*, 'Homestead Purple' starts flowering earlier and is more disease-resistant than many verbenas. It is at its best in hot weather. The plant is often grown as an annual (especially in mixed container plantings that are changed out every year), even in zones where it perennializes.

There are many other outstanding groups of verbena hybrids. Most are short-lived perennials hardy only in Zones 4–9, 12–24; H1, H2. They too are used as annuals in all zones. Most grow 6–12 in. high, 1½–3 ft. wide, with oblong, 2-to-4-in., bright green or gray-green leaves with toothed margins. Flowers grow in flat, compact clusters to 3 in. wide. Colors include white, pink, red, purple, blue, and combinations. Popular strains include the Aztec, Superbena, Tapien, and Temari series. All are low-growing plants available in a wide range of colors. In general, they are resistant to powdery mildew, free blooming, and heat-tolerant. Plants in the Babylon and Tapien series have more finely cut foliage. 'Sissinghurst' is perennial in Zones 3–24 and grows a few inches high, 4 ft. wide, with bright red flowers.

Verbena 'Homestead Purple'

HOW TO GROW IT

Soil Must be fast draining, especially in winter.

Planting Though many verbenas are available from seed, named varieties in nursery containers are usually more consistent and disease-resistant.

Care notes Cut back plants if they become too vigorous.

Yucca filamentosa

ADAM'S NEEDLE
Asparagus family (*Asparagaceae*)
PERENNIAL

ZONES 1–24

FULL SUN

REGULAR WATER

Terrific architecture, easy care, and a surprising degree of cold-hardiness earn these nearly stemless plants a place in the garden. Named for the stringy filaments on the edges of their tough, 18-in.-long, 1-in.-wide, sword-shaped leaves, they bear yellowish white, tulip-shaped flowers in hanging clusters on 4-to-7-ft. flowering stems in spring (warmer climates) or summer (cooler climates). The blooms are lightly fragrant in the evening. Plants grow to 2½ ft. high; over time, stolons make these grow into clumps up to 5 ft. wide. Varieties include 'Bright Edge', with yellow-striped leaves, and 'Color Guard', with leaves striped white and cream.

Adam's needle is so closely related to *Y. flaccida* (Zones 1–9, 14–24) that some botanists think the two species should be combined—and *Y. flaccida* selections are often sold as *Y. filamentosa*. The difference is that *Y. flaccida*'s flower clusters are somewhat shorter and leaves are less rigid, with straight fibers on the edges. 'Golden Sword' has yellow-variegated foliage; 'Ivory Tower' bears outward-facing rather than drooping flowers.

Cluster yuccas with cactus, agaves, or other succulents; or grow them with softer-leafed tropical foliage plants. Those mentioned here provide important vertical accents when in bloom. Because they have stiff, sharp-pointed leaves, it's best to keep them away from walks, terraces, and other well-traveled areas. (Some people clip off the sharp tips with nail clippers.)

TIP Yuccas die after flowering, but don't dig them out: offshoots around the base of the mother plant form new plants.

Yucca filamentosa '**Color Guard**'

HOW TO GROW IT

Soil Best in well-drained soil.

Planting Choose a location that is out of desiccating cold wind if you garden in a cold-winter zone.

Fertilizer Apply liquid fertilizer monthly during the growing season.

Water Cut back on watering during winter.

Bellis perennis

ENGLISH DAISY
Sunflower family *(Asteraceae)*
PERENNIAL OFTEN TREATED AS COOL-SEASON ANNUAL

✎ **ZONES 1–9, 14–24; ANYWHERE EXCEPT HAWAII AS ANNUAL**

☼ ☽ **LIGHT SHADE IN HOTTEST CLIMATES**

💧 **REGULAR WATER**

Bellis perennis

English daisies are the small, yellow-centered, single white or pinkish flowers that have naturalized in lawns throughout much of the West. Their cultivated forms are much bigger, with white, red, bicolor, or pink single or double flowers. Because English daisies bloom in winter or early spring, they're often effectively paired with daffodils or other spring-flowering bulbs. In legend, these are the "he loves me, he loves me not" oracles.

Dark green, 1-to-2-in.-long leaves form rosettes to 5 in. high and 8 in. wide. Plump flowers on 3-to-6-in. stems rise above the foliage, appearing year-round in mild weather, with peak bloom in late winter and early spring.

They grow so easily in lawns that they've become a mainstay of flowering lawns, which often also include crocuses, violets, chamomile, self-heal *(Prunella)*, and clover. They work well if the grass is cut at 3 or 4 in. high, but big cultivated kinds tend to die out after a few years; the species does better over the long term in lawns because its leaves are much smaller and lie closer to the ground. In garden beds, English daisies are good for edging or bedding out, either alone or with bulbs. They're also excellent in containers.

Good varieties include Galaxy (red, white), Habanera (white with red tips), and Tasso (red, red and white, white).

HOW TO GROW IT

Soil Plant in garden soil amended with compost. Richer soil makes bigger plants.

Planting Start any of these from nursery plants, usually sold in 4-in. pots in fall and spring; start nonsterile varieties from seed. To grow English daisies in the lawn, rough up the grass enough with a rake so that you can see soil; then sprinkle on seeds of the species (not named varieties), compost, and water well. To use as a groundcover, sprinkle seeds thinly on prepared, weeded soil, rake them in, tamp the soil down, and water.

Fertilizer Apply controlled-release fertilizer at time of planting.

Care notes To extend bloom, pick off faded flowers.

TIP Named varieties like 'Tasso Deep Rose' make very effective fillers paired with callas in big pots.

Cosmos bipinnatus

COSMOS
Sunflower family *(Asteraceae)*
WARM-SEASON ANNUAL

ZONES A1–A3; 1–24

FULL SUN

MODERATE WATER

These are among the garden's easiest, showiest, and most useful seed-grown flowers. Most grow 2–5 ft. tall, putting out abundant pink, white, or red flowers from summer through fall. Blooms can be single, semidouble, or double, crested or frilled; there are even varieties with rolled petals. Finely cut foliage creates a soft, even foil for adjacent flowers.

You can mass cosmos in borders or use them to fill spaces between shrubs.

Plants are open and branching in habit. Heights vary from 1½ to 6 ft., with widths usually in the 1½-to-2½-ft. range.

Blossoms are 3–4 in. wide, with tufted yellow centers and rays in shades of white, pink, rose, lavender, plum, or crimson. There are also several bicolors.

Among the best types to grow is the 2-to-4-ft.-tall Antiquity strain, with white-and-rose flowers. Double Click series, to 4 ft. tall, produces large, frilly, semidouble to double flowers in a range of colors. Psyche series, 3 ft. tall, comes in white, pink, or deep magenta single to semidouble flowers. Sea Shells', 3–4 ft. high, is grown for quilled ray flowers in creamy white, pink, rose, or carmine that look like long, slender cones. Sensation strain, 3–6 ft. tall, has a classic range of pink, white, and rose flowers. 'Sonata is a dwarf series 1½–2 ft. high. Versailles strain, bred for cut flowers, reaches 3½ ft. and bears its blossoms on long, strong stems.

TIP Cosmos is especially useful when sown among spring-flowering bulbs; as the bulb foliage withers, cosmos quickly overtops and hides it.

Cosmos bipinnatus

HOW TO GROW IT

Soil Needs good drainage. Plant in not-too-rich soil.

Planting Rake seeds into open prepared garden soil where plants are to grow, or set out transplants from spring to summer. Plants self-sow freely.

Fertilizer A light application of controlled-release fertilizer keeps plants blooming.

Care notes Though most cosmos won't bloom during Alaska's long summer days, the Sonata series and the Versailles strain will.

Helianthus annuus

SUNFLOWER
Sunflower family (*Asteraceae*)
WARM-SEASON ANNUAL

✎ **ZONES A1–A3; 1–24**

☼ **FULL SUN**

💧 **REGULAR WATER**

New gardeners (especially children) are usually surprised at how easy it is to grow giant sunflowers from seed. All annual kinds grow on sturdy plants whose familiar flowers come in summer and fall; most make great cut flowers.

The wild ancestor of today's sunflowers is a coarse, hairy plant with 2-to-3-in.-wide flowers. Breeders have transformed these into giant plants as well as a host of smaller varieties used for cut flowers. Blooms may be yellow, red, orange, or creamy white; some have several colors on each flower; others are frilled or doubled. Centers are brown, dark purple, or nearly black.

Giant forms grow 10–15 ft. tall and 2 ft. wide and typically produce a single huge head (sometimes more than a foot across) consisting of a circle of short rays with a brown central cushion of seeds. Sunflowers for cutting come on compact, branching plants and bear 4-to-8-in.-wide blooms in a wide variety of colors. They fall into two basic categories: pollen-bearing types and pollenless ones. Kinds without pollen have the advantage of not shedding on tabletops. Some annual sunflowers are bred to produce especially large seeds. New varieties and hybrids come to market each year.

Late in the season, the seeds can be harvested, roasted, and eaten, or left on the plants to feed birds as other sources of food disappear in fall and winter.

TIP Put a paper bag over the flower head when the petals drop to keep birds and squirrels from harvesting the seeds before you do.

Helianthus annuus

HOW TO GROW IT

Soil Large-flowered kinds need rich, moist soil. Smaller varieties thrive in ordinary garden soil. Give both kinds good drainage.

Planting Plant big sunflower seeds in prepared garden soil where plants are to grow, or set out transplants from spring to summer. Plants self-sow freely. Tall sunflowers may need staking.

Fertilizer Feed young plants while they're putting their energy into growing, but stop feeding as plants approach full size.

Care notes When seeds dry, they'll fall free as you rub them.

Impatiens

BUSY LIZZIE, NEW GUINEA IMPATIENS
Balsam family *(Balsaminaceae)*
PERENNIALS GROWN AS WARM-SEASON ANNUALS

⚡ ZONES VARY BY SPECIES

● ◑ ☀ EXPOSURE NEEDS VARY BY SPECIES

● REGULAR WATER

Just as *Impatiens walleriana* hybrids are famous for producing brightly colored flowers in shade, so New Guinea hybrid impatiens are becoming favorites for massed color in sun or light shade. All do well in both containers and garden beds.

These frost-intolerant, succulent-stemmed plants are perennials in their native tropics but annuals in all but the mildest parts of the West.

I. **New Guinea hybrids.** Perennials in Zones 24; I 11, H2. Upright to spreading, 1–2 ft. high and as wide or wider (some are much bigger or much smaller). Large leaves typically variegated with cream or red. Flowers usually large (3 in. wide) and held well above foliage; colors include lavender, purple, pink, red, orange, white, and bicolors. Give somewhat more sun than you would common impatiens *(I. walleriana).*

Popular strains include Celebration (with 3-in. flowers), ColorPower, and Infinity (which does well in sun or shade).

SunPatiens is the most robust, heavily flowering new strain. Bred to thrive in full sun, these grow 2–4 ft. tall and wide.

I. **walleriana.** BUSY LIZZIE. Perennial in Zones 17, 24; H1, H2. These are generally easier than New Guinea impatiens. Native to eastern Africa. Narrow, glossy dark green leaves. Five-petaled flowers 1–2 in. wide, in all colors but yellow and true blue. Space taller types 1 ft. apart, dwarfs 6 in. apart. If plants overgrow, cut them back to 6 in. aboveground. New growth emerges in days, with flowers in 2 weeks.

Most are just nuanced versions of the others. Among those in the 10-to-16-in. range are strains such as Blitz, Dazzler, and Stardust. Some that grow less than 12 in. include Accent, Super Elfin, and Swirl. Among doubles, try the Fiesta, Rockapulco, and Tioga strains; 'Victorian Rose' (frilly, rose-pink) is a semidouble.

Impatiens walleriana **'Fiesta Salmon'**

HOW TO GROW IT

Soil Plant in well-drained soil amended with 2–3 in. of compost.

Planting Set out nursery plants after average date of last frost.

Fertilizer Regular feeding.

Water Keep root zone moist.

Lathyrus odoratus

SWEET PEA
Pea family *(Papilionaceae)*
COOL-SEASON ANNUAL

✔ **ALL ZONES, EXCEPT AS NOTED**

☼ **FULL SUN**

● **REGULAR WATER**

◊ **SEEDS CONTAIN TOXIC AMINO ACIDS**

Sweet peas produce beautiful sprays of crisp-looking flowers with a clean, sweet perfume. Vining types climb several feet with tendrils that coil around strings or other supports; bush kinds grow 8 in. to 3 ft. high.

Each flower has one upright petal (the banner or standard), two side petals (wings), and two lower petals. Colors include deep rose, blue, purple, scarlet, white, cream, salmon, and bicolors. Good cut flowers.

Heirlooms. Not as showy as modern hybrids, these deliver powerful fragrance. Popular ones include 'America' (4 ft., white-striped crimson), 'Blanche Ferry' (5 ft., carmine-rose standard, pink wings), 'Cupani' (5–9 ft., deep blue standard, purple wings), 'Henry Eckford' (5–7 ft., red-orange), and 'Painted Lady' (8 ft., rose-and-white). Old Spice mix (5–6 ft.) includes eight old-fashioned varieties in white, pink, red, and purple.

Early-flowering. Early Spencer (5 ft.) and Early Multiflora (5–6 ft.) bloom in midwinter, when days are short. In Zones 12, 13, 17, 21–24; H1, H2, sow in late summer for winter bloom. Mixed colors.

Spring-flowering. Includes heat-resistant Cuthbertson types (6 ft.). Flowers come in pink, lavender, purple, white, cream, rose, salmon, cerise, carmine, red, and blue. Royal or Royal Family (5–6 ft.) are larger flowered, more heat-resistant. In Zones 7–9, 12–24, plant in fall. Elsewhere, as soon as soil can be worked.

Summer-flowering. Galaxy (6 ft.) is the most common. Wide color range. Blooms when days are long. Large flowered and heat-resistant, but not enough so for Zones 7–15, 18–21.

Bush type. Grow 8–36 in. high. Some are self-supporting. Flowers in all colors. Most are spring blooming; follow planting dates for early-flowering vining types. Bijou (to 1 ft., self-supporting); Cupid (4–6 in. by 1 ft., trailing); Jet Set (2–3 ft. high, needs support); Knee High (2½ ft., needs support); Little Sweethearts (8 in. high, self-supporting); Supersnoop (2 ft. high, self-supporting).

Lathyrus odoratus

HOW TO GROW IT

Soil Amend soil with compost before planting.

Planting To hasten germination, soak seeds for a few hours before planting.

Spacing Sow seeds 1 in. deep, 1–2 in. apart. When seedlings are 4–5 in. high, thin to 6 in. apart.

Fertilizer Feed monthly.

Water Keep soil moist.

Care notes Control slugs and snails.

Lobularia

SWEET ALYSSUM
Cabbage family *(Brassicaceae)*
COOL-SEASON ANNUAL

✎ **ALL ZONES**

☼ ☽ **BEST IN SUN; TOLERATES LIGHT SHADE**

◌ **MODERATE WATER**

Plant this classic, cool-season Mediterranean native once, and you'll probably always have it in your garden. Yet seedlings are easy to pull if they pop up where you don't want them. Plants are low and branching, to 1 ft. high and wide, with narrow or lance-shaped leaves ½–2 in. long. Crowded clusters of tiny, four-petaled, honey-scented flowers can bloom for months, and most self-seed. White is the most familiar color, but it also comes in pink or purple. In cold-winter regions, flowers can keep coming from spring until frost; in mild climates, self-sown seedlings supply all-year bloom. Sweet alyssum seeds are sometimes part of wildflower mixes.

These easy-to-grow mounds work well in containers or casual landscaping situations, especially along paths and in rock retaining walls.

L. maritima. Garden varieties are better known than the species, but when they self-sow, they tend to revert to taller, looser growth and bear smaller, paler blossoms than the parent. 'Carpet of Snow' (2–4 in. tall) is a good compact white. 'Rosie O'Day' (2–4 in.) has lavender-pink blooms. 'Snow Crystals' (10 in. high, trailing) and the Clear Crystal series (mounded 10 in. high, 14 in. wide; in white, rose, pink, lavender, peach, lemonade, or violet) are tetraploids whose genetics give them extra vigor and heat resistance. An increasing number of strains combine many colors in each seed packet.

L. 'Snow Princess'. This trailing hybrid grows 6–8 in. high, bearing a profusion of white flowers. Excellent in containers. Because it's sterile, it keeps blooming, even into the warm season. It is vigorous enough to overrun close neighboring plants, but never becomes a problem plant.

Lobularia maritima **'Worth Beyond Beauty'**

HOW TO GROW IT

Soil Ordinary garden soil.

Planting Sweet alyssum is sold as nursery transplants (that's the only way you can buy 'Snow Princess'), but most kinds are also very easy from seed, blooming about 6 weeks after sowing.

Fertilizer Plants need minimal fertilizer in good garden soil. Those growing in containers benefit from twice-monthly applications of liquid fertilizer.

Care notes If you shear back halfway 4 weeks after plants come into bloom, new growth will make another crop of flowers, and plants won't become rangy.

Petunia

Nightshade family *(Solanaceae)*
PERENNIAL GROWN AS WARM-SEASON ANNUAL

ALL ZONES
FULL SUN
REGULAR WATER

Because few other plants can produce as many flowers over as long a season, petunias consistently rank among the most popular annuals. Plants are bushy to spreading, with thick, broad leaves that are slightly sticky to the touch. Flowers vary from funnel-shaped single blooms to densely double, heavily ruffled ones; bloom diameters range from 1 to 6 in. They come in white and every color, from deep jewel tones to soft pastels. You can also buy bicolors, picotees (dark centers with light petal edges), and morns (light centers and darker edges). Still others have contrasting veins on the petals, or fringed or fluted edges.

Petunias are easy to grow, blooming throughout summer until frost in most climates. But they develop leaf spot in consistently smoggy areas and suffer where tobacco budworm is common. In desert Zones 12 and 13, grow them in winter and spring, before summer heat arrives.

Though petunias have been assigned many categories over the years, breeding advances have blurred the boundaries between them, and now many growers sell them by flower size—large, medium, or mini. You'll find a host of trailing or mounding varieties that grow as low as 6 in. and as wide as 6 ft. across. Your local nursery can help you find the color, bloom size, and plant habit best suited to your purposes.

Petunia

HOW TO GROW IT

Soil Plants thrive in rich, well-drained garden soil.

Planting Because petunia seeds are so tiny and hard to handle, it makes more sense to buy nursery plants. Space them 8–18 in. apart, depending on ultimate plant size (usually listed on the label).

Fertilizer Feed monthly with a complete liquid fertilizer; hungry trailing petunias do best when given controlled-release fertilizer at planting time in addition to weekly applications of liquid fertilizer.

Water To keep up with petunias' vigorous growth and constant flowering, never let plants dry to the wilt point.

Care notes After plants are established, pinch back halfway to encourage compact growth and maximize flowers. Repeat if plants become rangy after the main bloom period.

TIP For a popular petunia relative with smaller blooms, try the closely related *Calibrachoa*, which excels in containers.

Solenostemon
(Coleus × hybridus)

COLEUS
Mint family *(Lamiaceae)*
PERENNIAL USUALLY GROWN AS WARM-SEASON ANNUAL

⚡ **ZONES 24; H1, H2; ANYWHERE AS ANNUAL; OR INDOORS**

☼ ◐ ● **FULL SUN OR SHADE, DEPENDING UPON VARIETY**

💧 **REGULAR WATER**

Though its colorful leaves and tolerance for low light make coleus a natural houseplant, many new varieties are now available for planting outdoors in the garden's shady places; some tolerate full sun. They come in a kaleidoscopic color range; many have bigger leaves with more interesting margins. There are now coleus varieties for almost every imaginable situation that calls for bedding or edging plants. Most of these are hybrids bred from species native to the Old World tropics.

Seed-grown, large-leafed strains, such as Giant Exhibition and Oriental Splendor, grow 1½–2 ft. high and wide, with leaves 3–6 in. long. Plants in the Kong series have leaves up to 8 in. long. Dwarf strains such as Carefree, Fairway, and Wizard grow 8–12 in. high and wide, with leaves 1–1½ in. long. Colors include green, chartreuse, yellow, buff, salmon, orange, red, purple, and brown; a single leaf often shows many colors. The more red pigment the foliage has, the more sun-tolerant the plant tends to be. Most coleus perform best in strong indirect light or light shade, but the relatively new, cutting-grown "sun coleus" also thrive in sun; they come in a variety of leaf colors, shapes, and plant habits. The ColorBlaze series is late blooming and may not bloom at all in cool climates. Selections grow 2–3 ft. high, come in a huge range of colors and leaf shapes, and can be grown in sun or shade. Many coleus are useful for summer borders, containers, and hanging baskets.

TIP To maintain the attractive shape of coleus plants, pinch off the spikes of blue flowers as they emerge.

Solenostemon scutellarioides **'ColorBlaze Keystone Kopper'**

HOW TO GROW IT

Soil Give coleus rich, loose, warm, well-drained soil.

Planting Plant from nursery transplants after danger of frost is past in spring.

Fertilizer Feed regularly with high-nitrogen fertilizer.

Water Rather succulent stems and big leaves demand regular watering.

Care notes Even in frost-free zones where coleus is perennial, you'll typically get the best performance by starting new plants annually from seed or cuttings. Pinch stems often to encourage compact habit.

Tagetes

MARIGOLD
Sunflower family *(Asteraceae)*
WARM-SEASON ANNUALS

✎ **ALL ZONES**
☼ **FULL SUN**
🌢 **REGULAR WATER**

Among the easiest, most robust annuals you can grow, marigolds range from 6 in. to 4 ft. tall. Finely divided, ferny, usually strongly scented leaves give rise to flowers that bloom early summer to frost if old flowers are picked off; in the desert, they bloom best from fall until frost. Colors range from white and pale yellow through gold, orange, red, and brownish maroon. All make long-lasting cut flowers, but their aroma can be overpowering indoors; some odorless varieties are available. Good container plants.

T. erecta. AFRICAN MARIGOLD, AMERICAN MARIGOLD. Original strains were single-flowered plants 3–4 ft. tall, 2 ft. wide, but modern strains are more varied. Most have double flowers. Choices include Antigua (10–12 in.); Guys and Dolls, Inca, and Inca II series (12–14 in.); Lady and Perfection (16–20 in.); and Climax (2½–3 ft.). Novelty tall strains include Odorless (2½ ft.). Sweet Cream has creamy white flowers on 16-in. stems. Crosses between *T. erecta* and *T. patula*, such as Nugget (10–12 in. high) and Zenith (12–15 in. high), bear a profusion of 2-in. flowers over a long season.

T. patula. FRENCH MARIGOLD. These are 6–18 in. high and wide, yellow to rich maroon-brown. Blossoms may be single or double; many are bicolored. Excellent for edging are dwarf, very double strains such as Janie (8 in.), Bonanza (10 in.), and Little Hero (10–12 in.), with 2-in. flowers in yellow, orange, red, and brownish red. The 2½-in. flowers of Aurora and Sophia strains are not as double.

T. tenuifolia (T. signata). SIGNET MARIGOLD. Flowers are just 1 in. wide and single, but bloom is profuse. Finely cut foliage. Gem strain offers blossoms in golden yellow, lemon yellow, and tangerine on 10-to-12-in.-high plants.

Tagetes erecta **Sweet Cream**

HOW TO GROW IT

Soil Amended, well-drained garden soil; for container culture, use a soil-based mix.

Planting Fast and easy from seed or transplants.

Fertilizer Apply controlled-release fertilizer at planting; give containerized marigolds liquid fertilizer every week or two throughout the growing season.

Water Avoid overhead sprinkling on taller kinds; stems will sag and even break under weight of water.

Care notes To make tall types stand without staking, dig planting hole extra deep, strip any leaves off lower 1–3 in. of stem, and plant stripped part below soil line.

Tropaeolum majus

GARDEN NASTURTIUM
Nasturtium family (Tropaeolaceae)
WARM-SEASON ANNUAL

⊘ ALL ZONES

☼ ◑ FULL SUN OR LIGHT SHADE

● REGULAR WATER

Garden nasturtiums are among the garden's most gratifying plants. Chickpea-size seeds are easy to handle and quick to germinate; plants grow fast; and all varieties make good cut flowers. The young leaves, flowers, and unripe seedpods are edible, giving a peppery zing to summer salads. This old-fashioned favorite reaches peak performance where summers are mild and on the dry side.

There are two main kinds: climbing types, which trail over ground or climb to 6 ft. by coiling leafstalks, and compact, bushy, more widely sold dwarf kinds to 1½ ft. high and wide. Both are covered with eye-catching round, bright green leaves on long stalks. Long-spurred, 2½-in. flowers have a refreshing fragrance and come in colors including maroon, red-brown, orange, yellow, red, and creamy white. (Blossoms on the wild species are orange.) You can get seeds of mixed colors in several strains; some single colors are also sold. Both single- and double-flowered forms are available.

Don't confuse this popular flower with the little-known genus *Nasturtium*, a kind of watercress in the cabbage family.

Use climbing types to cover fences, banks, stumps, or rocks; use dwarf kinds for bedding, to hide fading bulb foliage, or for quick color. All kinds make excellent container plants.

HOW TO GROW IT

Soil Easy to grow in most well-drained soils but does best in sandy soil.

Planting Sow in early spring; plant grows and blooms quickly, reseeds (it has naturalized along parts of the central California coast). In mild-winter, hot-summer areas, sow in fall for winter and spring bloom.

Spacing Since nasturtiums come in both dwarf and trailing varieties, be sure you adjust spacing to accommodate each variety's ultimate size.

Tropaeolum majus 'Peach Melba'

Fertilizer A little controlled-release fertilizer or aged manure can get plants up to size quickly, but don't fertilize again: too much fertilizer makes plants produce leaves at the expense of flowers.

Water Somewhat drought-tolerant.

Care notes Black aphids may show up on nasturtiums. Plants sometimes grow through the problem, but in serious cases, rip the nasturtiums out. If they've been flowering, they'll self-sow.

Viola

VIOLA AND PANSY
Violet family *(Violaceae)*
PERENNIALS USUALLY GROWN AS COOL-SEASON ANNUALS

✎ **ALL ZONES**

☼ ◑ **FULL SUN OR PART SHADE**

🌢 **REGULAR WATER**

Deceptively delicate to look at, violas and pansies are tough, showy, cold-tolerant, and easy to grow. They grow generally bigger, have flatter faces, and tolerate more sun than violets, which are close cousins. Pansies commonly have bigger leaves and flowers and make bigger clumps than violas, but violas stand up better to blustery, rainy weather. Both have fragrant, five-petaled flowers, often with dark blotches or markings on side and bottom petals, and often with contrasting white or yellow eye. Pansy flowers tend to be round overall, while viola flowers are usually higher than wide.

Use them for mass color in borders and edgings, as covers for spring-flowering bulbs, and in containers. You can also scatter Johnny-jump-up seeds in your lawn, where they'll occasionally surprise you with flowers.

Viola. To 6–8 in. high and 8 in. wide, with smooth, wavy-edged leaves. Slender-spurred flowers of the original *V. cornuta* grow about 1½ in. across. Modern hybrids, strains, and varieties have larger, shorter-spurred flowers in solid purple, blue, yellow, apricot, red, and white—or with elaborate markings.

Johnny-jump-ups *(V. tricolor)* grow 6–12 in. high and wide, and freely self-sow. Oval leaves are deeply lobed. Pert, ½-to-¾-in., velvety purple-and-yellow or blue-and-yellow flowers are the original wild pansies. Hybridization has produced flowers in violet, blue, white, yellow, lavender, mauve, apricot, orange, and red—with or without markings.

English violas, which look very much like annual violas, form 2-ft.-wide clumps that are reliably perennial.

Pansy *(V. × wittrockiana).* These grow 6–10 in. high and 9–12 in. wide. There are dozens of strains with 2-to-4-in. flowers in white, blue, mahogany red, rose, yellow, apricot, and purple; also bicolors and multicolor blends. Most have dark blotches on the lower three petals. Shiny green leaves are oval to nearly heart-shaped, slightly lobed, 1½ in. or longer.

Viola cornuta **Penny series 'White Jump-Up'**

HOW TO GROW IT

Soil Amended garden soil.

Planting In cold-winter climates, set out nursery plants in spring for summer bloom; in mild climates, plant in autumn for winter-to-spring bloom.

Fertilizer Apply composted manure at planting time, with occasional feeding throughout the season.

Care notes To prolong bloom, pick flowers (with some foliage) regularly and remove faded blooms before they set seed.

Zinnia

Sunflower family (*Asteraceae*)
WARM-SEASON ANNUALS

ALL ZONES

FULL SUN

MODERATE TO REGULAR WATER

These longtime favorites come in a rainbow of flower colors, from solid to beautifully patterned. Blooms can be single to double on plants 1–4 ft. tall.

Z. angustifolia. To 16 in. high and wide, with very narrow leaves. Orange, inch-wide flowers; each ray has a paler stripe. Blooms in 6 weeks from seed; continues late into fall. The Classic and Star series bloom in shades of orange-yellow and white. 'Golden Eye' and 'Star White' have white rays, yellow centers.

Z. elegans. This has given rise to most cultivated zinnias. Grows from less than a foot high and wide to 4 ft. tall, half as wide. Oval to lance-shaped leaves to 5 in. long; summer flowers from about 1–7 in. across. Forms include double, cactus-flowered (with quilled rays), and crested (cushionlike center surrounded by rows of broad rays); colors are white, pink, salmon, rose, red, yellow, orange, lavender, purple, and multicolors. 'Envy' has lime green flowers.

Z. haageana. To 2 ft. high, 1 ft. wide. Narrow, 3-in. leaves. Persian Carpet (1 ft. high) and Old Mexico (16 in. high) have double blossoms with mahogany red, yellow, and orange mixed in the same flower. Long summer bloom.

Z. marylandica. These mildew-tolerant varieties are *Z. angustifolia* × *Z. elegans* hybrids. They include the Profusion and Zahara series, mostly in white, red, yellow, orange, and bicolors. Plants grow 1–1½ ft. high and wide, with 2½-in. flower heads containing more than one row of rays.

Z. peruviana (Z. pauciflora). PERUVIAN ZINNIA, BONITA ZINNIA. Grows to 3 ft. high and wide; leaves to 3 in. long and 1¼ in. wide. In summer, bears profuse, 1½-in. flowers in brick red or soft gold.

Zinnia elegans

HOW TO GROW IT

Soil Well-drained, rich garden loam.

Planting Easy from seed; just sow where plants are to grow (or carefully set out nursery plants) from late spring to early summer.

Fertilizer Feed generously.

Water Regular watering until plants reach blooming size, then moderate watering.

Care notes Tallest varieties need staking. Most varieties tend to mildew in foggy areas and at the end of the season. Good air circulation helps. Deadhead to extend bloom.

Festuca glauca

COMMON BLUE FESCUE
Grass family *(Poaceae)*
EVERGREEN GRASS

✦ ZONES 1–24

☼ ◑ BEST IN SUN; TOLERATES SOME SHADE

◗ ◖ MODERATE TO REGULAR WATER

A low, mounding grass, common blue fescue grows quickly to about 1 ft. high and nearly as wide, forming a dense tuft of very narrow, fine leaves that vary in color from blue-gray to silvery white. In summer, showy spikes of flowers rise above the foliage mass; these bloom in a frosty blue-green shade and slowly fade to buff. The uniform mounds are excellent for use as edging or groundcover, but they also work well as colorful accents dotted among flowers. Sometimes sold as *F. cinerea* or *F. ovina glauca*. Two tough, compact, long-lived selections with intensely silver-blue leaves are 'Boulder Blue' and 'Elijah Blue'. 'Golden Toupee' grows about 8 in. high and wide, with finely textured chartreuse foliage; does best in light shade.

For a more casual look in Zones 4–9, 14–24, try California fescue *(F. californica),* native to the Coast Ranges from Northern California to Oregon. It grows as a loose clump of semievergreen to deciduous blue-green leaves to 2–3 ft. high and 1–2 ft. wide. Airy flowers rise 1–3 ft. above the foliage in spring and early summer, blue-green at first, then turning purple and finally maturing to wheat. Tolerates part shade and works beautifully beneath oaks.

HOW TO GROW IT

Soil These grasses are not particular about soil.

In containers Common blue and California fescues grow well in containers.

Care notes Clumps may die out in the center after several years. Divide and replant in late winter or early spring, or simply replace with new plants from the nursery.

Festuca glauca **'Elijah Blue'**

TIP Common blue fescue combines beautifully with flowers in a mixed container composition.

Hakonechloa macra

JAPANESE FOREST GRASS
Grass family *(Poaceae)*
DECIDUOUS GRASS

✎ ZONES 2B–9, 14–24

☼ ◑ ● FULL SUN IN COOLER CLIMATES ONLY

● REGULAR WATER

This choice, shade-loving grass from Japan forms elegant mounds of bamboolike leaves. It grows 1–2 ft. high and somewhat wider, spreading slowly by underground runners but never becoming invasive. Leaves turn coppery orange in fall, then fade to an attractive wheat color during winter dormancy. New growth fills in quickly in spring.

Colored-leaf selections are more widely grown than the species. 'Albovariegata' ('Albostriata'), to 2 ft. high, has green leaves with longitudinal white stripes. The vigorous 'All Gold' has leaves of golden yellow. 'Aureola', the most widely grown variety, reaches 14 in. high and has green leaves with longitudinal yellow stripes that turn chartreuse in dense shade, pale creamy yellow in more sun; foliage is sometimes suffused with pink in fall. Leaves of 'Beni-kaze' are green in summer but turn various shades of red when weather cools. All tend to burn in full, hot sun or reflected heat.

HOW TO GROW IT

Soil Prefers rich, well-drained soil; add plenty of compost at planting time.

In containers Excellent in containers, where it can thrive for years. Use a moisture-retentive potting mix and feed with an all-purpose fertilizer in early spring.

Care notes Toward winter's end, clip or gently pull out the dormant leaves to make room for the emerging new growth. Let clumps spread naturally, or divide every 3 years or so.

Hakonechloa macra '**All Gold**'

TIP The weeping leaves of Japanese forest grass look great spilling over a wall or softening the edges of steps.

Helictotrichon sempervirens

BLUE OAT GRASS
Grass family *(Poaceae)*
EVERGREEN GRASS

ZONES 1–12, 14–24

FULL SUN

REGULAR WATER

Bright blue-gray, narrow leaves form a symmetrical fountainlike mound 2–3 ft. high and wide. Blue oat grass resembles a giant blue fescue *(Festuca glauca)* but is more graceful. In spring, stems to 2 ft. or higher rise above foliage, bearing wispy, straw-colored flower clusters. This grass is attractive in borders or among boulders. It is especially lovely in combination with white-blooming or silver-leafed plants, and it contrasts nicely with dark purple foliage too. Blooms best in colder areas but is partly deciduous there. Choose a spot with good air circulation.

HOW TO GROW IT

Soil Best in rich, well-drained soil. Heavy clay soils are not to its liking, but it is very tolerant of alkaline soils.

Care notes Pull out occasional withered leaves, and remove spent flowers and dead leaves in spring. Does not respond well to shearing.

TIP Use blue oat grass as a soft accent in a flower bed, or plant it in groups as a colorful evergreen groundcover.

Helictotrichon sempervirens

Miscanthus sinensis

EULALIA, JAPANESE SILVER GRASS
Grass family *(Poaceae)*
DECIDUOUS GRASS

✎ **ZONES 2–24**

☼ ☽ **FULL SUN OR PART SHADE**

◗ ◗ **MODERATE TO REGULAR WATER**

Spectacular in bloom, this highly ornamental plant forms a fountain of slender leaves in spring; these may be solid-colored, striped lengthwise, or banded cross-wise, depending on variety. In summer or early fall comes an impressive display of flowers held well above the foliage mass. Blooms open as tassels and gradually expand into silvery, pinkish, or bronze feathery plumes that usually last well into winter. They may be cut for fresh or dried arrangements. In fall and winter, foliage turns shades of yellow, orange, or reddish brown. It looks especially showy against snow or a background of dark evergreens. Stunning as an accent in a large pot or tub.

The species, which can reach 12 ft. tall, is seldom offered, but its many varieties are widely available, with new ones arriving on the market every year. The following are among the choicest. 'Adagio', to 5 ft. tall (in bloom) and 3 ft. wide, has silver-green foliage and pink plumes. 'Morning Light' is a little taller, with a narrow white stripe down the center of each leaf. *M. s. condensatus* 'Cabaret' can reach 9 ft. tall in bloom, with wide leaves broadly striped lengthwise in white; 'Cosmopolitan' is similar in size, but leaves are green in the center, with broad white edges. The foliage of 'Gold Bar' is decorated with horizontal yellow stripes; it's a compact, upright grower to 4–5 ft. tall. 'Little Kitten' reaches just 3 ft. high in bloom.

TIP Eulalia looks great in drifts or as a backdrop for a flower border.

Miscanthus sinensis **'Little Kitten'**

HOW TO GROW IT

Soil Tolerates most soils but grows best in moderately fertile, well-drained soil.

In containers Choose smaller varieties.

Care notes Needs no special care during growth and bloom. Cut old foliage back to the ground before new leaves sprout in early spring; in climates with a long growing season, cut back again in midsummer to keep compact and to freshen foliage. Divide every 2 or 3 years to limit clump size and prevent decline in vigor.

Muhlenbergia rigens

DEER GRASS
Grass family (*Poaceae*)
EVERGREEN GRASS

✎ **ZONES 4–24**

☼ ◑ **FULL SUN OR LIGHT SHADE**

◊ ◖ **LITTLE TO MODERATE WATER**

Although it's tough as nails, this big Western native grass manages to look light and airy, especially in bloom. Bright green leaves form a dense, tight clump to 4 ft. tall and at least as wide. Slender yellow or purplish flower spikes in autumn are erect at first, then lean out in every direction; they rise 2 ft. above the leaves. Deer grass is excellent massed along a drive or placed as an accent in a flower border. It is also good for erosion control on slopes.

A similar but smaller grass for Zones 3b, 7–24 is *M. dubia*, commonly called pine muhly or Mexican deer grass. It grows just 2–3 ft. high and wide and blooms in summer and fall.

HOW TO GROW IT

Soil Deer grass grows in almost any soil. Pine muhly does best in sandy, well-drained soil.

Spacing Be sure to give adequate room for each plant's mature size; they don't look good when crowded together.

Care notes Pull out the occasional dead leaf to keep grass looking neat. To freshen, cut back to 3 in. high in late winter.

Muhlenbergia rigens

TIP Deer grass is a good choice for the transition zone between formal and informal parts of the garden.

Pennisetum orientale

ORIENTAL FOUNTAIN GRASS
Grass family *(Poaceae)*
DECIDUOUS GRASS

✎ **ZONES 3–10, 14–24**

☀ ☽ **FULL SUN OR PART SHADE**

💧 💧 **MODERATE TO REGULAR WATER**

This elegant yet dependable plant forms a lush fountain of slender, green to gray-green leaves just 2 ft. high and 2½ ft. wide. In summer and fall, pinkish, foxtail-like plumes rise above the foliage and slowly mature to light brown; foliage turns straw-colored in winter. Unlike most other fountain grasses, this one seldom self-sows. A good choice for containers, for perennial or shrub borders, and as bank cover.

Two recommended selections grow taller. 'Karley Rose', to 4 ft., has an upright form with dark green foliage and deep pink plumes. 'Tall Tails', to 6 ft. tall and 3–4 ft. wide, is more open growing, with light tan plumes; it tolerates desert heat as well as coastal conditions.

For an even larger, more colorful choice, try *P. setaceum* 'Rubrum', purple or red fountain grass (Zones 8–24; H1, H2; often grown as an annual in colder climates). It hails from tropical Africa, southwestern Asia, and the Arabian peninsula and reaches 5 ft. tall and wide; it rarely reseeds. 'Rubrum' forms a dense clump of purplish red leaves and rose-colored plumes that fade to beige. It grows best in full sun and can take supplemental irrigation but doesn't need any. The dwarf variety 'Eaton Canyon' ('Red Riding Hood', *P. advena* 'Eaton Canyon') is similar in color but grows just 1½–3 ft. high and wide; it may be evergreen in frost-free areas.

HOW TO GROW IT

Soil Not particular about soil.

Care notes Cut back to about 3 in. high in late winter, before new growth emerges.

Pennisetum orientale

TIP The full, fluffy blooms of fountain grasses add interest to fresh arrangements. Cut plumes just as they begin blooming.

Sassy Grassy Accents

Sometimes a planting scheme needs a little pop, and the upright or arching foliage of ornamental grasses does the job.

But some of the easiest, most striking plants with this growth habit aren't true grasses at all; they're perennials with grasslike leaf blades. Their flowers are usually small and inconspicuous, a minor pleasure rather than a big show.

Listed here are top picks for a variety of garden situations. These easy-care plants are mostly evergreen, though some may die back in cold winters or benefit from a little springtime cleanup. All work beautifully in containers.

A / Japanese sweet flag (*Acorus gramineus*). Slender leaves grow in circular, 10-in.-high tufts to give a lush look. 'Ogon' has golden yellow leaves; those of 'Variegatus' are green with white stripes. Pretty beside ponds or as border edgings. Full sun or light shade. Give ample moisture; will grow in shallow water. Zones 3b–10, 14–24.

B / Evergold Japanese sedge (*Carex oshimensis* 'Evergold'). Forms a stunning fountain of thin, creamy white leaves edged in green. Grows 1–2 ft. high and 3 ft. wide. Plant in rich, well-drained soil in part to full shade. Regular water. Zones 3–9, 14–24.

C / Orange New Zealand sedge (*Carex testacea*). Soft-looking sedge with threadlike, olive green leaves that turn rich orange in cool weather. Grows 2 ft. high, 3 ft. wide. For a blast of fall color, plant it in an orange ceramic pot. Full sun to part shade. Give moderate water along the coast, regular water in hot inland areas. Zones 4–9, 14–24.

D / Cape rush (*Chondropetalum elephantinum*). Big, dramatic plant with thin, deep green stems up to 5 ft. tall, each tipped with chestnut brown flower heads. Moves beautifully in the breeze. Full sun or part shade. Regular to ample water. Cut old growth to ground when new shoots appear in spring. Zones 8, 9, 14–24.

E / California gray rush (*Juncus patens*). Like a soft exclamation point, this Western native rush forms a perfectly upright mass of wiry, gray-green stems to 2 ft. high. Cut to ground in late winter for fresh spring growth. Full sun or light shade. Regular to ample water. Zones 4–9, 14–24.

F / Orange libertia (*Libertia peregrinans*). Stiff, upright leaves resemble small, bright orange swords that positively glow when backlit. Plant grows 2 ft. high, 1 ft. wide, and spreads manageably to form colonies. Little white flowers appear in late spring or early summer. Full sun or light shade. Moderate to regular water. Zones 8, 9, 14–24.

G / Big blue lily turf (*Liriope muscari*). Bundles of narrow, rich green leaves up to 2 ft. high are joined in summer by dense spikes of purple or white blooms. Look for colored-leaf varieties, including the dependable 'Silvery Sunproof'. All do best with part shade and regular water. Zones 2b–10, 14–24; H1, H2.

H / Black mondo grass (*Ophiopogon planiscapus* 'Nigrescens'). The "little black dress" of grasslike accents, with a refined habit and shiny, slender, nearly black leaves that look great with any other color. Grows 8 in. high, 1 ft. wide. Full sun or part shade. Moderate to regular water. Zones 5–9, 14–24; H1, H2.

I / Red hook sedge (*Uncinia rubra*). Bring in some visual heat with this foot-high tuft of rich mahogany leaves touched with red accents. Seems to glow when lit from behind. Does not grow well in intense heat; mulch to keep roots cool. Full sun or part shade. Regular water. Zones 4–6, 15–17.

Adiantum

MAIDENHAIR FERN
Maidenhair family *(Pteridaceae)*

- ◤ **ZONES VARY BY SPECIES**
- ◑ ● **PART OR FULL SHADE**
- ◌ ◌◌ **REGULAR TO AMPLE WATER**

With a common name like "maidenhair," it's no surprise that these are among the most delicate-looking ferns for Western gardens. The majority of species in this large genus come from moist tropical areas, where they grow on forest floors, along streams and waterfalls, and in damp crevices among stones. All form spreading clumps over time, with dark, wiry stems that could be said to resemble a thick strand of hair. Fan-shaped leaflets are bright green and thin textured; new growth is often dusky pink. Most maidenhair ferns die back to some extent in winter.

Use these dainty but easy-to-grow ferns as accents among other shade-loving plants or as an edging along a woodland path or near a garden pool. Mossy rocks, especially when wet, make beautiful foils for these finely textured plants.

A. aleuticum. WESTERN FIVE-FINGER FERN. Zones 1–7, 14–21. Western native with forked fronds that make a fingerlike pattern atop stems 1–2½ ft. high. Excellent in containers and can take quite a bit of sun if moisture is abundant. *A. pedatum*, American maidenhair, is similar but even hardier, growing reliably in Zones A3; 1–7, 14–21. It spreads nicely beneath deciduous trees.

A. capillus-veneris. SOUTHERN MAIDENHAIR. Zones 5–9, 14–24; H1, H2. Grows about 1½ ft. high and wide, with twice-divided (but not forked) fronds. Light green leaflets are small and fan-shaped.

A. venustum. HIMALAYAN MAIDENHAIR. Zones 3–7, 14–17. Just 6–8 in. high, this one spreads slowly to form a lush colony to 5 ft. or wider.

Adiantum aleuticum

HOW TO GROW IT

Soil All need well-drained soil that is rich in organic matter. Amend with compost at planting time.

Fertilizer Sprinkle compost around maidenhair ferns in spring.

Water Don't let soil dry out.

In containers Western five-finger fern and Himalayan maidenhair grow well in containers filled with 2 parts standard potting soil to 1 part peat. For Southern maidenhair, use standard potting soil.

Care notes Bait for snails and slugs. Remove dead or damaged fronds in early spring.

Asplenium bulbiferum

MOTHER FERN
Spleenwort family *(Aspleniaceae)*

ZONES 14 (PROTECTED), 15–17, 20–24

PART OR FULL SHADE

REGULAR TO AMPLE WATER

This tropical-looking fern produces a fountain of graceful, arching, very finely cut fronds that look shiny and fresh year-round. The whole plant can reach 3–4 ft. tall and wide, large enough to hold its own among shrubs and perennials in a shady border or completely fill a large container. In a favorable spot, these plantlets can form a large colony. Hardy to 26°F (–3°C).

HOW TO GROW IT

Soil Does best in gritty, well-drained soil. Amend soil with a bit of compost and a few handfuls of sand or gravel.

Fertilizer Apply a half dose of general-purpose controlled-release fertilizer at planting time and again each spring.

Water Don't let soil dry out.

In containers Grows well in large containers. Add sand, gravel, or lava rock (available at garden centers) to standard potting soil. Start plantlets in small pots and move into larger containers as they grow.

Care notes Bait for snails and slugs.

Asplenium bulbiferum

TIP Mother fern is a favorite with kids, because each frond produces many tiny plantlets that can be picked off and planted once they've formed three or four leaves.

Blechnum spicant

DEER FERN
Chain fern family *(Blechnaceae)*

ZONES 2B–7, 14–19, 24

PART OR FULL SHADE

REGULAR WATER

This elegant, glossy, deep green plant, native primarily to the coastal forests of Northern California and the Pacific Northwest, grows 1–2 ft. high and up to 3 ft. wide, with two different kinds of fronds: spreading, sterile ones to 1¾ in. wide, and narrower, stiffly erect fertile ones, with slender, widely spaced leaflets. It partners well with other acid-loving plants like rhododendron and lily-of-the-valley shrub *(Pieris japonica)*. Looks great in a casual woodland garden tucked among boulders or beneath trees—or even lining a pathway.

HOW TO GROW IT

Soil Does best in rich, acidic, well-drained soil. Amend soil with peat moss or a bagged planting mix formulated for azaleas and camellias.

Fertilizer Sprinkle compost around the fern in early spring.

Water Don't let soil become too dry. Avoid overhead watering when air is humid or still.

In containers Grows well in a large pot. Use planting mix formulated for azaleas and camellias.

Blechnum spicant

TIP Surround deer fern with a drift of impatiens for an elegant composition in part shade.

Dryopteris erythrosora

AUTUMN FERN
Wood fern family *(Dryopteridaceae)*

✂ **ZONES 2–9, 14–24**

☼ ● **PART OR FULL SHADE**

💧 **REGULAR WATER**

This native of China and Japan is one of the few ferns with seasonal color variation. In spring, its expanding fronds are a lovely blend of copper, pink, and yellow; they turn dark green in summer, then rusty brown in fall. Bright red spores produced on the leaf undersides are an attractive winter feature. Erect, arching fronds form an upright plant to 2 ft. high and 1½ ft. wide. Evergreen in mild climates; may die back partially in colder zones. Works beautifully as a stand-alone specimen, massed as a groundcover, or grown as a colorful partner for flowers like impatiens or begonias. Choose a spot protected from strong winds. 'Brilliance' has especially bright coppery red new growth.

Two larger members of this genus are also popular and easy to grow. *D. dilatata,* broad buckler fern (Zones 2–7, 14–17), is a usually deciduous fern that hails from western and central Europe. It's a vigorous grower to 3–4 ft. tall and wide, with rich green fronds that are broadly triangular. *D. filix-mas,* male fern (Zones 2–9, 14–17), is native to much of the Northern Hemisphere. Usually evergreen, it grows 2–5 ft. tall and wide, with finely cut, medium green fronds to 1 ft. wide.

HOW TO GROW IT

Soil All thrive in rich, well-drained soil. Amend soil with plenty of compost at planting time.

Fertilizer Sprinkle a little compost around the plant's base in early spring.

Water Best with regular water, but all will tolerate considerable drought when grown in full shade.

Dryopteris erythrosora

TIP Try planting these striking ferns beneath deciduous trees, where fallen leaves will provide a natural layer of mulch.

Polystichum munitum

WESTERN SWORD FERN
Wood fern family *(Dryopteridaceae)*

ZONES A3; 2–9, 14–24

PART OR FULL SHADE

REGULAR WATER

This hardy, symmetrical, easy-to-grow plant is among the most useful and widely planted ferns. Native from California to Alaska and Montana, Idaho, and South Dakota, it is the most common fern of Western forests, particularly recognizable as a companion to redwood trees. Plants reach 2–4 ft. tall and wide, with leathery, lustrous evergreen fronds that are erect, then spreading. Each leaflet is dagger-shaped, with toothed edges and a base that looks rather like a sword hilt. Old plants may have as many as 100 fronds.

Sturdy, deep green Western sword fern combines well with other plants, and when mature it is substantial enough to function as a small shrub. Use it in shady beds, along house walls, and in mixed woodland plantings.

HOW TO GROW IT

Soil Does best in well-drained soil amended at planting time with compost.

Fertilizer Sprinkle a little compost around the base of the fern in early spring.

Water Give regular water for the first year or two. Established plants get by with reduced moisture.

Care notes If plant looks untidy or thrips attack, snip off old fronds at their base in early spring, just as new ones start to unfurl.

Polystichum munitum

TIP The sturdy, deep green fronds last a long time in fresh arrangements. Snip them near the base and strip off leaflets that would be submerged in the vase.

Woodwardia fimbriata

GIANT CHAIN FERN
Chain fern family *(Blechnaceae)*

ZONES 2B–9, 14–24

PART OR FULL SHADE

REGULAR TO AMPLE WATER

This dramatic plant is among the largest of the native Western ferns, topping out at 9 ft. in mild, wet coastal regions; in gardens, it typically reaches 4–5 ft. tall and 3 ft. wide. Thick, leathery, apple green fronds are upright but spread gracefully toward the top. Foliage is twice cut but still somewhat coarse. The common name refers to the distinctive chainlike pattern of spores that form beneath the frond segments.

Use this bold-textured fern alongside a stream, against a shaded wall, or in a garden with a tropical or woodland theme. Giant chain fern is fast growing and vigorous, but not invasive.

HOW TO GROW IT

Soil Grows best in moist, organically enriched soil with a thick layer of mulch.

Fertilizer Sprinkle compost around the base in late winter or early spring.

Water Looks best with consistent deep watering and occasional spraying to keep dust and pests off the fronds.

Care notes Snip off any old, ragged fronds in late winter. They'll be quickly replaced by the new spring growth.

Woodwardia fimbriata

TIP To keep the huge fronds looking fresh during the dry season, wash them off with an occasional sprinkle from a hose.

Allium sphaerocephalon

DRUMSTICKS, ROUND-HEADED GARLIC
Onion family (*Alliaceae*)
PERENNIAL FROM BULB

✎ **ZONES 1–24**

☼ **FULL SUN**

◗ **REGULAR WATER DURING GROWTH AND BLOOM**

This is among the easiest and best alliums you can grow in your garden. Unlike most fall-planted bulbs, *A. sphaerocephalon* flowers from early to midsummer, after spring-flowering bulbs have faded. Egg-shaped, dense, 1-in. flower clusters (umbels) rise on 2-ft. stems. Wine red color develops first on the top of the green flower head, giving it a two-toned look, then gradually infuses the whole thing. *A. sphaerocephalon* is a great naturalizer; lift and divide only after clumps become crowded.

Several other alliums are useful in the same climate zones for late spring color. *A. caeruleum (A. azureum)*, blue allium, has cornflower blue umbels on 1-to-2-ft. stems. *A. cristophii*, star of Persia, has very large, round clusters (6–12 in. across) of lavender to deep lilac, starlike flowers with a metallic sheen. Stems grow 12–15 in. high. Leaves are long, white, and hairy beneath. *A. moly* 'Jeannine', golden garlic, produces bright, shining yellow flowers in open, 3-in.-wide clusters on stems 6–10 in. high. Flat leaves, to 2 in. wide, are almost as long as flower stems.

Though alliums mix well with other perennials, they are easily disturbed when you pull adjacent weedy grasses. Avoid trouble by treating soil with corn gluten–based herbicide at planting, then mulch well.

TIP Flowers can be cut and used fresh, or dried by hanging them upside down.

Allium sphaerocephalon

HOW TO GROW IT

Soil All alliums do best in well-drained soil (preferably on the sandy side), enriched before planting with organic matter.

Planting In fall or spring, plant bulbs as deep as their height or width, whichever is greater.

Spacing Plant *A. cristophii* and *A. sphaerocephalon* 8–12 in. apart. Plant *A. caeruleum* and *A. moly* 4 in. apart.

Water Even watering helps growth and flower production. After bloom, when foliage begins to yellow, cut back on watering or let soil go dry; foliage dies to the ground, even in mild-winter areas.

Canna

CANNA
Canna family *(Cannaceae)*
PERENNIALS FROM RHIZOMES

🖊 **ZONES 6–9, 12–24; H1, H2; OR DIG AND STORE**

☼ **FULL SUN**

💧💧 **REGULAR TO AMPLE WATER DURING GROWTH AND BLOOM**

Bold leaves, imposing size, and tropical colors make cannas a focal point in the perennial border or in big pots. Most are hybrids, with large, lance-shaped leaves that are rich green, bronzy red, striped, or variegated. Spikes of large, irregularly shaped flowers come in red, orange, yellow, pink, cream, white, or bicolors, flowering in summer and fall.

All show well in groups of single colors against plain backgrounds.

The following are among those in the 4-to-6-ft. range: 'Bengal Tiger' ('Striata', 'Pretoria') has yellow-striped green leaves, orange blossoms; 'Tropicanna' produces hot orange blooms over purple foliage striped with green, yellow, pink, and red; *C. indica* 'Tropicanna Gold' has yellow-orange flowers flecked with dark orange over green-and-gold-striped leaves; 'Tropicanna Black' has deep bronzy chocolate leaves and red flowers that fade to orange; and 'Black Knight' has blackish bronze foliage and velvety, deep red flowers. 'Ermine' ('Ermine White') has white flowers on a 3-to-4-ft. plant; 'President' has scarlet blooms; 'Intrigue' has orange flowers on a 6-to-8-ft. plant.

For dwarf varieties that grow 24–30 in. high, try 'Red Futurity', with red flowers and dark-striped green leaves, and 'Yellow Futurity', with yellow flowers against green foliage.

Water cannas *(C. glauca)* love wet soil. Try 'Erebus', salmon-pink, 4–6 ft. tall, with slender stems and small (for a canna) blue-green leaves.

Best adapted to warm-to-hot-summer climates, cannas are also successful in mild-summer areas, like the Pacific Northwest. Keep them out of wind, which shreds their leaves. Where soil freezes deeply, treat these as annuals, or lift and store rhizomes over winter.

Canna **'Bengal Tiger'**

HOW TO GROW IT

Soil Should be rich and moist.

Planting Plant in spring after danger of frost is past, setting rhizomes 2–4 in. deep, 1½–2 ft. apart. In colder regions, start rhizomes indoors 4–6 weeks before last frost date; then plant out.

Fertilizer Apply controlled-release fertilizer at planting, then high-phosphorus fertilizer monthly.

Water Regular watering is essential.

Care notes Cut stems to ground after bloom; new stems will continue to grow into early fall. Divide clumps every 3 or 4 years. ❯❯

Canna 'Tropical Rose'

Cannas in Containers

It has been said that you need three kinds of plants to make containers come alive: thrillers (tall focal points), fillers, and spillers. Cannas make near-perfect thrillers: they have the imposing stature for it, showy flowers, and (in many cases) multicolored leaves that pick up the colors of fillers and spillers. Use large containers—16-in. diameter minimum, but 18 in. is better—placed out of the wind, which can shred canna leaves. Choose a glazed container, since it won't dry out as fast as terra-cotta (cannas are thirsty). Pick fillers and spillers at the same time you buy your canna, so you can choose colors that complement each other and work with the canna leaves. Bidens can make a good filler, while *Mecardonia* 'Gold Dust' and golden creeping Jenny (*Lysimachia nummularia* 'Aurea') can make impressive spillers. Water often and feed every 2 weeks for strong growth and flowering. Plant your canna at the back of any pot seen only from one side.

Top: *Canna* 'Pfitzer's Salmon Pink'
Bottom: *Canna* 'Picasso'

Crocosmia

CROCOSMIA, MONTBRETIA
Iris family *(Iridaceae)*
PERENNIALS FROM CORMS

🌡 **ZONES VARY BY TYPE**

☼ ☽ **FULL SUN OR SOME SHADE IN HOTTEST CLIMATES**

💧 **REGULAR WATER DURING GROWTH AND BLOOM**

As much a delight for hummingbirds as for the gardeners who grow them, garden crocosmias are nearly all hybrids of species native to tropical and southern Africa. They were formerly called tritonia and are related to freesia, ixia, and sparaxis. Small orange, red, or yellow flowers bloom in summer (spring in hottest areas) on branched stems, rising above basal clumps of sword-shaped leaves.

There are two important hybrid groups:

C. × crocosmiiflora (Tritonia crocosmiiflora). MONTBRETIA. Zones 5–24; H1, H2. A favorite for generations, montbretias can still be seen in older gardens where they have spread freely, producing orange-crimson flowers 1½–2 in. across on 3-to-4-ft. stems. Leaves grow 3 ft. high and ½–1 in. wide. Many once-common named forms in yellow, orange, cream, and near-scarlet are making a comeback. Good for naturalizing on slopes or in fringe areas. Can be invasive in mild parts of the Pacific Northwest; has established itself in wildlands throughout the Hawaiian Islands. Among 2-ft.-high choices are 'Citronella', light yellow flowers with dark eye; 'Emily McKenzie', orange with red eye; and 'Solfatare', bronze foliage and yellow flowers. In the 2-to-3-ft. range are 'Babylon' (orange flowers with scarlet throats) and 'Voyager' (bright yellow).

C. hybrids. Zones 4–24. These more complex hybrids are slightly hardier than *C. × crocosmiiflora*. In the 2-to-3-ft. range try 'Emberglow' (scarlet), 'Jenny Bloom' (golden yellow), and 'Walberton Yellow'. 'Lucifer' grows 4 ft. tall with red blossoms.

TIP Plant behind a low boxwood hedge or a low wall to keep bloom-heavy tops from falling over.

Crocosmia 'Lucifer'

HOW TO GROW IT

Soil Well-drained, enriched soil is optimal for large plants and flowers, but most will naturalize even in unamended soil.

Planting Set corms 2 in. deep, 3 in. apart.

Fertilizer One application of controlled-release fertilizer early in the growing season is sufficient.

Care notes Where winter lows range from 10°F to –5°F (–12°C to –21°C), provide winter mulch. In colder areas, dig and store over winter; or, to stay true to the theme of this book, save yourself work and plant something hardier, like iris. Divide clumps only when vigor and flower quality begin to decline.

Dietes iridioides

FORTNIGHT LILY, AFRICAN IRIS
Iris family *(Iridaceae)*
PERENNIALS FROM RHIZOMES

✎ **ZONES 8, 9, 12–24; H1, H2**

☼ ☽ **FULL SUN OR PART SHADE**

◐ ● **MODERATE TO REGULAR WATER**

These classic mild-winter perennials (also known as *D. vegeta* and *Moraea iridioides*) form dense, long-lasting clumps and flower for months. Evergreen plants resemble Siberian iris, with upright fans of stiff, narrow leaves, while the flowers are reminiscent of small Japanese irises. They appear on branched stalks throughout spring, summer, and fall—sometimes well into winter in mild climates. Bloom bursts seem to occur at 2-week intervals, hence the common name "fortnight lily." Each flower lasts only a day, but the supply is seemingly endless. Excellent in permanent landscape plantings with pebbles, rocks, shrubs, and other long-lived perennials.

Stems on this East African plant grow 2–3 ft. high. Waxy white flowers to 3 in. across have yellow-orange blotches, with a few orange marks at bases of inner three segments; three appendages radiating from the flower's center are usually pale violet. Deadhead flowers to prolong bloom, but don't cut flower stems (they last for more than a year) until they have clearly stopped producing blooms; then cut back to a leaf joint near base of stem.

'John's Runner' is a dwarf form growing only 1–2 ft. high and 2–3 ft. wide with white flowers marked with yellow and purple. Spent flower stalks produce plantlets that root as the stalks fall over, allowing the plant to spread.

The plant sold as *D. iridioides* 'Johnsonii' is actually *D. grandiflora*, a slightly larger plant with longer leaves, brown markings at the base of inner segments, and yellow beards on outer segments. Flowers last 3 days.

HOW TO GROW IT

Soil Rich, well-drained soil gets plants off to the best start, but even lean soil is acceptable if drainage is good.

Planting Plant from containers (bare rhizomes are not sold) at any time of year.

Dietes iridioides

Spacing Plant 2 ft. apart.

Fertilizer A little fertilizing is helpful during the growing season.

Water Regular watering the first year, then moderate watering.

Care notes Clumps can remain undisturbed for years; when you need to divide, do so in fall or winter, and go back to a regular watering schedule until divisions are well established.

Hemerocallis

DAYLILY
Daylily family *(Hemerocallidaceae)*
PERENNIALS FROM TUBEROUS ROOTS

✎ **ZONES 1–24; H1, H2; EXCEPT AS NOTED**

☼ ◐ **FULL SUN, OR PART SHADE IN HOTTEST CLIMATES**

● **REGULAR WATER**

◆ **TOXIC TO CATS**

At a distance, daylilies make easy, effective summer borders, while up close, the flowers are perfect specimens for the vase. All grow in large clumps of arching, sword-shaped leaves that emerge from tuberous, somewhat fleshy roots and produce clusters of mostly warmtoned, lilylike flowers that rise well above foliage at the ends of generally leafless stems. Each bloom lasts for only a day, but replacements are plentiful.

Dwarf varieties are available.

Deciduous types go dormant in winter and survive without protection to about −35°F (−37°C); where the winters are very mild, however, they may not get enough chill to perform well. Evergreen kinds succeed in mild-winter regions as well as in colder areas, but they need a 4-to-6-in. layer of protective mulch (straw, for example) where temperatures dip below −20°F (−29°C). Semi-evergreen sorts may or may not retain their leaves, depending on climate.

Use in flower beds, under high-branching deciduous trees, among evergreen shrubs near water, or as groundcovers.

To use as cut flowers, choose stems with well-developed buds; these open on successive days, though each flower is slightly smaller than the preceding one. Arrange individual blooms in low bowls.

Hybrids (of which there are thousands) generally grow 2½–4 ft. tall and 2–3 ft. wide; some selections reach 6 ft. tall. Dwarf types grow 1–2 ft. high and wide. Flowers of standard kinds are 4–8 in. across; those of dwarfs 1½–3½ in. wide. Some have broad petals, others narrow, spidery ones; many are ruffled. Colors range far beyond the basic yellow, orange, and rusty red to pink, vermilion, buff, apricot, plum, lilac-purple, cream, and near-white, often with contrasting eyes or midrib stripes that yield a bicolor effect. Many varieties are sprinkled with tiny iridescent dots known as diamond dust. Selections with semidouble and double flowers exist. Tetraploid varieties have petals that are unusually heavy textured.

Hemerocallis **'Pink Damask'**

Bloom usually begins in mid- to late spring, but early and late bloomers are also available. By planting all three types, you can extend bloom period. Scattered bloom may occur during summer, and reblooming types put on a second display in late summer to midautumn. Some varieties bloom throughout warm weather. These include the 3-ft.-high Starburst series, which comes in a variety of colors, as well as 2-ft.-high dwarf varieties 'Black-eyed Stella' (yellow with red eye), bright yellow 'Happy Returns' and 'Stella de Oro', and red 'Pardon Me'.

New hybrids appear in such numbers that no book can keep up. To get the ones you want, visit daylily specialists, buy plants in bloom at your local nursery, study catalogs, or visit the website of the American Hemerocallis Society *(daylilies.org)*. ❯❯

Among species, you may come across two, both deciduous. The Chinese *H. lilioasphodelus (H. flava)*, lemon daylily, grows 3 ft. high and wide, with 2-ft.-long leaves; 4-in., fragrant, pure yellow flowers bloom in mid- to late spring. The East Asian *H. minor*, grass-leaf daylily (Zones A1–A3; 1–9, 14–17), grows 2 ft. high and wide, with slender leaves. Fragrant, bright golden yellow flowers appear for a relatively short time in late spring or early summer. They stand just above the foliage.

HOW TO GROW IT

Soil Daylilies adapt to almost any kind of soil, but for best results, provide well-drained soil amended with organic matter.

Planting Set out container plants at any time during the growing season; spring and summer are better in cold-winter zones, while fall and winter are preferred where winters are warm. Plant from nursery containers at any time from early spring through midautumn (year-round in mild-winter areas).

Spacing Plant 1 to 2 ft. apart.

Fertilizer Apply balanced fertilizer in late winter before new growth starts, and feed again monthly with liquid fertilizer until bloom starts.

Water Give regular moisture from spring through autumn.

Care notes When clumps become crowded (usually after 3 to 6 years), divide them in fall or early spring in hot-summer areas, during summer in cool-summer regions or where growing season is short.

TIP Dwarf daylilies shine in rock gardens.

Top: *Hemerocallis* **'Marion Vaughn'**
Bottom: *Hemerocallis* **'Bela Lugosi'**

Iris

Iris family (*Iridaceae*)
PERENNIALS FROM RHIZOMES

✎ **ZONES VARY ACCORDING TO SPECIES OR TYPE**

☼ ☽ **FULL SUN OR PART SHADE IN HOT-SUMMER CLIMATES**

◦ ◦ ◦◦ **WATER NEEDS VARY BY SPECIES**

◈ **TOXIC KINDS NOTED IN ENTRIES**

Spring bloom wraps up with a spectacular rainbow of irises. Few perennials are more reliable, and few have as many variants. From over 250 species, three deserve space in any good garden.

All have grassy or swordlike foliage and flower parts in threes. The three inner segments (the standards) are petals; they are usually upright or arching but, in some kinds, may flare to horizontal. The three outer segments (the falls) are really petal-like sepals; they are held at various angles, from nearly horizontal to drooping. Bearded iris, which comes in the widest color range, is named for the caterpillar-like ornaments in the center of each fall. The falls on beardless iris are smooth.

TALL BEARDED IRISES

Zones 1–24. Among the choicest perennials for borders, massing, and cutting, these hybrids are the most widely sold irises. Ingestion causes gastric upset, and plants have poisoned livestock; in addition, some people get contact dermatitis from handling the rhizomes.

Mid- to late-spring flowers appear on branching, 2½-to-4-ft. stems and come in all colors but pure red and green. Color combinations and elaborately ruffled or fringed flowers produce infinite variety. Countless named selections are available.

Variegated-foliage selections include 'Pallida Variegata' ('Zebra'), with green leaves striped with cream, and 'Argentea', whose green leaves have white stripes. Both bear smallish blue-lavender flowers on 2-ft. stems but are grown primarily for their leaves.

Reblooming tall bearded irises flower in spring, then again in mid- to late summer, fall, or winter, depending on variety and climate. In mild climates, some are nearly everblooming. These types need continued feeding and regular moisture for best performance.

Tall bearded iris 'Flammenschwert'

PACIFIC COAST IRISES

Best in Zones 4–9, 14–24. Eleven species native to Pacific Coast states have been bred into a hybrid group that comes in a broad range of colors and patterns. Flowers may be white, blue shades, pink, copper, brown, maroon, or violet—many with elaborate veining or patterning. Foliage is narrow, grassy. Slender flower stems reach 8–24 in., depending on variety.

I. douglasiana is native to the California coast from Santa Barbara into Oregon. Evergreen leaves are 1½–2 ft. long; stems are 1–2 ft., sometimes branched; flowers come in purple and blue shades to white and cream. Tolerates less-than-perfect conditions. *I. innominata* comes from northwestern California and southwestern

Oregon. Evergreen leaves; 8-to-12-in. stems bear flowers in yellow, orange, lavender, purple, brown, many attractively veined. Best in mild-summer regions, in woodland or rock garden. *I. tenax*, from Washington and Oregon, makes grassy clumps of foot-high deciduous leaves. Flowers may be white, blue, purple, pink, or cream, often veined in purple or brown. Best with mild winter chill.

SIBERIAN IRISES

Zones A2, A3; 1–10, 14–23. The most widely sold members of this group are named hybrids derived from *I. sibirica* and *I. sanguinea* (formerly *I. orientalis*)—species native to Europe and Asia. Clumps of narrow, almost grasslike deciduous leaves produce slender stems to 4 ft. tall (depending on variety), each bearing two to five blossoms with upright standards and flaring to drooping falls. Colors include white and shades of blue, lavender, purple, wine red, pink, and light yellow.

HOW TO GROW IT

Soil Well-drained soil is a must. Siberian iris needs neutral to acid soil.

Planting Container stock can be planted anytime. For rhizomes, July to October is the best planting period for tall bearded (earlier in cold-winter areas, later in hot-summer regions), while September to October is best for Siberian and Pacific Coast irises.

Spacing Space rhizomes 1–2 ft. apart, with tops just beneath the soil surface. Spread roots well. Growth proceeds from the leafy end of rhizome, so point that end in the direction you want growth initially to occur.

Fertilizer Feed plants with moderate-nitrogen commercial fertilizer as growth begins in spring, then after bloom has finished.

Water From the time growth starts in late winter or early spring, water regularly until about 6 weeks after flowers fade; buds for next year's flowers form during post-bloom period. During summer, plants need much less water.

Care notes Divide only when vigor and flower quality begin to decline. Make divisions at the best planting time for your area.

Top: *Iris douglasiana* 'On the Edge'
Bottom: *Iris sibirica*

Lilium

LILY
Lily family *(Liliaceae)*
PERENNIALS FROM BULBS

🪧 **ZONES VARY BY SPECIES OR TYPE**

☼ ◑ **ROOTS COOL, TOPS IN SUN OR FILTERED LIGHT**

⬤ **REGULAR WATER, EXCEPT AS NOTED**

Though it might seem that anything this elegant would be hard to grow, that isn't the case. Breeding advances have given us strong, disease-resistant plants that grow well in the ground or in containers. Most are in the 3-to-5-ft. height range and have large, colorful, often fragrant flowers. All make splendid cut flowers. Lily species range wild across Asia, Europe, and North America, but the following two groups are hybrids optimized for fragrance, color, habit, and garden performance.

ORIENTAL LILIES

Oriental hybrids. Zones 1–9, 14–22. These bloom midsummer to early fall, with big (to 9 in.), fragrant flowers of white or pink, often banded with gold or red on the center of each petal, and spotted with red. Most are 3–5 ft. tall, with flowers that face upward or outward (a few have nodding blooms). If you live where summer temperatures routinely rise above 90°F (32°C), plant these in dappled afternoon shade. Examples are 'Casablanca', pure white; 'Mona Lisa', pink, intensifying toward the center, with darker pink center lines and freckles, 1½–2 ft. high; 'Muscadet', white with pink freckles and pink center lines; 'Salmon Star', pink flushed with salmon toward the center and base of each petal, 2–3 ft. high; and 'Stargazer', rose-red with white margins. Double-flowered selections all require dappled sun or afternoon shade because they have thin petals.

OT hybrids (also called Orienpets). Zones 1–9, 14–23. This group blends China's trumpet lilies with Japan's Oriental lilies to produce heavy-stemmed, 3-to-5-ft. plants. They tolerate a little more heat and demand less winter chill than their Oriental parents, and most have a light, sweet fragrance with lemony overtones. The color range is mostly in shades of yellow but also includes reds and pinks; "whites" are really cream-colored. Examples include 'Black Beauty', very deep wine color edged with a white line, strongly curled petals; 'Conca d'Or' (heady perfume), lemon yellow petals with

OT hybrid 'Miss Freya'

pale edges; 'LaVern Freimann' ('Miss Freya'), maroon-red, 6–7 ft. tall, late-summer bloom; and 'Scheherazade', genetically very robust, rose-red with creamy yellow margins, light fragrance.

ASIATIC LILIES

Asiatic hybrids. Zones A1–A3; 1–9, 14–24. These early-summer-bloomers are the most reliable for the average garden, so breeders produce them by the score. Flowers are usually unscented. Some of the hybrids have upward-facing flowers, while others have horizontal or drooping blooms. Stems are strong and erect, and range in height from short (1½ ft.) to moderate (4½ ft.). Flowers (mostly singles) come in virtually every color but blue,

Top: Oriental lily
Bottom: LA hybrid 'Kentucky'

many with dark spots or contrasting bands of color. Noteworthy examples include 'Fata Morgana', double yellow; 'Graffity', greenish yellow petals with maroon speckles coalescing into a deep maroon center; 'Landini', plum black; 'Orange Cocotte', clear orange, upward facing, and pollen-free; and 'Red Velvet', dark red, with pendant flowers.

LA hybrids. Zones A2, A3; 1–9, 14–24. Hybrids between Easter lilies *(L. longiflorum)* and Asiatic hybrid lilies, these grow quickly to 3–4 ft., bloom early, and make great cut flowers. Blooms face up and are available in yellow, pink, red, white, and orange. Examples include 'Eyeliner', petals white with black edge and a few black freckles; 'Kentucky', whose fragrant, early-summer flowers have an orange-yellow base with paprika speckles, 3 ft. high; and 'Red Alert', deep, shiny red. Along with OT hybrids, LA hybrids are among the best-performing lilies for Southern California.

HOW TO GROW IT

Soil Dig amendment into the top 16 in. of soil before planting; good drainage is essential.

Planting Plant bulbs in fall or spring. Dig a planting hole the depth of your shovel blade, then place enough soil at bottom of hole to bring it up to proper level for bulb, which should be buried 2½ times as deep as its diameter. Set bulb with its roots spread; fill in hole with soil, firming it around bulb to eliminate air pockets.

Spacing Ideal spacing is 1 ft. apart, but you can plant as close as 6 in.

Fertilizer In fertile garden soil, fertilizer may be unnecessary. In leaner soil, apply controlled-release fertilizer when first spears emerge in spring.

Water In the morning, water when the top 2 in. of soil has dried out. Cut back on watering somewhat after tops turn yellow in fall, but never let roots go completely dry. Flooding is preferable to overhead watering. If you use drip irrigation, keep the emitter 8 in. from the stem.

Care notes Sometimes lilies get viruses that mottle leaves and stunt growth. Remove and discard such plants.

Narcissus

DAFFODIL, NARCISSUS
Amaryllis family *(Amaryllidaceae)*
PERENNIALS FROM BULBS

✿ **ZONES A2, A3; 1–24**

☀ ☽ **FULL SUN DURING BLOOM, PART SHADE AFTER IN HOT CLIMATES**

💧 **REGULAR WATER DURING GROWTH AND BLOOM**

⬧ **POISONOUS IF CONSUMED, AND BULBS CAN CAUSE CONTACT DERMATITIS**

These cheery spring bulbs are great naturalizers, popping up year after year and increasing over time. All have the same basic flower structure. Each bloom has six outer "petals" (the perianth) that surround a cup or trumpet (the corona) in the blossom's center. Flowers may be borne singly or in clusters. Colors are basically yellow and white, but there are many variations—shades of orange, red, apricot, pink, and cream. Some are fragrant. Leaves may be straight and flat (strap-shaped) or narrow and rushlike. All are natives of Europe and North Africa.

Given minimum care at planting, they thrive with virtually no further attention. These plants need only infrequent division (and will survive without it) and are unappetizing to gophers and deer. They bloom in late winter or spring.

All plants known by the names "daffodil" and "narcissus" are properly *Narcissus*. In gardeners' terms, however, "daffodil" refers to large-flowered kinds, while "narcissus" denotes small-flowered (usually early blooming) types bearing blossoms in clusters.

Daffodils perform well in containers. They also make fine cut flowers, though freshly cut stems release a substance that causes other flowers in the same vase to wilt. To prevent this, let cut daffodils soak in cool water overnight, rinse stem ends, and then combine with other flowers.

Plant in sweeping drifts if space is available. In hot-summer regions, daffodils are often planted beneath high-branching deciduous trees, where they receive full sun while they are blooming; after bloom, dappled shade. Flowers usually face the sun—another factor to keep in mind when selecting planting locations.

Of the 13 generally recognized divisions of daffodils, the following are recommended for the 20-minute garden.

Narcissus **'Mount Hood'**

Trumpet daffodils. Trumpet is as long as or longer than surrounding perianth segments; one flower to each stem. Best known are yellow 'King Alfred' (an old name improperly applied to newer varieties) and 'Dutch Master', but newer yellow-flowered 'Marieke' and 'Primeur' are superior. 'Mount Hood' is pure white. Bicolors with white segments and yellow trumpet include 'Bravoure', 'Las Vegas', and 'Topolino'. Among those with yellow segments and some white on the trumpet are 'Pay Day' and 'Pistachio'.

Large-cupped daffodils. Cup is shorter than perianth segments but always more than one-third their length; one flower per stem. Varieties include 'Stainless' (white), and 'Carlton' and 'Saint Keverne' (both yellow). Varieties with white perianth segments and colored cup

include 'Ice Follies' (yellow cup); 'Accent' and 'Salome' (pink cup); 'Fragrant Rose' (reddish pink cup); and 'Redhill' (reddish orange cup). 'Ambergate', 'Ceylon', and 'Fortissimo' all have yellow perianth segments and orange or red cup. Those with yellow segments and white cup include 'Altun Ha' and 'Fellows Favorite'.

Small-cupped daffodils. Cup no more than one-third the length of perianth segments; one flower per stem. Varieties include 'Audubon' (white segments, pale yellow cup banded pink) and 'Barrett Browning' (white segments, orange-red cup).

Triandrus hybrids. Cup at least two-thirds the length of perianth segments; several flowers to each stem. White 'Thalia' is an old favorite. Others include 'Hawera' (yellow) and 'Kate Heath' (white segments, pink cup).

Cyclamineus hybrids. Early bloomers with one flower per stem. Perianth segments are strongly recurved. Yellow 'February Gold' is best known. Yellow 'Rapture' has an especially long trumpet. 'Jack Snipe' and 'Wisley' have white segments, yellow trumpets. 'Jetfire' has a butter yellow perianth and red-orange trumpet.

Miscellaneous. This category contains all types that don't fit the other divisions. 'Tête-à-tête' and fragrant 'Tiny Bubbles' (both yellow) are rock garden dwarfs to about 6 in. high.

HOW TO GROW IT

Soil Daffodils are not fussy about soil as long as it is well drained.

Planting In mid- to late fall, set bulbs approximately twice or three times as deep as they are tall. Water newly planted bulbs thoroughly.

Spacing Space bulbs at least 6–8 in. apart (or three times their width for smaller varieties).

Fertilizer Usually unnecessary, but in poor soil apply mild liquid fertilizer the spring after planting.

Water In many regions, fall and winter rain and snow provide all the moisture that daffodils require. If precipitation fails before bloom period ends and leaves begin to yellow, irrigate. Summer watering is not needed.

Care notes As long as the leaves are green, they are using sunlight to rebuild the bulbs' energy for next year's growth. After foliage has turned yellow, remove it and lightly cultivate the soil so that insects will not have an easy way in.

Top: *Narcissus* **'Barrett Browning'**
Bottom: **Triandrus hybrid 'Thalia'**

Zantedeschia aethiopica

COMMON CALLA, CALLA LILY
Arum family *(Araceae)*
PERENNIALS FROM RHIZOMES

ZONES 5, 6, 8, 9, 12–24; H1, H2

FULL SUN OR PART SHADE

REGULAR TO AMPLE WATER

POISONOUS TO CATS AND DOGS

Large, graceful white flowers (really flower bracts) rise above clumps of big, fleshy, arrow-shaped leaves, making these favorite spring pot plants, especially around Easter. (And while these are sometimes mis-labeled as such, they aren't Easter lilies, *L. longiflorum*.) They're also standouts in partially shaded garden borders, and even in shallow streams or ponds.

Common callas have shiny green, stalked, unspotted leaves that can grow 18 in. long and 10 in. wide. Each flower bract (spathe) surrounds a fingerlike, yellow central spike (spadix) that is tightly covered with tiny true flowers. Spathes can reach 8 in. long and appear on stems slightly taller than the foliage.

Varieties include robust 'Green Goddess', with large spathes that are white at the base, green toward the tip, and 'Hercules', which is larger than the species, with big spathes that open flat and curve backward. Dwarf types include 'Childsiana', which grows about 1 ft. high.

Where summers are hot, grow in light shade; in milder climates, give full sun or light shade.

Zantedeschia aethiopica **'Green Goddess'**

HOW TO GROW IT

Soil Tolerates a wide range of soil, but thrives in fertile, moist (even boggy) ground.

Planting From fall through early spring, set rhizomes 4 in. deep, 1 ft. apart.

Fertilizer Regular feeding helps maintain steady growth. In containers, apply half-strength liquid fertilizer weekly.

Water Needs year-round moisture.

In containers These are great container subjects anywhere and pair well with English daisies in spring. In cold-winter climates, container gardening is the only option. Bring containers inside every fall to protect from hard freezes.

Care notes Dig and divide only when performance declines.

Azalea

Heath family *(Ericaceae)*
SHRUBS (EVERGREEN TYPES)

✎ **BEST IN ZONES 4–6, 15–17**

☼ **FILTERED SUNLIGHT**

💧 💧 **REGULAR TO AMPLE WATER**

⬦ **LEAVES ARE POISONOUS IF INGESTED**

Evergreen azaleas are show-stoppers in early spring, when flowers practically cover the plant. They look good out of bloom, too, with handsome small leaves and a pleasing overall shape. Most are dense little shrubs that grow slowly to about as wide as they are high.

Azaleas may be deciduous or evergreen, but evergreen types are particularly easy to grow. They fall into more than a dozen groups and species; an increasing number of hybrids have such mixed parentage that they don't fit into any category. Your best bet is to visit a local nursery to find out which evergreen azaleas are best suited to your area. Then you can choose the color and size that fit your garden.

HOW TO GROW IT

Soil These plants need excellent drainage and much air around their roots. Amend soil with plenty of organic matter.

Planting In clay or alkaline soil, plant in bed raised 1–2 ft. above original soil level. Mix a generous amount of organic material into the top foot of native soil; then fill bed above it with a mixture of 50 percent organic matter, 30 percent native soil, and 20 percent sand. Plant evergreen azaleas with top of rootball slightly above soil level. Then add a generous layer of mulch such as pine needles, oak leaves, or bark or wood chips. Never dig around the plants.

Fertilizer Some experts dig fertilizer into the soil to get new plantings off to a good start. Feed established plants with commercial acid fertilizer well before bloom, as buds swell (in early spring, except for the earliest bloomers). Feed again when new leaves begin to grow, just as blooms are fading. Sprinkle a little compost around the base of the plant in early fall.

'Congratulatory Light' azalea

In containers Compact varieties grow well in containers filled with acidic soil mixes specially formulated for azaleas, camellias, and rhododendrons.

Care notes Evergreen azaleas are dense, usually shapely plants; snipping off the occasional wayward branch restores symmetry. To keep bushes compact, tip-pinch frequently, starting after flowering ends and continuing until July. Azaleas can even be sheared into formal hedges.

To prevent the accumulation of salt in the soil, periodically leach the planting by watering heavily enough to drain through the soil two or three times. If leaves turn yellow while veins remain green, plants have iron chlorosis; apply iron chelates to soil or spray foliage with an iron solution.

Buddleja davidii

BUTTERFLY BUSH
Figwort family *(Scrophulariaceae)*
SEMIEVERGREEN OR DECIDUOUS SHRUB

/ ZONES 2–24; H1

☼ ☽ FULL SUN OR LIGHT SHADE

◐ ● MODERATE TO REGULAR WATER

Beloved for its incredible display of summertime flowers, this upright, fountain-shaped shrub is sometimes called summer lilac. It can put on several feet of growth in a season, maturing at 5–15 ft. tall and wide. Tapering leaves are up to 1 ft. long, dark green above, white and felted beneath. Lilac-like, 4-to-24-in. inflorescences of fragrant flowers (lilac with orange eye) appear in dense, arching clusters.

Choose from the many excellent varieties with a range of flower colors, dark to light blue, many shades of pink and purple, and white. Variegated 'Harlequin' has reddish purple flowers and leaves edged in creamy white. Dwarf *B. d. nanhoensis* selections grow just 5–8 ft. tall and 6 ft. wide and come in white, deep blue, or reddish purple flowers.

The species is invasive in mild parts of the Northwest. Its sale in Oregon is limited to sterile varieties like 'Asian Moon', 'Blue Chip', and 'Purple Haze' (all dwarfs), and sterile interspecific hybrids like 'Blue Cobbler', 'Peach Cobbler', 'Tangerine Dream', and 'Vanilla' (all in the Flutterby Grande series).

Also popular is *B.* 'Lochinch' (Zones 3b–9, 14–24). It grows 5–8 ft. (or taller) and as broad, with gray foliage and sweetly fragrant, light lavender-blue flowers over a long season in late summer and fall.

TIP As you might guess from its common name, this shrub is a magnet for butterflies—but hummingbirds find it irresistible too.

Buddleja davidii **'Harlequin'**

HOW TO GROW IT

Soil Not particular about soil, as long as it is well drained. If in doubt, amend before planting with plenty of organic matter.

Care notes Cut back heavily (as low as 6–12 in.) before spring growth begins. Top may die in freezing weather but will regrow from roots and bloom the same year.

Callistemon viminalis

WEEPING BOTTLEBRUSH
Myrtle family (*Myrtaceae*)
EVERGREEN SHRUB

✎ ZONES 6–9, 12–24

☼ FULL SUN

💧💧 MODERATE TO REGULAR WATER

The bright red flowers of this Australian native look just like bottlebrushes held at the end of pendulous branches—hence the common name. The brushes appear from late spring into summer, then sporadically year-round. Blooms are followed by curious woody capsules that can last for years. Narrow, light green leaves tend to concentrate at branch ends. Choose a somewhat protected spot for planting, as bottlebrushes don't do well in windy, dry areas.

Plants grow quickly to 20–30 ft. tall, 15 ft. wide. If that's too large for your space, look for 'Little John', a superior dwarf form to 3 ft. high and wide, with dense growth pattern and blood red flowers in fall, winter, and spring. 'Captain Cook' is dense and rounded, to 6 ft. tall and wide, suitable for a border, low hedge, or screen. 'Red Cascade' grows to a similar height with large, abundant, rosy red blooms. 'McCaskillii', to 20 ft. tall, is denser, with better flower color and form.

A commonly grown cousin is *C. citrinus,* lemon bottlebrush, for Zones 8, 9, 12–24; H1, H2. It is quite tolerant of heat, cold, and poor soils. Grows naturally into a shrub 10–15 ft. tall and wide, with narrow, vivid green leaves that smell lemony when bruised. Bright red, 6-in.-long brushes appear in waves throughout the year. Look for these cutting-grown selections with good flower size and color: 'Violaceus' ('Jeffersii'), about 6 ft. tall and 4 ft. wide, has stiffer branching; narrower, shorter leaves; and reddish purple flowers fading to lavender. 'Mauve Mist' is the same but can reach 10 ft. 'Perth Pink', 10 ft. tall, has pink flower clusters.

Callistemon viminalis

HOW TO GROW IT

Soil Endemic to moist sites, bottlebrush can withstand waterlogged soil. Tolerant of saline or alkaline soils, though it may suffer from chlorosis.

Care notes After bloom or before spring growth, remove weak or dead branches. Don't cut into bare wood beyond leaves—plant may not resprout.

Camellia sasanqua

Tea family *(Theaceae)*
EVERGREEN SHRUB

🔆 **ZONES 4–9, 12, 14–24**

◑ **BEST OUT OF STRONG SUN**

◌◌ **MODERATE TO REGULAR WATER**

This elegant shrub is among the most useful broad-leafed evergreens for espaliers, informal hedges, screening, and containers. Plants vary in form from spreading and vinelike to upright and densely bushy; sizes range from 1½ ft. high and 6 ft. wide to 12 ft. tall and wide, depending on variety. The shiny, dark green leaves make a nice backdrop for the flowers, which are heavily produced in autumn and early winter. Blooms are short-lived and rather flimsy, but so numerous that plants make a show for months. Some are lightly (and pungently) fragrant.

Most sasanquas tolerate much sun in cooler climates, and in fact flower best in winter sun; some even thrive in full year-round sun with the right soil and regular water. The following are among the best varieties sold.

'Apple Blossom'. Single white flowers blushed with pink, from pink buds. Upright, somewhat leggy plant.

'Cleopatra'. Rose-pink semidouble flowers with narrow, curving petals. Growth is erect and fairly compact. Takes clipping well.

'Jean May'. Double, shell pink flowers. Compact, upright grower with glossy foliage.

'Kanjiro'. Large semidouble flowers of rose-pink shading to rose-red at petal edges. Erect growth habit.

'Mine-No-Yuki' ('White Doves'). Large, full peony-form flower. Drops many buds. Spreading, willowy growth; effective espalier.

'Setsugekka'. Large, white semidouble flowers with fluted petals. Blossoms have substance; cut sprays hold well in water. Upright and rather bushy shrub.

'Yuletide'. The best of these, with its profusion of small, single, bright red flowers with yellow anthers on a dense, compact, upright plant. Bloom comes in late fall, early winter.

Camellia sasanqua 'Yuletide'

HOW TO GROW IT

Soil Provide moist, well-drained soil high in organic content. Commercial soil amendments formulated for rhododendrons and azaleas work well.

Fertilizer Feed with a commercial acid plant food after bloom.

In containers Use a planting mix containing at least 50 percent organic material, such as a commercial mix for rhododendrons and azaleas.

Care notes Plants benefit from a thick layer of organic mulch, but keep it a few inches away from the trunk. Prune away dead or weak wood, and thin when growth is too dense for flowers to open properly.

Choisya ternata

MEXICAN ORANGE
Citrus family *(Rutaceae)*
EVERGREEN SHRUB

✎ **ZONES 6–9, 14–24; BORDERLINE IN ZONES 4, 5**

☼ ☽ **FULL SUN IN COOLER CLIMATES ONLY**

⬤ **MODERATE WATER**

The lustrous, rich green leaves of this shrub are divided into fans of three leaflets, giving it a textured, almost tropical look. It's sometimes called mock orange for its clusters of fragrant white flowers, like small orange blossoms, which open in late winter or early spring. Bloom is continuous for at least two months and then intermittent through summer.

Mexican orange grows quickly to 6–8 ft. tall and often slightly wider. Makes a great informal hedge or screen and serves beautifully as a backdrop for a flower border. Foliage of 'Sundance' is yellow when young, gradually turning green. 'Aztec Pearl' is a more compact hybrid with narrower leaves and white flowers opening from pink buds in spring and sometimes again in summer.

HOW TO GROW IT

Soil Plant in fertile soil with good drainage; suffers in alkaline soils or where water is high in salts. Under such conditions, amend the soil as for azaleas.

Care notes Protect from snails and slugs. During growing season, thin older branches in plant's center to force leafy new interior growth.

Choisya ternata

TIP With its glossy green leaves and fragrant flowers, you might think deer would browse Mexican orange, but they rarely do.

Cistus

ROCKROSE
Rockrose family (*Cistaceae*)
EVERGREEN SHRUBS

✎ **ZONES 4–9, 14–24**

☼ **FULL SUN**

◊ **LITTLE OR NO WATER**

These carefree Mediterranean natives are covered with flowers for at least a month in spring or early summer and may give bonus blooms at other times. In some rockroses, the leaves are coated with a perfumed resin; others have foliage covered with gray wool. Out of bloom, their soft green, silver, or grayish foliage and mounded form add subtle color and texture to the landscape.

Rockroses thrive in ocean winds, salt spray, and even desert heat. Fast growing and sun loving, they are perfect for controlling erosion on a dry bank. They are also useful in big rock gardens, rough areas along drives, and wild plantings. Many species and hybrids are available, mostly in the range of 2–5 ft. tall and usually wider than tall. Flowers range from white through every shade of pink to nearly purple, often with strongly contrasting marks at the petal bases.

HOW TO GROW IT

Soil Rockroses tolerate poor soil, but it must be well drained if they will be watered.

Planting Don't plant rootbound stock, especially in unirrigated places; cut encircling roots and spread out the mass so that roots can find moisture deeper in the soil.

In containers Smaller types grow well in containers filled with standard potting soil.

Care notes To keep plants vigorous and neat, periodically cut out a few old stems. Tip-pinch young plants to thicken growth, or lightly shear new summer growth. When plants become woody and old, it is often easier to replace than rejuvenate them.

Cistus purpureus

TIP Rockroses grow well even in the garden's hottest spots, such as at the base of a south-facing wall or beside a heat-reflecting sidewalk.

Coleonema pulchellum

PINK BREATH OF HEAVEN
Citrus family *(Rutaceae)*
EVERGREEN SHRUB

🔪 **ZONES 7–9, 14–24**

☀ ◐ **FULL SUN OR LIGHT SHADE**

💧 💧 **MODERATE TO REGULAR WATER**

This popular and easy-to-grow shrub has a delicate look and a wonderfully soft texture. Slender branches are packed with soft, narrow, heathlike leaves that have a "heavenly" fragrance when brushed or bruised. Tiny pink, starlike flowers are borne freely over a long season in winter and spring, with scattered bloom at any time of year.

Plants reach about 5 ft. tall and wide but can get twice that large with great age. Good on banks or hillsides; also nice as a soft filler for flower beds. 'Sunset Gold' has yellow foliage and grows 1½–2 ft. high and 4–6 ft. wide.

C. album, white breath of heaven, is quite similar to *C. pulchellum*, but with white blooms.

HOW TO GROW IT

Soil Plant in light soil; fast drainage is a must.

In containers Young plants grow well in pots filled with fast-draining potting soil.

Care notes To control size and promote compactness, shear lightly after main bloom is over. For an even filmier look, thin out some interior stems.

Coleonema pulchellum

TIP Plant this soft shrub along paths where you can break off and bruise a twig to enjoy the wonderful fragrance.

Coprosma

Madder family *(Rubiaceae)*
EVERGREEN SHRUBS

✐ ZONES VARY BY SPECIES

☼ ☽ FULL SUN OR PART SHADE

◐ ◑ ● LITTLE TO REGULAR WATER

Prized for their handsome, glossy foliage, these New Zealand natives are also very easy to grow, even in difficult situations. All do particularly well near the coast. Many offer shiny, colorful berries in autumn if male and female forms are grown near each other.

C. hybrids. Zones 8, 9, 14–24. These hybrids were developed for their brightly colored foliage. They grow 4–5 ft. tall and wide, and make dramatic accents for borders or pots. 'Evening Glow' has glossy green leaves that are variegated gold during the growing season and turn orange-red in fall and winter. 'Rainbow Surprise' bears leaves variegated with cream and pink, washed with red in fall and winter. The compact 'Tequila Sunrise' produces shiny green new growth edged with gold and maturing through shades of gold and orange before turning bright red and orange in winter. 'Coppershine', to 6 ft. tall, has leathery, bright green leaves heavily shaded with copper; entire plant is bright copper in winter. For something really different, try 'Black Cloud', with dark brownish green leaves that turn nearly black in winter.

C. × kirkii. Zones 14–24; H1, H2. Growing only 1–3 ft. high and spreading 4–6 ft. wide, this tough plant is good in the foreground of a shrub border or as a bank cover that spills attractively over a wall. Long, straight stems slant outward from the base and are closely set with narrow yellow-green leaves just ½–2 in. long. Needs part shade in hot inland gardens. The popular 'Variegata' (6–24 in. high and up to 5 ft. wide) has white-edged gray-green leaves and translucent white berries. It's a good trailing plant for large planters and hanging baskets.

C. repens. MIRROR PLANT. Zones 14–24; H1. The common name refers to the oval, 3-in.-long leaves, which are dark to light green and exceptionally shiny. Plant grows rapidly to 10 ft. tall and 6 ft. wide, but it's much lower and more compact when subjected to seacoast conditions. Inland, it's an open, straggly shrub if neglected, but it takes on a beautiful, dense form if pruned twice yearly (at any height desired). Easy to

Coprosma repens **'Marble Queen'**

maintain as a hedge, screen, or informal espalier; can even be grown as a houseplant. Yellow or orange fruits may appear on female plants if male forms are grown nearby.

Several variegated forms are available, including 'Argentea', with green leaves flecked silvery white; 'Marble Queen', just 2–3 ft. high, with creamy white leaves splashed and dotted with green; 'Marble King', slow grower with cream-colored leaves heavily speckled in lime green; 'Picturata', green leaves blotched creamy yellow in the middle; 'Exotica', female version of 'Picturata' with orange-yellow fruits; 'Marginata', with green leaves irregularly edged in creamy white; 'Pink Splendor', green leaves with yellow margin that takes on a pink edging with maturity. **»**

Coprosma 'Tequila Sunrise'

Kaleidoscopic Coprosma Colors

Even though they're evergreen, many coprosmas are anything but "plain green." Variegated selections of *C. repens* and the many flamboyant *C.* hybrids appear in a rainbow of incredibly vivid hues—from yellow and orange through pinks and reds to nearly black, often with several colors present on each leaf. And the colors of many take turns deepening as the seasons change. Cooler temperatures bring out the red in most types, giving the whole plant a warm, rosy glow that is particularly welcome in winter.

Top: *Coprosma* 'Evening Glow'
Bottom: *Coprosma* 'Rainbow Surprise'

HOW TO GROW IT

Fertilizer For best leaf color, apply a general-purpose fertilizer—or a generous sprinkling of compost—in early spring.

Care notes Prune to shape anytime except during hot summer months. *C. × kirkii* needs regular pruning to stay dense.

Cotinus coggygria

SMOKE TREE
Cashew family *(Anacardiaceae)*
DECIDUOUS SHRUB OR SMALL TREE

✄ ZONES 2–24

☼ FULL SUN

💧 MODERATE WATER

This unusual and colorful shrub creates a broad, urn-shaped mass of stems about 12–15 ft. tall and wide—though it may reach 25 ft. and function as a spectacular small tree. The common name is derived from the dramatic puffs of "smoke" from fading flowers: as the tiny greenish blooms wither, they send out elongated stalks clothed in a profusion of fuzzy lavender-pink hairs.

The roundish, ½-to-3-in. leaves are bluish green in the species, but purple-leafed types are more commonly grown. Leaves of 'Purpureus' emerge purple, then gradually turn green; 'Royal Purple' and 'Velvet Cloak' hold their purple color through most of the summer. Those with purple foliage have richer purple "smoke puffs" than the species. 'Golden Spirit' reaches about 7 ft. tall and 6 ft. wide, with leaves that are lime green in spring and turn golden yellow in summer. 'Pink Champagne' is a green-leafed selection with pinkish tan puffs. Leaves of all types change in autumn, taking on colors from yellow to orange-red.

C. 'Grace', a popular hybrid, grows 15 ft. tall and wide, with blue-green foliage shaded purple in summer and turning orange and purple-red in fall. It has large, deep pink puffs.

HOW TO GROW IT

Soil Smoke trees are at their best under stress in poor or rocky soil. Give them fast drainage and avoid overly wet conditions.

Care notes For a smaller plant with fresher, brighter leaves, you can cut all stems to 1 ft. high in late winter or early spring—but in doing so, you'll sacrifice that year's flowers. Another option is to shape into a small tree by removing a few lower branches each year.

Cotinus coggygria

TIP Smoke tree is great as a focal point in a shrub border or an out-of-the-way part of the garden.

Hydrangea macrophylla

BIGLEAF HYDRANGEA
Hydrangea family *(Hydrangeaceae)*
DECIDUOUS SHRUB

ZONES 3B–9, 14–24; H1

☼ ☽ **PART SHADE IN HOTTEST CLIMATES**

💧 **REGULAR WATER**

With its bold leaves and outsize clusters of distinctive, long-lasting flowers, bigleaf hydrangea is as impressive as it is familiar. The plant has a symmetrical, rounded shape, growing 4–8 ft. tall (or more) and as wide. Leaves are thick, shiny, and coarsely toothed. Flowers of white, pink, red, or blue are held in big clusters in summer and fall. Best known are mophead types, with round clusters composed of sterile flowers, but lacecap types (with a cluster of small, starry-petaled, fertile flowers surrounded by a ring of larger sterile ones) have their own charm. The sterile flowers last for a long time, often holding up for months as they gradually fade to beige.

Bigleaf hydrangeas are good-looking as single plants, massed, or in tubs on the patio. Most bloom on old wood, but a few (mostly recent introductions) bloom on the current season's growth as well, significantly lengthening the bloom season. All kinds do well where winters are fairly mild. Those that bloom only on old wood are disappointing in cold-winter climates where plants freeze to the ground every year. Those that bloom on new wood can freeze to the ground (or be pruned hard) every winter, and they'll still flower if the season is long enough. The varieties that follow bloom only on old wood unless noted.

Mophead varieties. These include 'Glowing Embers', which grows 6 ft. tall, 8 ft. wide, with deep pink flowers; especially cold-hardy 'Madame Emile Mouillère', which grows 6 ft. tall, 6–8 ft. wide, producing white flowers with blue or pink eye, and fall foliage in the red and orange range; compact 'Merritt's Supreme', with deep rose-purple blooms; 'Nigra', with dark purple-black stems bearing light green leaves and flowers that vary from soft pink to blue; 'Nikko Blue', with large blue blossom clusters; and 'Pia' ('Pink Elf'), just 1½ ft. high and 2 ft. wide, with deep pink flowers. Those that produce pink or blue flowers on new wood include 'All Summer Beauty', 'Endless Summer', and 'Penny Mac'. 'Blushing Bride' has white flowers that age to pink.

Hydrangea macrophylla **'Nikko Blue'**

Lacecap varieties. These include 'Blue Wave', with light blue to pink sterile flowers and darker fertile flowers; 'Lanarth White', just 3–4 ft. tall and wide, with white sterile flowers and fertile flowers of blue or pink; 'Shooting Star' ('Hanabi'), with fully double blooms of pure white; 'Teller Red' ('Teller Rot'), with a double row of rose-red sterile flowers surrounding pink-and-blue fertile ones; and old favorites 'Maculata' ('Variegata') and 'Mariesii Variegata', with dark green leaves marked with cream and light green. 'Twist-n-Shout' blooms blue or pink, depending on soil pH, on both new and old wood.

Hydrangea macrophylla 'Merritt's Supreme'

Hydrangea macrophylla 'Shooting Star'

HOW TO GROW IT

Soil All grow and bloom best in rich, porous soil. Add plenty of organic matter at planting time.

Fertilizer A healthy dose of compost in spring ensures strong growth.

Care notes Prune bigleaf hydrangeas as needed to control form—in late dormant season for those producing blooms on new growth, after bloom for those flowering on previous year's growth. For types that bloom on both new and old wood, prune dead wood out when new growth starts in spring, then prune for shape after bloom.

TIP To make hydrangea flowers more blue, apply aluminum sulfate to the soil in early spring. To make them more pink, apply lime or superphosphate. White varieties stay white.

Lavandula angustifolia

ENGLISH LAVENDER
Mint family *(Lamiaceae)*
EVERGREEN SHRUB

◢ **ZONES 2–24**

☀ **FULL SUN**

💧 **MODERATE WATER**

Lavandula angustifolia **'Martha Roderick'**

This is the legendary lavender whose colorful, sweetly fragrant flowers are used for perfume, soap, and sachets; it's also the hardiest, most widely planted lavender species. Most varieties are fairly low growing, forming mounds of narrow, smooth-edged, gray-green or silvery gray leaves. Unbranched flower stems rise 4–12 in. above foliage and are topped with 1-to-4-in.-long flower spikes in white, pink, lavender-blue, or various shades of purple. Plants bloom mainly from early to midsummer, but some varieties repeat in late summer or autumn.

Use English lavender as an informal hedge or edging, in herb gardens, in containers, or in borders with plants that also thrive in full sun and no more than moderate water. (If you live in an area with hot, humid summers, you'll have better luck with one of the two lavenders listed at the end of this entry.) The following is a sampling of many named selections.

'Arctic Snow'. Grows 1½–2 ft. high and wide, with slender gray-green leaves and a profusion of very fragrant pure white blooms.

'Blue Cushion'. To 1½ ft. high, 2 ft. wide. Profuse bright violet-blue flowers above medium green foliage.

'Buena Vista'. Repeat bloomer to 1½–2 ft. high and wide. Deep violet-blue flowers with superb fragrance.

'Compacta'. To 1½ ft. high and wide; good dwarf hedge plant. Light violet flowers; gray-green leaves.

'Hidcote'. Deep violet flowers and medium green foliage on a plant 1½–2 ft. high. 'Hidcote Blue' (with deep blue flowers) and 'Hidcote Superior' (compact, uniform, 16 in. high and 18 in. wide) are popular selections.

'Jean Davis'. To 1½–2 ft. high and wide. Flowers in pale lilac-pink; gray-green foliage.

'Martha Roderick'. Compact growth to 1½–2 ft. high and wide. Dense gray foliage. Profuse bright violet-blue blossoms from late spring to early summer.

'Melissa'. Dense, compact grower to 1½ ft. high and wide. Good pink flower color, fading to white in hottest sun. Gray-green leaves.

'Munstead'. The original is 1½ ft. high, 2 ft. wide, with bright lavender-blue flowers and medium green foliage. Long bloomer; makes a good low hedge.

'Nana Alba'. Dense and compact, to just 1 ft. high and wide, with narrow gray-green leaves and short spikes of white flowers.

'Rosea'. To 1½–2 ft. high and wide. Light mauve-pink flowers; light green foliage.

'Thumbelina Leigh'. Very compact mound of medium green leaves to just 6 in. high and 12 in. wide. Bright violet-blue flowers rise 6 in. above foliage.

Another easy-to-grow lavender is *L.* 'Goodwin Creek Grey' (Zones 8, 9, 12–24), a silver-leafed hybrid that grows into a dense mound 2½–3 ft. high, 3–4 ft. wide. Though prized for its beautiful foliage, it produces an abundance of deep violet-blue flowers from spring to late fall,

Lavandula angustifolia 'Arctic Snow'

Lavandula 'Goodwin Creek Grey'

year-round in mild-winter climates. Its piney scent is more medicinal than sweet. Tolerates heat and humidity well.

A final group of low-maintenance lavenders is *L. × intermedia*, often called lavandin or hedge lavender (Zones 4–24). These summer-blooming hybrids are a bit larger than the English lavenders and are vigorous, fragrant plants that make great low hedges. They are almost as hardy as English lavender and more tolerant of warm, humid summers.

HOW TO GROW IT

Soil Lavenders require well-drained soil; they'll quickly succumb to root rot in heavy clay.

Planting Choose a spot with good air circulation, and add organic amendments at planting time. If your soil tends toward clay, add a generous handful or two of round river rock of up to ¾-in. diameter. Mix all together to form a planting mound about 1½ ft. wide and several inches high. Plant in the center of the mound, and mulch around the plant with pea gravel, decomposed granite, or sand rather than organic materials.

In containers Lavenders thrive in clay pots and light, well-drained potting mix. Apply a balanced, controlled-release fertilizer in spring.

Care notes To keep plants neat and compact, shear back by one-third to one-half (even by two-thirds) every year immediately after bloom.

Loropetalum chinense

Witch-hazel family *(Hamamelidaceae)*
EVERGREEN SHRUB

✎ ZONES 6–9, 14–24

☼ ☽ PART SHADE IN HOTTEST CLIMATES

💧 REGULAR WATER

This elegant shrub grows naturally into a neat, compact mound 6–10 ft. tall and wide, with tiers of arching or slightly drooping branches. The roundish, soft-textured leaves are light green, but throughout the year an occasional leaf turns yellow or red, providing a nice touch of color. Odd little white to greenish flowers, each with four narrow, twisted, inchlong petals, appear in clusters of four to eight at branch tips. Flowering is heaviest in spring, but some bloom is likely at any time.

This is a subtly beautiful plant; good in raised beds, woodland gardens, and large containers. Young plants are particularly attractive spilling from hanging baskets.

If you're looking for more color, try the following varieties, all with purple foliage and pink to purple flowers: 'Blush', 'Burgundy', 'Fire Dance', 'Pippa's Red', 'Razzleberri', 'Ruby', 'Sizzlin' Pink', and 'Suzanne'. Check the size on the nursery label, as some of these are lower growing than the species.

HOW TO GROW IT

Soil Provide rich, well-drained soil.

In containers Don't let soil become completely dry, as plant may wilt and not recover.

Care notes Doesn't need pruning but can take any amount of it (best done after flowering).

Loropetalum chinense **'Razzleberri'**

TIP For a charming hanging-basket composition, plant a young loropetalum with a couple of white or pink bacopas.

Nandina domestica

HEAVENLY BAMBOO
Barberry family *(Berberidaceae)*
EVERGREEN OR SEMIEVERGREEN SHRUB

☀ **ZONES 4–24; H1, H2**

☀ ☽ **SOME SHADE IN HOTTEST CLIMATES**

◊ ◑ ● **LITTLE TO REGULAR WATER**

♦ **BERRIES CAN BE TOXIC, ESPECIALLY TO LIVESTOCK**

Want the look of a delicate bamboo without the worry of rampant spreading? Plant this finely textured shrub with lightly branched, canelike stems and lacy-looking foliage. It grows rather slowly to 6–8 ft. tall and 3–4 ft. wide. It makes a light, airy-looking hedge, screen, or tub plant, especially suited to narrow, restricted spaces. Dramatic with night lighting. Low-growing types make a pretty, low-maintenance groundcover when planted close together. In climates where summers are very hot, heavenly bamboo requires some shade; in milder climates, it can take sun or shade.

Foliage emerges pinkish and bronzy red, then turns to soft light green; it takes on purple and bronze tints in fall and often turns fiery crimson in winter, especially in a sunny location and with some frost. Leafy stems make a good filler in bouquets. In late spring or early summer, clusters of small pinkish white or creamy white blossoms appear at branch ends. If plants are grouped, shiny red berries follow the flowers; isolated plants seldom fruit heavily.

Many varieties are available, most with improved foliage color in spring and fall. Dwarf varieties include 'Fire Power' (2 ft.), 'Gulf Stream' (3–4 ft.), 'Harbor Dwarf' (2–3 ft.), and 'Sienna Sunrise' (3–4 ft.). Taller varieties include 'Moyers Red' (6–8 ft.), 'Plum Passion' (4–6 ft.), and 'Royal Princess' (6–8 ft.). 'Filamentosa' (1–3 ft.), also sold as 'San Gabriel', has very finely cut leaves.

Nandina domestica

HOW TO GROW IT

Soil Does best in rich soil with regular water but can even compete with tree roots in dry shade.

In containers Grows well in pots with occasional feeding during warm months.

Care notes In time, unpruned clumps become top-heavy and bare at the base; to encourage denser foliage lower down, cut oldest canes to the ground each year before new growth begins in spring. May suffer damage from very cold weather but usually recovers quickly.

Phormium tenax

NEW ZEALAND FLAX
Daylily family *(Hemerocallidaceae)*
PERENNIAL

◢ **ZONES 7–9, 14–24; H1, H2; REGROWS AFTER FREEZES IN ZONES 5, 6**

☼ ◐ **FULL SUN OR PART SHADE**

◌ ◖ ● **LITTLE TO REGULAR WATER**

Though technically a perennial, this dramatic evergreen plant is substantial enough to be used as a shrub in the garden. Swordlike, bronzy green leaves can reach 9 ft. long and 5 in. wide; they grow in an upright fan pattern to form a slowly expanding clump to 6–8 ft. wide. On established plants, branched clusters of tubular flowers appear in late spring or early summer, rising to twice the height of the foliage clump in some kinds. This is a sturdy and fast-growing plant that takes almost any soil and does well at the seacoast. Excellent massed or used as focal points, providing year-round color in perennial and shrub borders, on hillsides, near swimming pools. More commonly sold than the species are the following varieties, selected for colorful foliage and smaller stature. Cool weather intensifies foliage colors, and bronze-leafed varieties take on a deeper color in full sun.

'Atropurpureum', 'Bronze', 'Rubrum', Purpureum Group. These names are used interchangeably for plants with purplish or brownish red foliage that grow 6–8 ft. tall and wide.

'Atropurpureum Compactum' ('Monrovia Red'). To 5 ft. tall and wide, with burgundy-bronze foliage.

'Chocolate' ('Chocolate Dream'). To 4–5 ft. tall and wide, with rich brown leaves.

'Radiance'. To 5–6 ft. tall, 7 ft. wide. Green leaves have a central yellow stripe, lime green margins with a thin orange edge.

'Variegatum'. To 6–8 ft. tall and wide, with ¾-in.-wide, grayish green leaves that have creamy yellow stripes along edges.

'Wings of Gold'. Resembles 'Variegatum' but reaches just 2–3 ft. high and wide. Ideal for containers.

An attractive relative with more arching leaves is *P. cookianum*, mountain flax. It requires a bit more water, and in hot areas it needs afternoon shade to prevent burning. Leaves curve gracefully, drooping at the tips; they grow 4–5 ft. long, 2½–3 in. wide. Mature clumps are 4–5 ft. tall, spreading to 8–10 ft. or more. 'Black Adder' grows 3–4 ft. tall and wide, with glossy, deep burgundy-

***Phormium tenax* 'Atropurpureum'**

black leaves. 'Flamingo' grows just 1–2 ft. high and wide, with leaves in shades of orange, rose, light green, and yellow. *P. c. hookeri* 'Cream Delight' has leaves with a broad, creamy yellow central stripe and narrow green margins edged in dark red. *P. c. h.* 'Tricolor' has green leaves margined in cream and red; foliage is flushed with rose in cool weather.

There are dozens of hybrids between *P. cookianum* and *P. tenax* that were selected for distinctive leaf color, from nearly black through shades of green to yellow, cream, orange, pink, and red. Leaves of many are vertically striped in several colors, and some have a thin edge that glows when backlit. Plants range from 1 to 8 ft. tall and wide. New ones come on the market frequently, so visit your local nursery to see the latest selections.

Phormium cookianum **'Black Adder'**

Phormium cookianum hookeri **'Cream Delight'**

HOW TO GROW IT

Planting Be sure that the plant's crown is at or slightly above soil level. Crown rot can be a problem if plant is placed too low in poorly drained soil.

Spacing Nursery plants in containers are deceptively small; when you plant, allow enough room to accommodate a mature specimen.

In containers Smaller types are easy to grow in good-size containers with regular feeding.

Care notes Cut out flower stalks when blossoms wither. As leaves age, colors fade; cut out older (outer) ones as close to base as possible to maintain best appearance. In variegated sorts, watch for reversions to solid green or bronze; remove reverted crowns down to root level before they take over the clump.

Pittosporum tobira

TOBIRA
Pittosporum family (*Pittosporaceae*)
EVERGREEN SHRUB

◪ **ZONES 8–24; H1, H2; WORTH TRYING IN ZONES 4–7**

☀ ◐ **FULL SUN OR PART SHADE**

◖ ● **MODERATE TO REGULAR WATER**

Mostly grown for its foliage and form, this attractive plant also bears clusters of small, creamy white flowers with a strong fragrance reminiscent of orange blossoms. Blooms appear in early spring and are followed by fairly conspicuous fruits the size of large peas. Ripe fruits split open to reveal sticky seeds; fallen fruit can be a nuisance on lawns and paving. The leathery, shiny, dark green leaves look good year-round.

A basic, dependable shrub, tobira grows into a dense, rounded mass 6–15 ft. tall and wide. You can remove lower limbs from an older plant to make a small tree, or you can hold plant to 6 ft. by careful heading back and thinning (it doesn't look good sheared). Very tolerant of seacoast conditions.

'Variegatum' grows 5–10 ft. tall and wide and has smaller leaves in gray-green and gray with an irregular creamy white margin.

Several compact selections are available. The most common is 'Wheeler's Dwarf', to 2–3 ft. high and 4–5 ft. wide, with the same handsome leaves as *P. tobira*. It is a choice plant for foreground, low boundary, or even small-scale groundcover. 'Turner's Variegated Dwarf' is the size of 'Wheeler's Dwarf' but has foliage like that of 'Variegatum'. 'Cream de Mint' grows just 2–2½ ft. high and wide and has mint green leaves with a creamy white border.

HOW TO GROW IT

Care notes Prune periodically to enhance form, thinning out weak branches and wayward shoots. Aphids and scale insects may attack; sooty mold on leaves is a sign of infestation. Spray with insecticidal soap to control both pests.

Pittosporum tobira **'Variegatum'**

TIP In coastal gardens, a tobira hedge makes an excellent windbreak. It's so undemanding that it is often seen in commercial landscapes and street medians.

Rhododendron

Heath family *(Ericaceae)*
EVERGREEN SHRUBS

✎ ZONES 4–6, 15–17

◐ FILTERED SUNLIGHT

● ◖◗ REGULAR TO AMPLE WATER

◊ LEAVES ARE POISONOUS IF INGESTED

A rhododendron in full bloom is among a garden's most eye-catching sights. Big, rounded clusters of blossoms in colors ranging from white through pink, apricot, salmon, orange, red, yellow, near blue, and purple appear in winter, spring, or summer, depending on variety.

There are more than 800 species in the genus, but the most popular ones are small to medium-size shrubs with large, leathery leaves and a pleasingly mounded shape. Most fare best in filtered sunlight beneath tall trees; east and north sides of house or fence are next best. Where summers are mild or foggy, they can take more sun, but the sunnier or hotter the climate, the more protection plants will need.

For more information on rhododendrons, including lists of those best suited to your area, refer to the helpful website of the American Rhododendron Society *(rhododendron.org).*

HOW TO GROW IT

Soil Rhododendrons need excellent drainage. Amend soil liberally with organic material before you plant.

Planting If you have clay or alkaline soil, plant in bed raised 1–2 ft. above original soil level. Mix a generous amount of organic material into the top foot of native soil; then fill bed above it with a mixture of 50 percent organic matter, 30 percent native soil, and 20 percent sand. Plant with top of rootball slightly above soil level, and mulch with pine needles, oak leaves, or bark or wood chips. Never cultivate around these plants.

Fertilizer Feed established plants with commercial acid fertilizer in early spring. Feed again when new leaves begin to grow, just as blooms are fading. Sprinkle compost around base of plant in early fall.

Rhododendron **'Fragrantissimum Improved'**

Care notes Tip-pinch young plants to shape them and make them bushy; prune older, leggy plants to restore desired shape. Do extensive pruning in late winter or early spring (wait until danger of frost is past in colder areas). Clip or break off spent flowers, taking care not to damage growth buds at base of each truss. To prevent the accumulation of dissolved salts in the soil, periodically leach the planting by watering heavily enough to drain through the soil two or three times. If leaves turn yellow while veins remain green, plants have iron chlorosis; apply iron chelates to soil or spray foliage with an iron solution.

Ribes sanguineum

FLOWERING CURRANT
Currant family *(Grossulariaceae)*
DECIDUOUS SHRUB

🌿 **ZONES A3; 4–9, 14–24**

☼ ☽ **FULL SUN IN COOLER CLIMATES ONLY**

💧 **MODERATE WATER**

This strong grower reaches 5–12 ft. tall and wide in just a few years. It begins blooming when young, producing a profusion of drooping, 2-to-6-in.-long clusters of small deep pink, red, or white flowers in early spring. Medium to dark green leaves resemble those of maple and are pleasantly aromatic. The blue-black fruit has a whitish bloom, but birds may collect it all before you have time to enjoy the show.

Most commonly sold is *R. s. glutinosum* (more southerly in origin than the species); its blossoms are typically deep or pale pink, carried in clusters of 15 to 40.

'Barrie Coate', 'Elk River Red', 'King Edward VII', and 'Pulborough Scarlet' are red-flowering selections.

Pink varieties include 'Brocklebankii', with gold foliage; 'Claremont', with two-tone blossoms aging to red; 'Poky's Pink'; and 'Spring Showers', with 8-in. flower clusters.

'Album' and 'White Icicle' are good white varieties.

HOW TO GROW IT

Care notes Adaptable and easy, flowering currant needs little care once established. Pruning isn't necessary, but you can cut out a few of the oldest stems after flowering to make room for new growth.

Ribes sanguineum

TIP This Western native produces loads of flowers even at a young age, and the blooms attract butterflies and hummingbirds.

Rosa

ROSES (LANDSCAPE OR SHRUB TYPES)
Rose family *(Rosaceae)*
DECIDUOUS SHRUBS

✔ ALL ZONES

☀ ◐ FULL SUN OR LIGHT SHADE

● REGULAR WATER

The rose is so beloved and widely planted, it's sometimes called the queen of flowers. Thousands of varieties are grown for their gorgeous, often scented blooms. Roses are divided into three main categories: modern roses, old roses, and the wild species and their hybrids. The last two groups can be a bit tricky to grow, but many modern roses—and particularly "landscaping roses" or "shrub roses"—are easy enough to include in low-maintenance gardens. These new plants have been developed for prolific bloom over a long season and abundant disease-resistant foliage.

Shrub roses are natural choices for flower beds and shrub borders, whether planted as accents or in groups—and because they bloom almost continuously, they pair well with perennials. The following modern shrub rose varieties are among the best choices for Western gardens. Most of these grow 3–6 ft. tall and wide; check plant labels for size estimates when purchasing.

Red: 'Alexander Mackenzie', 'Carefree Spirit', 'Champlain', 'Darcey Bussell', 'Double Knock Out', 'Linda Campbell', 'Munstead Wood', 'Oso Easy Cherry Pie'.

Pink: 'Ballerina', 'Blushing Knock Out', 'Bonica', 'Carefree Delight', 'Carefree Wonder', 'Erfurt', 'Gertrude Jekyll', 'Harlow Carr', 'John Cabot', 'Pink Home Run', 'Pink Meidiland', 'Sunrise Sunset', 'Wisley 2008'.

Orange/warm blend: 'Coral Cove', 'Lady Elsie May', 'Oso Easy Honey Bun', 'Oso Easy Paprika', 'Watercolors'.

Yellow: 'Baby Love', 'Carefree Sunshine', 'Graham Thomas', 'Happenstance', 'Lemon Splash', 'Molineux', 'Sunny Knock Out'.

White: 'Buff Beauty', 'Macy's Pride', 'Sally Holmes' (shrub rose in the Northwest, climber in California), 'Sea Foam', 'Snowdrift', 'White Meidiland'.

Lavender/mauve/purple: 'Midnight Blue', 'Outta the Blue'.

Another group of landscaping roses, referred to as "groundcover roses," grow around 2–2½ ft. high and spread 3½–6 ft. wide; they're large enough to count as shrubs in smaller gardens. Vigor, disease resistance, and

***Rosa* 'Molineux'**

a profusion of bloom from late spring until frost are the hallmarks of this category. Groundcover roses are perfect for covering slopes, planting at the front of borders, spilling over a wall, or growing in pots. Here are some of the best for the West.

Red: 'Crimson Meidiland', 'Fire Meidiland', 'Red Drift', 'Red Flower Carpet', 'Red Meidiland', 'Red Ribbons', 'Scarlet Flower Carpet', 'Scarlet Meidiland'.

Pink: 'Appleblossom Flower Carpet', 'Coral Flower Carpet', 'Peach Drift', 'Pink Drift', 'Pink Flower Carpet', 'Roseberry Blanket', 'Sweet Drift'.

Orange/coral: 'Electric Blanket'.

Yellow: 'Happy Chappy', 'Sunrise Vigorosa', 'Yellow Flower Carpet'.

White: 'Icy Drift', 'White Flower Carpet', 'White Meidiland'. **»**

Top: *Rosa* **'Sally Holmes'**
Bottom: *Rosa* **'Crimson Meidiland'**

HOW TO GROW IT

Soil Needs to be reasonably well drained. Don't plant too close to trees or large shrubs, which can steal water and nutrients.

Planting Dig soil deeply and add plenty of organic matter such as compost. Add a small amount of complete fertilizer as well as supplemental phosphorus and potassium. Set the plant in the hole so that the bud union is just above or right at soil level. Add a 3-in. layer of mulch around the rose, but leave a few inches of space around the base of the stem.

Fertilizer Most landscaping roses do not need regular fertilizer, but if growth and bloom are not satisfactory, feed monthly with a commercial rose food according to package directions. Stop feeding in late summer or fall in cold zones, in mid-October in mild-winter zones.

In containers Choose a smaller variety; groundcover roses are ideal. When it comes to the container size, bigger is better. One roughly the size of a 5-gallon nursery can is the smallest you should consider. Wooden half-barrels offer plenty of space for most shrub roses. Standard commercial potting mixes work well. Fertilize regularly, as nutrients wash out of the soil when you water.

Care notes Prune conservatively, removing dead or nonproductive old branches and weak growth in the plant's center; then cut back the previous season's growth by about one-fourth. Do the job at the end of the dormant season (mid-January in mild climates, early April in colder ones).

For local help with pests and diseases, consider joining the American Rose Society *(ars.org)*. Its consultants advise member gardeners on rose problems at no cost. Your local garden center can also help with identification and treatment of common challenges such as aphids, powdery mildew, rust, and black spot.

Rosa rugosa

RAMANAS ROSE
Rose family *(Rosaceae)*
DECIDUOUS SHRUB

✎ **ZONES A1–A3; 1–24**

☼ ☽ **FULL SUN OR LIGHT SHADE**

💧 **MODERATE WATER**

This vigorous rose is so tough and dependable, it's in a class all its own. It withstands hard freezes, wind, aridity, and salt spray—and still delivers wonderfully fragrant flowers in spring, summer, and early fall. Blooms are 3–4 in. across and, in the many varieties, range from single to double and from pure white and creamy yellow through pink to deep purplish red. Prickly stems hold glossy bright green leaves with distinctive heavy veining that gives them a crinkled appearance. Bright red, tomato-shaped hips, 1 in. or more across, appear in fall; they're striking enough to give this plant another common name: "sea tomato."

All rugosas grow 3–6 ft. tall and wide. They make fine hedges, and plants grown on their own roots will make sizable, spreading colonies and help prevent erosion. Foliage remains quite free of diseases and insects, except possibly aphids.

Among the most widely sold rugosas and rugosa hybrids are 'Blanc Double de Coubert', double white; 'Frau Dagmar Hartopp', single pink; 'Hansa', double purplish red; and 'Wildberry Breeze', single, clove scented, lavender-pink.

HOW TO GROW IT

Refer to care notes on the previous page.

Rosa rugosa **'Rubra'**

TIP This durable rose is native to the seashore, so it grows well in even the sandiest soils and can handle salt spray without a problem.

Sarcococca ruscifolia

SWEET BOX
Box family *(Buxaceae)*
EVERGREEN SHRUB

ZONES 4–9, 14–24, EXCEPT AS NOTED
PART OR FULL SHADE
MODERATE TO REGULAR WATER

Though its small white flowers are nearly hidden among its leaves, sweet box has a fragrance that can perfume much of the winter garden. The dense evergreen foliage is dark green and waxy, with a polished, elegant look year-round. Small red fruits decorate the branches after the flowers fade.

Sweet box grows slowly to 4–6 ft. tall and 3–7 ft. wide. If grown against a wall, it will form a natural espalier, with branches fanning out to create patterns. Plants maintain gradual, orderly growth even in deepest shade. Its tolerance for low light gives this handsome shrub special value under overhangs, in entryways, and beneath low-branching evergreen trees. Sweet box will also tolerate sun in cool-summer climates if the soil is not allowed to become too dry.

S. confusa is similar to *S. ruscifolia* and generally sold as such. However, *S. confusa* has black fruit rather than red.

S. hookeriana humilis (S. humilis), for Zones 3–9, 14–24, is low growing, seldom more than 1½ ft. high; it spreads by underground runners to 8 ft. or more. Its branches are thickly set with pointed leaves, and its glossy blue-black fruit is especially attractive. Good along a shady path or massed as a groundcover.

HOW TO GROW IT

Soil All grow best in organically enriched soil.

Care notes Rarely bothered by pests or diseases, though scale may require treatment with insecticidal soap or horticultural oil.

Sarcococca ruscifolia

TIP Sweet box looks refined but is quite resilient, tolerating deep shade, air pollution, and even browsing deer.

Westringia fruticosa

COAST ROSEMARY
Mint family *(Lamiaceae)*
EVERGREEN SHRUB

⚡ **ZONES 8, 9, 14–24**

☼ **FULL SUN**

◊ ◊ **LITTLE TO MODERATE WATER**

This Australian native, sometimes sold as *W. rosmarini-fomis,* looks something like a softer version of rosemary, with spreading, rather loose growth to 3–6 ft. tall and 5–10 ft. wide. Its medium green to gray-green leaves have white undersides and are slightly finer and filmier in texture than rosemary leaves. Small white or very pale blue flowers with tiny dark freckles bloom from mid-winter through spring in colder areas, practically all year in milder climates. This wind-tolerant shrub is an excellent choice for coastal gardens.

'Wynyabbie Gem', possibly a hybrid, has light lavender flowers. 'Morning Light' grows 3–4 ft. tall and a little wider, and has white flowers and white-edged leaves. 'Smokey' is similar but slightly more upright with an overall grayer tint.

HOW TO GROW IT

Soil Needs light, well-drained soil.

Care notes Looks great when allowed to grow naturally but can be trimmed to control size or shape in late spring and again in summer.

Westringia fruticosa **'Smokey'**

TIP Coast rosemary takes shearing well, making it an excellent subject for topiary. Just clip during the warm months to shape it into a ball, a box, or any form you like.

Shrubs for Hedges

Need to block an unpleasant view or create a privacy screen? Plant a row of easy-care shrubs and let them grow into a "green wall."

Or to edge a path or to divide space between different areas of the garden, choose small, slow-growing shrubs and give them an occasional clipping to keep them in shape. The nine low-maintenance hedge plants listed here are evergreen, so they look good in all seasons. Most have the added bonus of flowers or fruit. All can be clipped into formal shapes or left to grow naturally.

A / Compact strawberry tree (*Arbutus unedo* 'Compacta'). Red-brown branches hold dark green leaves and clusters of white flowers followed by yellow (young) or red (mature) fruits that resemble strawberries. Grows 10 ft. tall and wide. 'Oktoberfest' is slightly smaller, with pink flowers. Full sun or part shade. Moderate water. Zones 4–24.

B / Common boxwood (*Buxus sempervirens*). Classic choice for low hedges, with dense, uniform, fresh green leaves. Many varieties sold, including 'Suffruticosa', a slow grower to 4–5 ft. tall and wide, and 'Variegata', with leaves edged in creamy white. Sun or shade. Regular water. Zones 3b–6, 15–17.

C / Purple hopseed bush (*Dodonaea viscosa* 'Purpurea'). Fast grower to 10–15 ft. tall and nearly as wide. Dark, bronzy red leaves are long and willowy. Clusters of papery, pinkish seed capsules are showy and long lasting. Full sun or light shade (color is darker in full sun). Little to regular water. Zones 7–24; H1, H2.

D / Red escallonia (*Escallonia rubra*). Glossy, dark green leaves make a nice backdrop for the bright red, butterfly-attracting flowers. Grows 6–15 ft. tall and wide. Just one of several escallonias good for hedging. Full sun; part shade in hottest climates. Regular water. Zones 4–9, 14–24.

E / Armstrong juniper (*Juniperus* × *pfitzeriana* 'Armstrongii'). Compact, upright growth to 4–5 ft. tall and wide, with arching, feathery, medium green foliage. Tough plant that thrives at almost any site. Columnar types like *J. chinensis* 'Spartan' are good for narrow strips. Full sun or part shade. Little to moderate water. Zones 1–24.

F / Japanese privet (*Ligustrum japonicum*). Compact, dense plant to 10–12 ft. tall and 8 ft. wide. Leaves are dark green and glossy; varieties with wavy-edged or white-variegated leaves are available. Profuse, scented white flowers appear in late spring. Full sun or part shade. Regular water. Zones 4–24; H1, H2.

G / Myrtle (*Myrtus communis*). Rounded, densely foliaged shrub to 5–6 ft. tall and nearly as wide (larger with great age). Bright green leaves are aromatic, and white flowers have a sweet perfume. Bluish black berries follow blooms. Full sun or part shade. Little to moderate water. Zones 8–24; H1, H2.

H / Kohuhu (*Pittosporum tenuifolium*). Fast grower to 15–25 ft. tall and 10–15 ft. wide, but easily kept smaller. Species has deep green leaves, but many colorful and smaller varieties are offered. 'Silver Sheen' has shiny, bright green leaves; 'Marjorie Channon' (to 8–10 ft.) has light green leaves bordered in white. Full sun or part shade. Moderate to regular water. Zones 9, 14–17, 19–24.

I / Germander (*Teucrium* × *lucidrys*). Sturdy sub-shrub with small, dark green leaves and spikes of red-purple or white flowers in summer. Grows just 1 ft. high and 2 ft. wide, perfect for edging a path or flower bed. Shear back once or twice a year to keep neat. Full sun. Moderate water. Zones 2–24.

Groundcovers

Sometimes you need to fill in areas of exposed soil in your garden. You could cover those with mulch to keep weeds from taking up the vacant real estate, but why not plant low, spreading plants to do the job more attractively?

Listed here are 9 of the easiest groundcovers for Western gardens, including those that take hot sun and others for cool, damp shade. Some are short, wide shrubs; some are leafy perennials; some are scrambling succulents; and others hug the ground as tightly as a green carpet. All are evergreen in mild climates, and most have pretty flowers or fruit. Plant widths (or specific instructions) are given as a guide to spacing.

A / Kinnikinnick (*Arctostaphylos uva-ursi*). Glossy, bright green leaves clothe this ground-hugging, wide-spreading shrub. White or pinkish flowers are followed by bright red fruits. Plant 2–3 ft. apart in acidic soil and surround with mulch. Full sun or light shade. Little to moderate water. Zones A1–A3, 1–9, 14–24.

B / Powis castle artemisia (*Artemisia* 'Powis Castle'). This foolproof perennial quickly forms a mound of lacy, silvery gray, fragrant foliage to 3 ft. high and 6 ft. wide. Great on sunny slopes or as a backdrop for colorful beds. Cut back moderately in spring. Full sun or part shade. Little to moderate water. Zones 2–24.

C / Sweet woodruff (*Galium odoratum*). This charming spreader has delicate emerald green leaves and tiny white flowers with a sweet perfume. Usually stays under 1 ft. high; spreads indefinitely in rich soil. Part or full shade. Regular to ample water. Zones A2, A3; 2–6, 15–17.

D / Creeping juniper (*Juniperus horizontalis*). Flat-growing, spreading shrub with feathery-looking foliage. Many fine varieties offered in shades of green, blue, and silvery gray; most are under 1 ft. high and reach about 8 ft. wide. Full sun or part shade. Little to moderate water. Zones 1–24 (some varieties grow in A1–A3 as well).

E / Japanese spurge (*Pachysandra terminalis*). Shiny dark green leaves and small white flowers on a plant about 1 ft. high that spreads slowly but surely. Good choice under trees and alongside shady paths. Part or full shade. Moderate to regular water. Zones 2–10, 14–21.

F / Scotch moss (*Sagina subulata*). Resembles bright green moss, but grows in sun rather than shade and produces tiny white flowers. Good between steppingstones. Plant in rich, well-drained soil and feed occasionally. Full sun or part shade. Regular water. Zones 1–11, 14–24.

G / Angelina stonecrop (*Sedum rupestre* 'Angelina'). Bright yellow, needlelike leaves give this the look of a golden spruce—but one that grows just 16 in. high and 1–2 ft. wide. Lovely spilling from a container or over a stone wall. Full sun or part shade. Little to moderate water. Zones 2–24.

H / Lamb's ears (*Stachys byzantina*). Soft, thick, woolly white leaves grow in clumps under 1½ ft. high, spreading to about 3 ft. In late spring and summer, tall stalks bear small purple flowers that are attractive to bees. Nice edging for a path. Full sun or light shade. Moderate water. Zones 1–24.

I / Creeping thyme (*Thymus polytrichus britannicus*). Tiny fragrant leaves and pink flowers make this a favorite choice between steppingstones. Just 3 in. high, it spreads slowly to 3 ft. wide. Woolly thyme (*T. serpyllum*) is similar, but with soft, woolly leaves. Full sun in cooler climates only. Little to moderate water. Zones A2, A3; 1–24.

Aeonium arboreum

Orpine family *(Crassulaceae)*

☒ ZONES 15–17, 20–24

☼ ☽ FULL SUN IN COOLER CLIMATES ONLY

◖ MODERATE WATER

Looking like something from the imagination of Dr. Seuss, this upright grower reaches 3 ft. high and wide, its branches tipped with rosettes of fleshy, bright green leaves. Each rosette grows 6–8 in. wide and, after several years, may produce a single large stalk of yellow flowers in spring or summer. Branches that have flowered die, but new ones are continually produced. 'Atropurpureum', with magenta-and-green rosettes, is more striking and more widely grown than the species.

A. haworthii is more shrubby, growing about 2 ft. high and 4 ft. wide. Rosettes of blue-green, red-edged leaves are 2–3 in. wide; flowers are cream-colored.

Several colorful hybrids are popular. 'Kiwi' forms a low, tight mound to about 2 ft. high and wide. Its flowers are pale yellow, and its leaves are tricolored: light green with pale yellow variegation and bright red edges. 'Starburst' and 'Sunburst' show off with 12-in.-wide rosettes of green leaves variegated in light yellow or creamy white and edged with red; flowers are cream-colored. They usually grow 1½–2 ft. high and wide but can mound up to 4 ft. tall; these two don't respond well to pruning. 'Zwartkop', sometimes called black rose, has very dark purple (nearly black) rosettes up to 10 in. across; it can reach 5 ft. tall.

HOW TO GROW IT

Soil Plant in well-drained soil.

In containers Aeoniums grow well in containers filled with commercial cactus mix. Feed potted plants in early spring with a balanced liquid fertilizer.

Care notes These cool-season growers go dormant in warmest months to save water, so cut back on irrigation in summer. During dormancy, plants may appear sick and lose leaves—but when the weather cools and they get a little water, they perk up and regrow leaves. With age, most types grow leggy. To encourage branching, cut back branches several inches below rosettes anytime except during summer dormancy.

Aeonium arboreum 'Zwartkop'

TIP Cuttings are easily rooted: let dry for a few days, then plant in sandy soil kept barely moist until new growth appears.

Agave attenuata

FOX TAIL AGAVE
Asparagus family *(Asparagaceue)*

🗡 **ZONES 13, 20–24; H1, H2**

☼ ☽ **SOME SHADE IN HOTTEST CLIMATES**

💧💧 **MODERATE TO REGULAR WATER**

💧 **JUICE FROM CUT LEAVES CAUSES SKIN IRRITATION**

Use this large, architectural plant as a dramatic focal point in a tropical or drought-tolerant garden; it also makes a statuesque container subject and looks great near water. Plant forms a huge rosette of fleshy leaves that are soft green or gray-green and up to 2½ ft. long. Clumps grow to 6–8 ft. across, and older plants develop a stout trunk to 5 ft. tall. After many years, a flower stalk resembling a giant asparagus emerges from the rosette's center; after flowering, the rosette dies, usually leaving behind plenty of suckers that make new plants.

Look for colorful varieties like 'Nova' ('Boutin Blue'), with broader and bluer leaves than the species, and 'Variegata', a showstopper with pale green leaves broadly marked with yellow stripes. Both are smaller and slower growing than the species.

A. americana 'Mediopicta Alba' (Zones 10, 12–24; H1, H2) grows about 4 ft. tall and 6 ft. wide. It has blue-green leaves with a broad central stripe of creamy white. Each leaf has spiny edges and a sharp terminal spine, so site this plant away from paths.

A. 'Blue Glow' (Zones 9, 13–24; H1) is a compact, colorful hybrid that grows 1–2 ft. high and 2–3 ft. wide, with blue-green leaves edged in red and yellow and tipped with a short red spine.

A. victoriae-reginae (Zones 10, 12, 13, 15–17, 21–24) forms a distinctive, solitary rosette 12–15 in. across. The stiff, thick leaves are dark green with narrow white lines and sharp black tips. Excellent in containers.

HOW TO GROW IT

Soil Provide fairly rich soil and excellent drainage.

In containers Use standard cactus potting mix, and apply a low-nitrogen fertilizer monthly during summer. Keep as dry as possible during winter; moving pots under an overhang also provides frost protection.

Care notes Protect from frost and—except along the coast—provide shade from hottest sun.

Agave attenuata

TIP Most agaves have leaves with toothed margins and a wickedly sharp terminal spine, but this big softy has neither.

Crassula ovata

JADE PLANT
Orpine family *(Crassulaceae)*

✎ ZONES 8, 9, 12–24; H1, H2

☼ ☽ FULL SUN OR PART SHADE

◖ LITTLE TO NO WATER

Well known as a top-notch houseplant, jade plant also performs beautifully as a landscaping shrub or large container plant in mildest climates. It has a stout trunk and sturdy limbs, and can reach 9 ft. tall and half as wide, but is usually smaller (especially when grown in a pot). Leaves are thick, oblong, fleshy pads 1–2 in. long, glossy green, often with red-tinged edges that are more prominent with more sun. Clusters of small star-shaped, pink or white flowers bloom in profusion from fall into spring. Good near swimming pools. May not survive winter without overhead protection in Zones 8, 9, 12–15, 18–21.

'Crosby's Dwarf' is a low, compact grower. Among the best variegated kinds are 'Sunset' (yellow-tinged red) and 'Tricolor' (green, white, and pinkish). 'Gollum' and 'Hobbit' have reddish, concave leaf tips.

For something otherworldly, try *C. perfoliata falcata* (*C. falcata*). It grows 4 ft. tall and 2½ ft. wide, with thick, fleshy, gray-green, sickle-shaped leaves that are vertically arranged in two overlapping columns on erect stems. Dense clusters of scarlet flowers are held well above the leaves in late summer.

HOW TO GROW IT

Soil Grows in any well-drained soil.

In containers Excellent in containers filled with standard cactus potting mix. In spring, summer, and fall, apply a balanced liquid fertilizer monthly. Cut back on watering during winter.

Care notes Easily pruned to any shape: Just clip or snap off unwanted branches. These branches (or even a single leaf) will root readily in sandy soil in spring or summer and provide you with new plants.

Crassula ovata

TIP To protect jade plant from extreme summer heat in Zones 12 and 13, grow it in patio containers with overhead shade or in the coolest sites, such as a northern exposure.

Echeveria elegans

HEN AND CHICKS
Orpine family *(Crassulaceae)*

🌿 **ZONES 8, 9, 12, 14–24**

☼ ☽ **FULL SUN IN COOLER CLIMATES ONLY**

💧 **MODERATE WATER**

This little charmer forms tight grayish white rosettes to 4 in. across, spreading freely by offsets (hence the common name). Clusters of rosettes can mound up to 8 in. high and spread to form a solid foot-wide cover. In late winter or early spring, clusters of bell-shaped pink-and-yellow flowers dangle above the foliage. For an instant rock garden, bury a few small boulders halfway and surround them with hen and chicks. Also great for edging and for filling low, wide containers.

    E. hybrids generally have large, loose rosettes of big leaves on single or branched stems. They do well in open ground in mild-summer areas and are splendid potted plants. Leaves are crimped, waved, and/or heavily shaded with red, bronze, or purple. 'Imbricata' is very common—it resembles *E. elegans* but forms slightly larger rosettes and loose clusters of orange-red flowers. 'Afterglow' has powdery, pinkish lavender leaves edged with brighter pink. 'Big Red' has large triangular leaves that start light green and turn rose-red. 'Black Prince' grows just 3 in. wide and has dark reddish purple leaves. 'Blue Curls' has frilly-edged, blue-green leaves. 'Domingo' has powder blue leaves. 'Perle von Nürnberg' has pearly lavender-blue foliage.

    E. nodulosa, called painted echeveria (Zones 8, 9, 13–24), grows 1–2 ft. high and 2–3 ft. wide, with green leaves brightly marked in red. Light yellow summer flowers are also marked in red.

HOW TO GROW IT

Soil Grow in well-drained soil.

Planting Away from the coast, choose a spot with some shade, as plants can burn in hot summer sun.

In containers Grow in pots filled with commercial cactus potting mix. During warm months, apply a half-strength balanced liquid fertilizer once per month. Reduce watering during winter.

Echeveria elegans

TIP Echeverias look fabulous planted in containers. Make sure the pot has drainage holes, and top the soil with a layer of gravel or decorative pebbles.

× Graptoveria 'Fred Ives'

Orpine family *(Crassulaceae)*

ZONES 17–24

FULL SUN OR PART SHADE

LITTLE TO MODERATE WATER

This fast-growing succulent forms rosettes that look like big, bronzy pink flowers. It's beautiful, dependable, and very easy to grow. Fleshy leaves are arranged in rosettes 8 in. high and nearly 1 ft. across; rosettes multiply to form mounding, spreading, shrublike clumps. In summer, a slender, branched stem rises 1–2 ft. above the leaves to hold small, pale yellow flowers with orange centers and dotted petals.

Fine choice for containers, as an edging, or as a repeated element in a succulent garden. Takes considerable shade, but color fades to blue-gray in low light.

HOW TO GROW IT

Soil Plant in well-drained soil.

In containers Grow in pots filled with commercial cactus potting mix. During warm months, apply a balanced liquid fertilizer monthly. Reduce watering during winter.

Care notes When watering, try not to wet leaves. Control slugs and snails. If a rosette breaks off, let it dry for a day or two, then plant the stem in sandy soil kept barely moist until new growth appears.

× *Graptoveria* **'Fred Ives'**

TIP Plant this bold succulent with English lavender and common blue fescue for a drought-tolerant composition of contrasting colors and textures.

Sedum spathulifolium

PACIFIC STONECROP
Orpine family *(Crassulaceae)*

🌿 **ZONES 2–9, 14–24**

☼ ☽ **FULL SUN OR PART SHADE**

◊ ◖ **LITTLE TO MODERATE WATER**

This diminutive succulent grows just 4 in. high but can spread to an eventual 2 ft. wide. Its spoon-shaped, ½-to-1-in., silvery blue-green leaves are tinged with reddish purple and packed into rosettes on short, trailing stems. Bright yellow, star-shaped flowers sprinkle the plant in spring and summer. 'Cape Blanco' is a selected form with light gray leaves; those of 'Purpureum' are suffused with purplish red.

Use Pacific stonecrop as a groundcover (set plants 1–1½ ft. apart) in areas with no foot traffic or as a filler between larger plants in a succulent composition. Looks great in containers, whether alone in a teacup-size pot or with other succulents in a shallow bowl.

S. × *rubrotinctum* (Zones 8, 9, 12–24; H1, H2), known by the common name "pork and beans," is a larger relative with a distinctive look. Sprawling, leaning 6-to-8-in. stems are set with ¾-in. leaves that look like jelly beans; they are green with reddish brown tips, often entirely bronze-red in sun. These detach easily and root readily. Springtime flowers are yellow. Looks great in a rock garden, in pots, or as a small-space groundcover (set plants 8–10 in. apart). Leaves of 'Aurora' are bright pink.

HOW TO GROW IT

Soil Plant in well-drained soil.

In containers Grow in pots of commercial cactus potting mix. During spring and summer, apply a balanced liquid fertilizer at half strength monthly. Reduce watering during winter.

Care notes If a piece of stem breaks off, just bury it partway in sandy soil and keep moist until new growth appears.

Sedum spathulifolium **'Cape Blanco'**

TIP In its natural setting, stonecrop grows in rocky crevices, so it's perfect for tucking into a dry-stacked stone wall or planting at the base of boulders.

Sempervivum tectorum

HOUSELEEK
Orpine family *(Crassulaceae)*

⚡ ZONES 2–24

☀ ◑ LIGHT SHADE IN HOTTEST CLIMATES

◊ ● LITTLE TO MODERATE WATER

Known for its tightly packed rosettes of fleshy, evergreen leaves, this low grower spreads by little offsets that cluster around the parent rosette (another common name is "hen and chickens"). Gray-green leaves tipped in reddish brown form symmetrical rosettes 2–5 in. wide; these spread quickly to form clumps to 2 ft. or wider.

Clustered, star-shaped flowers are borne on thick, leafy stems to 2 ft. high in summer. The red or reddish blooms are pretty in detail but not showy. After blooming and setting seed, individual rosettes die, but offsets (easily detached and replanted) carry on.

Good choice for rock gardens, in pots, and even in pockets in boulders or pieces of porous rock.

Colored-leaf varieties and hybrids in red, purple, chartreuse, and silvery blue are popular. *S. arachnoideum*, cobweb houseleek, is similar, but with leaves joined by fine hairs. It spreads slowly to form a dense mat 1 ft. wide or wider. Bright red flowers are held on 4-to-6-in. stems.

HOW TO GROW IT

Soil These do best in very well-drained, gritty soil. Add sand or gravel to ensure perfect drainage.

In containers Grow in low bowls filled with commercial cactus potting mix.

Care notes Water only to prevent shriveling. When blooming stems begin to brown and shrivel, snip them off at the base.

Sempervivum tectorum **'Royal Ruby'**

TIP The Latin name for this genus means "live forever," which gives you a clue about its durability and easy care.

Senecio mandraliscae

Sunflower family *(Asteraceae)*

✎ **ZONES 12, 13, 16, 17, 21–24; H1, H2**

☼ ☽ **PART SHADE IN DESERT, FULL SUN ELSEWHERE**

◊ ◖ **LITTLE TO MODERATE WATER**

This colorful, textural succulent is equally at home spilling from a large container or spreading as a groundcover. Plant grows about 1–1½ ft. high and 2–3 ft. wide, with upright, cylindrical, slightly curved leaves to 6 in. long. The leaves are an appealing shade of blue-gray that blends well with many other colors. The shape, color, and powdery white coating of the leaves have earned this plant a few different common names, like "blue chalk sticks," "blue fingers," and even "blue fries." Small white flowers appear in summer, but the foliage is the real show. Sometimes listed as *Kleinia mandraliscae*.

Great choice for edging a path, filling in a drought-tolerant bed, or carpeting the ground beneath larger succulents like agaves or jade plants.

HOW TO GROW IT

Soil Needs well-drained soil.

In containers Good in pots filled with commercial cactus potting mix.

Care notes If stems become rangy, clip back for fresh new growth. Be careful not to overwater in summer.

TIP Fleshy, water-filled leaves make this a good choice for a fire-resistant groundcover near the house.

Senecio mandraliscae

Vines as Colorful Cover-Ups

Vines can dress up fences, walls, trellises, and arbors. The nine listed here are fast and easy to grow; six are evergreen, two are deciduous (they lose their leaves in winter), and one is semievergreen (it keeps some foliage in winter).

Twining vines, as well as those with tendrils and coiling leafstalks, are perfect for covering a chain-link fence or climbing a trellis. Clinging vines hold firmly onto flat surfaces like walls or wood-slat fences. Most vines are exuberant growers; it's better to keep them in shape as they grow than to wait until they've gotten out of control. Trim wayward branches as needed during the growing season. After flowers fade (except as noted), prune more heavily, sorting out any tangled growth and shaping the vine to its support.

A / Violet trumpet vine (*Clytostoma callistegioides*). Evergreen. Produces sprays of violet or lavender trumpet-shaped flowers with golden throats from late spring to fall. Glossy, dark green leaves. Climbs quickly by tendrils to about 30 ft. Prune in late winter. Full sun or part shade. Moderate to regular water. Zones 8, 9, 12–24.

B / Carolina jessamine (*Gelsemium sempervirens*). Evergreen. Twining growth to about 20 ft., with shiny, light green leaves on long, thin branches that cascade beautifully. In late winter or early spring, plant is covered with bright yellow trumpets. All parts are poisonous if ingested. Full sun or part shade. Regular water. Zones 4–24.

C / Lilac vine (*Hardenbergia violacea*). Evergreen. Clusters of sweet-pea-shaped flowers in lilac, rose, or white (depending on variety) appear in late winter or early spring. Handsome dark green foliage. Grows by twining to about 10 ft. fall. Full sun; part shade in hottest climates. Moderate water. Zones 8–24.

D / Pink jasmine (*Jasminum polyanthum*). Evergreen. Dense clusters of highly fragrant white blossoms that open from pink buds. Blooms heavily in late winter and spring, with occasional flowers year-round. Fast, strong-growing twiner to 20 ft., with attractive dark green leaves. Full sun or light shade. Moderate to regular water. Zones 5–9, 12–24; H1.

E / Goldflame honeysuckle (*Lonicera × heckrottii*). Semievergreen. Twining growth to about 15 ft., with blue-green leaves and clusters of flowers from spring to frost. Coral pink buds open to fragrant, tubular flowers that are bright pink outside and rich yellow inside. Full sun or part shade. Moderate to regular water. Zones 2–24; H1, H2.

F / Bower vine (*Pandorea jasminoides*). Evergreen. Blooms from late spring to early fall, producing loads of pink-throated white flowers. Some varieties are pure white; others are darker pink. Great-looking foliage is rich, glossy green. Twining growth to 20–30 ft. Full sun; part shade in hottest climates. Regular water. Zones 16–24; H1, H2.

G / Boston ivy (*Parthenocissus tricuspidata*). Deciduous. Prized for its big, glossy leaves that are bronzy when new, maturing to dark green, then turning reliably orange to wine red in fall. Clings tightly by suction disks and makes a dense, uniform wall or fence cover to 50 ft. Prune during winter dormancy. Sun or shade; needs some shade in hottest areas. Moderate water. Zones 1–24.

H / Star jasmine (*Trachelospermum jasminoides*). Evergreen. Delightfully fragrant white flowers bloom in spring and early summer. Twining growth can reach 20–30 ft. Leaves are glossy light green when new, maturing to lustrous dark green. Prune in early spring. Full sun; light shade in hottest climates. Regular water. Zones 8–24; H1, H2.

I / Chinese wisteria (*Wisteria sinensis*). Deciduous. Footlong clusters of white or violet-blue, slightly fragrant flowers put on quite a show in spring. This twining, woody vine can get quite large (to 30 ft.) and heavy, so grow it on a sturdy support. Prune in winter. Full sun or part shade. Little to moderate water. Zones 3–24.

Apple

MALUS HYBRIDS
Rose family (Rosaceae)
DECIDUOUS FRUIT TREES

✏ **ALL ZONES, EXCEPT AS NOTED**

☼ **FULL SUN**

💧 **REGULAR WATER**

Tree-ripened apples have incomparable flavor and are easy to grow. Hybrids of southwest Asian species, most grow to 5–20 ft. tall and wide. Trees bear large, fragrant, white or pink blossoms in midspring, and fruit from midsummer through fall.

With important exceptions, earlier varieties such as 'Chehalis', 'Summerred', and 'Yellow Transparent' don't keep long, so they're favored for cooking. Late apples such as 'Braeburn' and 'Shizuka' are better keepers. Midseason apples such as 'Golden Delicious', 'Gravenstein', and 'Jonagold' are excellent fresh and cooked.

There are also many apples bred for specific reasons: 'Honeycrisp' for cold climates, 'Liberty' for overall disease resistance, and 'Pink Pearl' for pink flesh.

In regions with balmy winters, choose apples with low winter chill requirement: 'Anna', 'Dorset Golden', 'Gordon', and 'Winter Banana' are examples.

Although apples such as 'Golden Delicious', 'Mollie's Delicious', and 'Chehalis' are fairly self-fruitful, most do best when cross-pollinated. Some varieties have pollenizers grafted in. Nurseries can tell you which varieties are pollen compatible.

'Liberty' apple

TREE SIZE AND FORM

Natural growth habit and rootstock determine each tree's ultimate size.

Dwarf apple trees. Reaching 5–8 ft. tall and wide, these grow on rootstocks such as M9, EMLA27, and P22. They bear at a younger age than standard apples, but have shallow roots that demand good soil, attention to feeding and watering, and physical support. They are not reliable in coldest climates. Great in half wine barrels.

Semidwarf apple trees. These grow on rootstocks such as MARK, M26, and M7, which reduce normal tree height by about half. These trees may be espaliered or trellised if planted 12–16 ft. apart and allowed to grow 8–12 ft. tall. Semidwarfing rootstocks MM106 and MM111 reduce height by 15 to 25 percent.

Spur apples. All apple trees bear fruit on spurs (short branches), but a category called spur apples is distinct. Their spurs form within 2 years after planting (versus 3–5 years for regular apples) and grow closer together on shorter branches, giving more apples per foot of branch. Spur apple trees grow about two-thirds the size of standard apple trees. They can be further dwarfed by grafting onto dwarfing rootstocks. Some apples, such as 'Winter Banana', are sold in both regular and spur forms.

Columnar apple trees. These grow 8–10 ft. tall and 2 ft. wide. Look for varieties such as 'Crimson Spire', 'Emerald Spire', 'Golden Sentinel', 'Northpole', 'Scarlet Sentinel', 'Scarlet Spire', and 'Ultra Spire'. Two varieties are necessary for pollination.

'Golden Delicious' apple

'Winter Banana' apples

HOW TO GROW IT

Soil Deep, well-drained soil is best.

Planting Plant from bare-root stock in winter or early spring, or plant containerized apples anytime.

Spacing Spur types: 12–14 ft. apart; on EMLA27, M9, P22 rootstocks, 6–8 ft. apart; on MARK rootstock, 8 ft. apart. Semidwarf trees: On MM106 or MM111 rootstocks, 15–17 ft. apart; on MARK, M26, or M7 rootstocks, 10 ft. apart. Dwarf trees: On EMLA27, M9, or P22 rootstocks, 5–8 ft. apart. Columnar types: 1½–2 ft. apart.

Fertilizer Give newly planted trees ¼ pound of 10-10-10 fertilizer as buds start to open the first year. In every subsequent year, add ¼ pound until dwarf trees

and columnar types are getting 2½ pounds, semidwarfs 5 pounds.

Water Regular water is critical as fruit develops.

Pruning, training Encourage widely angled branches to grow in spiral placement around the trunk. Keep tree centers open to some sun. Grow dwarf trees as espaliers tied to fences or other supports. On columnar apples, remove wayward growth. Thin fruit after June drop, when the tree thins itself. Remove all but one apple in each cluster, and keep apples about 6 in. apart.

Challenges Codling moth (apple worm) and apple maggots can be controlled with an organic spray called spinosad. Timing is critical; follow label instructions. Avoid disease by buying resistant varieties.

Artichoke

CYNARA CARDUNCULUS (SCOLYMUS GROUP)
Sunflower family *(Asteraceae)*
PERENNIAL VEGETABLE SOMETIMES GROWN AS ANNUAL

✎ **ZONES 8, 9, 14–24; AS ANNUAL IN ZONES 2B–7, 10–13**

☼ ◑ **FULL SUN OR PART SHADE**

💧 **REGULAR WATER**

If the world's most delectable flower buds weren't reason enough to grow it, artichoke's ornamental foliage and flowers would be. This Mediterranean native is big and ferny-looking, with a fountainlike form to 4 ft. tall, 8 ft. wide. Leaves are silvery green. The flower buds—the artichokes you cook and eat—form at tops of stalks. Purple flowers follow if buds aren't harvested.

In most of California Zones 8, 9, 14–24, artichoke is a perennial, producing edible buds in early summer. But in central California coastal Zone 17, where it is grown commercially, artichoke can produce fine, tender artichokes from early fall to late spring.

In Southwest desert Zones 11–13, artichoke is usually treated as an annual and planted in fall for spring harvest, but it may hang on to be a perennial.

In Zones 2b–7 and 10, plant in spring—you will get foliage for sure and a crop if the weather cooperates. A deep organic mulch in fall may carry it through winter if freezes are not deep or long.

Favored varieties include standard 'Green Globe' and 'Imperial Star'; among those with violet-tinged buds, try 'Purple Italian' and 'Violetto'. 'Northern Star' has survived 0°F (–18°C), so it is popular in chilly-winter climates.

HOW TO GROW IT

Soil Dig in 4–6 in. of compost along with ½ pound of complete fertilizer per 100 square ft.

Planting Start dormant roots or containerized plants in winter or early spring, at least a month before average date of last spring frost. Set roots vertically, with buds or shoots just above soil level. Where artichokes are grown as perennials, space them 4–6 ft. apart in rows; where they are grown as annuals, space them 18 in. apart in rows 2–3 ft. wide.

Fertilizer Give plants monthly doses of high-nitrogen fertilizer starting 4 weeks after transplant.

Artichokes

Water After active growth starts, water plants thoroughly once a week, wetting the entire root system.

Harvest Cut off buds with 1½ in. of stem while they are still tight and plump.

TIP If you admire the artichoke for its architectural good looks, try cardoon, an ornamental form of the same species.

Asparagus

ASPARAGUS OFFICINALIS
Asparagus family (*Asparagaceae*)
PERENNIAL VEGETABLE

✎ **ZONES A1–A3; 1–24**

☼ **FULL SUN**

💧 **REGULAR WATER**

Probably the most permanent and dependable of home garden vegetables. Plants take 2–3 years to come into full production but then furnish delicious spears every spring for 10–15 years. They take up considerable space but do so in the grand manner: plants are tall, feathery, graceful, highly ornamental. Use along a sunny fence or as background for flowers or other vegetables.

Asparagus seeds and roots are sold as "traditional" ('Mary Washington' and others) and "all-male" ('UC 157', 'Jersey Giant', and 'Jersey Knight'). The latter are more productive because they don't have to put energy into seed production.

'Jersey Supreme' is an all-male variety that comes to harvest more than a week ahead of the others.

'Millennium F1' is a cold-hardy all-male variety bred for the Far North.

Among purple-tinged varieties, look for the all-male 'Marte' and a high-sugar variety sold as 'Purple Passion' or 'Sweet Purple'.

HOW TO GROW IT

Soil Must be well drained, deeply dug, rich. Where drainage is poor, plant in raised beds.

Planting Make trenches 1 ft. wide, 8–10 in. deep; space trenches 4–6 ft. apart. Heap loose, manure-enriched soil at bottom of trenches and soak. Set out roots in fall or winter in mild-winter climates, in early spring in cold-winter areas. Cover with 2 in. of soil and water again. As young plants grow, gradually fill in the trench, taking care not to cover growing tips. Space plants 1 ft. apart.

Fertilizer Feed generously after harvest.

Water Soak deeply whenever the soil begins to dry out at root depth.

Asparagus

Pruning, training Don't harvest any spears the first spring; the object at this time is to build a big root mass. The following spring, you can cut spears for 4–6 weeks or until appearance of thin spears indicates that roots are nearing exhaustion. Cut spears when they are 5–8 in. long.

Care notes Clean up debris from asparagus beds in fall to help get rid of overwintering asparagus beetles. Use row covers over beds in spring. If fusarium and rust are a problem where you garden, buy resistant varieties.

Blueberry

VACCINIUM SPECIES
Heath family *(Ericaceae)*
DECIDUOUS FRUIT SHRUBS

✎ **ZONES VARY BY TYPE**

☀ **FULL SUN**

💧 **AMPLE WATER**

Handsome enough for a place in shrub borders and hedges, blueberries do double-duty as ornamentals and edibles. Leaves, to 3 in. long, are bronze when new, maturing to dark green, turning scarlet or yellow in fall. Tiny, urn-shaped spring flowers are white or pinkish.

Blueberries are available bare-root or in containers. Plant two varieties for best pollination.

Northern highbush *(V. corymbosum).* Zones 2–9, 14–17. These are the blueberries found in grocery stores. From the Northeast, they grow to 6 ft. and require definite winter cold to ripen fruit from late spring to late summer. Early: 'Earliblue', 'Ivanhoe', and 'Spartan'. Midseason: 'Blueray', 'Chandler', 'Olympia', 'Tophat' (dwarf), and 'Toro'. Late: 'Darrow' (huge fruits), 'Elliott', and 'Legacy' (evergreen). 'Rubel' bears from early to late.

Southern highbush *(V. darrowii × V. corymbosum).* Zones 8, 9, 14–24). To 6 ft. These are better adapted to mild-winter climates, and ripen their fruit in mid- to late spring. Very early: 'Misty' and 'O'Neal'. 'Jubilee' is early, and 'Sharpblue' is early to midseason. Midseason: 'Southmoon', and the very compact, self-fruitful 'Peach Sorbet' (18–24 in.) and 'Sunshine Blue' (3 ft.) varieties.

Rabbiteye blueberries *(V. virgatum).* Zones 8, 9, 14–24. From 4½ to 12 ft. Native to southeastern United States, these heat-tolerant plants can be grown in mild-winter areas if given acid soil conditions. They ripen large, light blue berries from May to July. Midseason: 'Bluebelle'. Late midseason: 'Southland' and 'Tifblue'.

Hardy half-high varieties *(V. corymbosum × V. angustifolium).* Zones A2, A3; 1–3. To 4 ft. tall. Early: 'Polaris' and 'St. Cloud'. Early midseason: 'Northcountry'. Midseason: 'Chippewa' and self-fruitful 'Jelly Bean' (1 to 2 ft.). Midseason to late: 'Northblue' and 'Northsky' (to 18 in. tall).

'Chippewa' blueberries

HOW TO GROW IT

Soil Well-drained and acidic (pH 4.5 to 5.5). If your soil isn't acidic, amend it with peat.

Planting Plant in early spring in cold-winter regions, spring or autumn in mild climates, with the crown ½ in. or less below the ground. Mulch. In containers: Grow small kinds in containers at least 18 in. deep and wide, larger ones in half wine barrels.

Fertilizer Don't feed the first year, and feed only lightly in following years.

Water During the first 3 years, give plants 1 in. water every week during the growing season. In subsequent years, keep plants moist during the growing season.

Fig

FICUS CARICA
Mulberry family *(Moraceae)*
DECIUOUS FRUIT TREE

✎ **ZONES 4–9, 12–24; H1, H2; OR ANYWHERE IN POTS**

☼ **FULL SUN**

◖◖ **MODERATE TO REGULAR WATER**

With two crops of fruit per year, ornamental leaves, and minimal problems, fig is a standout among fruit trees. Native to western Asia and the eastern Mediterranean, it grows quickly 15–30 ft. tall, and easily as wide. Can be held to 10 ft. in a large container or trained as espalier.

Heavy, smooth gray trunks are picturesque in silhouette. Rough bright green leaves with three to five lobes are 4–9 in. long and nearly as wide. Casts dense shade. In areas where temperatures fall below 15°F (–9°C), fig wood freezes and plants grow like big shrubs. In hot-summer regions, paint trunks of newly planted figs with white latex paint to prevent sunburn.

Plant where fallen fruit won't make a mess on path or patio.

The following varieties don't need pollinating, and most bear one early-summer crop on last year's wood, and a second in late summer or early fall on current year's growth.

The most widely adapted figs include 'Desert King' (green-skinned, red-fleshed fruit; one crop), 'Improved Brown Turkey' (brownish purple fruit), and 'Mission' (purple-black figs with pink flesh).

In warm climates, try 'Black Jack' (purple skin, pink flesh), 'Celeste' (violet-tinged bronzy skin, rosy amber flesh), 'Kadota' (tough-skinned, greenish yellow fruit; excellent in Hawaii), 'Panachée' (striped, greenish yellow skin, strawberry flesh; one crop), and 'Peter's Honey' (greenish yellow skin, amber flesh).

'Osborn Prolific' (dark reddish brown skin; amber flesh) does well in cool-summer climates; 'Genoa' (greenish yellow skin, strawberry to yellow flesh) is excellent in coastal valleys; 'Texas Everbearing' (mahogany to purple skin, strawberry flesh) produces well in short-season parts of the Southwest.

'Panachée' figs

HOW TO GROW IT

Planting Set out container plants anytime except during hot weather; plant bare-root trees in late winter or spring. Cut back tops hard at planting.

Fertilizer Feed as new growth starts.

Water Irrigate regularly for the first 2 years, then deeply every 2 weeks during the growing season.

Harvest Ripe figs detach easily when lifted and bent back toward the branch. If the fig's milky white sap irritates your skin, wear gloves.

Challenges Avoid deep cultivation over roots. If your garden has gophers, plant fig trees in ample wire baskets.

Grape

VITIS SPECIES
Grape family *(Vitaceae)*
DECIDUOUS FRUIT VINES

⁄ ZONES VARY BY VARIETY

☼ FULL SUN

◖ MODERATE WATER

Grapes are beautiful and useful, bearing much fruit with little care. Climbing by tendrils, a single grapevine can quickly roof an arbor or form a leafy wall. Big, textured leaves have good fall color and create welcome shade.

The following varieties are seedless, and none need pollination from another variety.

American grapes *(V. labrusca).* These are slip-skin grapes. Blue 'Concord' (Zones 2b, 3, 6–9, 14–23) makes classic juice and jelly. Use red 'Canadice' (Zones 2b–9, 11–21) or black 'Campbell Early' ('Island Belle', Zones 5–22) fresh or juiced; both ripen well even in cool-summer climates.

European grapes *(V. vinifera).* These have tight skin, need more heat. They include wine grapes and the table grapes of the market. 'Black Monukka' (Zones 3, 6–16, warm parts of 17, 18–24) is purple-black, all-purpose. 'Crimson Seedless' (Zones 6–9, 12–16, 18–22) and 'Flame' (Zones 6–9, 11–16, warm parts of 17, 18–24) have red fruit. 'Thompson Seedless' (Zones 7–14, 18–19) produces amber-green grapes. The last three are good fresh or dried.

American hybrid grapes. Crossed with European grapes, these have a mix of their parents' characteristics. Try white 'Himrod' (Zones 3–9, 11–21) for fresh eating.

Plant grapes in an open, sunny spot with free air movement. Cut bunches only when grapes are sweet, since they stop ripening at harvest.

HOW TO GROW IT

Soil Provide deep, moderately fertile, well-drained soil.

Planting Plant bare-root vines in holes spaced 8–10 ft. apart after trimming roots to 6 in.

Fertilizer Apply balanced fertilizer each spring.

Water Avoid splashing water on leaves; drip irrigation is ideal.

'Campbell Early' grapes

Training For the 20-minute gardener, simply train your grapevines over an arbor or along a fence, tying them loosely in place.

Pruning Though sophisticated pruning yields the highest-quality fruit, the vines still produce good grapes with little attention. The purpose of yearly pruning, done in winter, is to limit the amount of fruiting wood so that plants won't overproduce. Fruit grows on stems that formed the previous season.

Care notes Pierce's disease, spread by the sharp-shooter insect, is a mortal threat to grapes in parts of California. For more information, contact your cooperative extension office.

'Improved Meyer' lemon

CITRUS HYBRID
Citrus family *(Rutaceae)*
EVERGREEN FRUIT TREE

✎ **ZONES 8, 9, 12–24; H1, H2; OR INDOORS**

☼ **FULL SUN; BRIGHT LIGHT**

💧 **REGULAR WATER**

'Improved Meyer' lemons

Topping out at around 12 ft., 'Improved Meyer' lemon fits easily into most gardens. And on a dwarf rootstock, it can be held to half that size, in a container or in the ground. Either way, it's much smaller than a standard lemon tree but still has an attractive form and glossy deep green foliage. Because this is a hybrid of *C. limon* (lemon) and *C. sinensis* (orange), it is hardier than a lemon and needs less heat to ripen than an orange. Fruit hangs on the tree nearly year-round in mild coastal climates.

The word "improved" in the name means that this variety is disease-free. It is the only Meyer lemon that can be sold in California and Arizona, and is the best lemon for Hawaii. Fruit is quite different from a commercial lemon: rounder, thinner skinned, and orange-yellow in color. Its aroma is tangy, but the flavor is less acidic than a standard lemon's. Very juicy. Bears at an early age.

HOW TO GROW IT

Soil Fast drainage is essential. If soil drains slowly, plant above soil level in raised beds or on a soil mound.

Planting Plant trees from containers. Trunks of newly planted trees are subject to sunburn in hot climates. Protect the trees by painting with white latex paint diluted 50/50 with water, or apply commercial trunk-wrapping bands.

Fertilizer Apply complete fertilizer several times during the growing season each year. In freeze-prone areas, start feeding in late winter and stop in late summer. Citrus may suffer from chlorosis due to iron, manganese, or zinc deficiency. Commercial products containing chelates of all three nutrients are available as foliar sprays. In Hawaii, add lime to acidic soils and phosphate to soils low in phosphorus, at planting time.

Water Trees need moist soil but never standing water. Water newly planted trees twice a week in normal summer weather, more frequently during hot spells. Water established trees at least every other week during summer. Be sure to wet the entire root zone to a depth of 3–4 ft., and be consistent: fluctuating soil moisture can aggravate fruit splitting—a problem that can affect all citrus (typically in autumn).

Orange

CITRUS SINENSIS
Citrus family *(Rutaceae)*
EVERGREEN FRUIT TREE

✎ **ZONES 8, 9, 12–24; H1, H2; OR INDOORS**

☼ **FULL SUN; BRIGHT LIGHT**

◆ **REGULAR WATER**

Just two kinds of oranges—'Washington' navel and 'Valencia'—can keep you in fruit for 10 months of the year. Both are also ornamental, growing 20–25 ft. tall and bearing sweetly scented white flowers and decorative fruit in season.

The two types, 'Valencia' and navel, come to harvest at different seasons and have different characteristics.

'Valencia'. With the lower heat requirement of the two, 'Valencia' grows well near the Southern California coast, with fruit ripening into spring and summer. This is the standard commercial juice orange and the most widely planted orange in the world. Widely adapted in California, it is a poor risk in Arizona; if you plant it there, select a warm location or provide some protection to fruit, which must overwinter on tree. 'Valencia' oranges can store on tree for months, improving in sweetness. This is a vigorous tree, fuller growing than 'Washington' navels, both as standard and as dwarf. 'Campbell', 'Delta', and 'Midknight' are early-ripening, nearly seedless selections of 'Valencia'.

Navel. Because navel oranges demand even more warmth, they are better suited to inland regions. Their fruit-development period is shorter than that of 'Valencia', so trees will produce palatable fruit between winter frosts if summer heat is high. Skin is thick and peels easily.

'Washington'. The most widely available. It is widely adapted except in desert regions and is best in warm interiors. Standard tree is a 20-to-25-ft. globe. On dwarf stock, it grows 8–12 ft. tall. Bears early to midwinter. 'Tabata' is identical (or nearly so) to 'Washington'; it is grown in Hawaii, as is the standard 'Washington'.

'Cara Cara'. First rosy-fleshed navel; bears at the same time as 'Washington'. Rich flavor.

'Lane Late'. Late-ripening navel, extending the season well into summer.

'Robertson'. Smaller variant of 'Washington'. Fruit is identical but earlier by 2 to 3 weeks. Tends to carry fruit in clusters. Dwarf trees produce amazing amounts of fruit.

'Valencia' oranges

All citrus fruit is damaged at several degrees below freezing—hence the importance of choosing early-ripening varieties in freeze-prone areas.

HOW TO GROW IT

See "How to Grow It" section for 'Improved Meyer' lemon, page 245.

Plum and prune

PRUNUS SPECIES
Rose family *(Rosaceae)*
DECIDUOUS FRUIT TREES

✒ **ZONES VARY BY TYPE**

☀ **FULL SUN**

💧 **MODERATE WATER**

Few fruits yield a bigger harvest for less care than plums. We recommend several, all self-fruitful and all easy to keep under 15 ft. with annual pruning. Like apricots, cherries, and peaches, these are stone fruits that bloom in late winter or early spring. Fruit ripens at some point from May into September, depending on variety and climate.

European plums *(Prunus × domestica).* Bred from European and west Asian species. Best in cooler climates where winter chill is higher and late-spring frosts (or rain) aren't as likely to interfere with pollination. These have firm flesh and can be cooked or eaten fresh. Prunes also belong here: they're varieties with a high enough sugar content for sun drying without fermentation. Prunes can be eaten fresh if you like their very sweet flavor.

Good varieties for fresh eating include 'Green Gage' (Zones 2–22, H1; greenish yellow skin, amber flesh) and 'Mt. Royal' (Zones 2–12, 14–18; blue skin, yellow flesh). For prunes, try 'French Improved' (Zones 2, 3, 7–12, 14–22; reddish purple skin, greenish yellow flesh), 'Italian Prune' (Zones 2–12, 14–18; purple-black skin, yellow-green flesh), and 'Stanley' (Zones 2–12, 14–22; purple-black skin, yellow-green flesh).

Japanese plums *(P. salicina).* Native to Japan and China, these are large and juicy, with a pleasant blend of acid and sugar. Most fresh market plums sold in the United States are Japanese types.

Some of the best are 'Burgundy' (Zones 7–12, 14–24; dark red skin and flesh), 'Golden Nectar' (Zones 2, 3, 7–12, 14–20; yellow skin and flesh), 'Kelsey' (Zones 2, 3, 7–12, 14–18, H1; greenish yellow skin splashed red, yellow flesh), and 'Santa Rosa' (Zones 2, 3, 7–23; purplish red skin with heavy blue bloom, yellow flesh that's dark red near skin).

'Santa Rosa' plums

HOW TO GROW IT

Soil Almost any soil with good drainage.

Planting Plant bare-root stock in winter, early spring.

Fertilizer Before spring leafout, apply ½ pound of 10-10-10 fertilizer for each year of the tree's age, up to 6 lbs.

Water Irrigate moderately but consistently.

Care notes Thin Japanese plums to 4–6 in. apart as soon as fruit forms, or crop may break branches.

Strawberry

FRAGARIA × ANANASSA
Rose family (*Rosaceae*)
PERENNIAL FRUIT

✎ **ZONES A1–A3; 1–9, 14–24; H1, H2; DIFFICULT IN ZONES 10–13**

☼ **FULL SUN, EXCEPT AS NOTED**

💧 **REGULAR WATER**

Probably the most versatile fruit, strawberries can be used as a groundcover, grown in hanging baskets where snails and slugs can't reach them, or planted in wide rows. Standard market strawberries are hybrids. Plants have toothed, roundish, medium green leaves and white flowers. They grow 6–8 in. high, spreading by runners to about 1 ft. across. Strawberries of one variety or another can be grown in every part of the West, though it is hard to succeed with them in areas where soil and water salinity are high.

June-bearing types produce one crop per year in late spring or early summer; in general, they are the highest-quality strawberries you can grow, and deliver the whole crop at once for freezing or cooking. Everbearing and day-neutral kinds can fruit over a longer season. Ever-bearers produce one crop in early spring and one in fall, while day-neutrals come to peak harvest in early summer and continue to bear fruit (often unevenly) through fall. The exact fruiting pattern for both types depends on variety and temperature: plants stop flowering when the temperature rises above 85°F (29°C). Everbearers and day-neutrals put out fewer runners than June bearers and generally have smaller fruit. The quality of day-neutral fruit is higher than that of everbearing strawberries.

'Chandler' strawberries

JUNE-BEARING VARIETIES

'Benton'. Flavorful, somewhat soft berries. Virus-tolerant, mildew-resistant. Outstanding in the North-west, especially in mountain and intermountain areas.

'Camarosa'. Huge, conical berries over a long season. Susceptible to mildew. Adapted to California, especially southern areas.

'Chandler'. Large, juicy berries over long period. Excellent flavor, good texture. Some resistance to leaf spot. Best in California, particularly Santa Barbara area and south.

'Guardian'. Large, all-purpose fruit with good flavor. Disease-resistant. Good in cold-winter regions.

'Honeoye'. Large, symmetrical, bright red fruit with sweet-tart flavor. Recommended for cold-winter regions.

'Hood'. Large, conical to wedge-shaped berries for fresh eating and processing. Excellent flavor and early ripening. Resists mildew. Good in Pacific Northwest.

'Jewel'. Large, firm, bright red berries. Best in cold-winter regions.

'Puget Reliance'. Large crop of big, tasty berries; excellent flavor when processed. Vigorous. Virus-tolerant. Adapted to Pacific Northwest.

'Puget Summer'. A heavy-yielding, late-season variety. Holds its fruit up off the ground, avoiding rot. Susceptible to powdery mildew; otherwise disease-resistant. Excellent, sweet flavor. Best in the Pacific Northwest.

'Rainier'. Good-size berries with fine flavor. Vigorous. Fair tolerance to root rot. Best in Pacific Northwest, west of Cascades.

'Sequoia'. One of the tastiest strawberries. Bears for many months. Resistant to alkalinity, yellows, and most leaf diseases. Developed for coastal California but widely adapted, even to cold winters.

'Shuksan'. Soft, mealy berries. Excellent frozen; good fresh. Tolerant of alkalinity. Resistant to botrytis, viruses, red stele. Good east of Cascades in Northwest.

EVERBEARING AND DAY-NEUTRAL VARIETIES

'Albion'. Day-neutral. Long, conical fruit with excellent flavor. Resists verticillium wilt and crown rot. For California.

'Fort Laramie'. Everbearing. Good yield of berries over long season. Excellent flavor. Tolerates −30°F (−34°C) without mulch. Hardy in mountain states, High Plains, milder parts of Alaska. Also good in Southern California.

'Ozark Beauty'. Everbearing. Medium-size red berries; excellent flavor in cold-winter areas, just fair where winters are mild. Vigorous.

'Quinault'. Everbearing. Large, attractive berries are very flavorful, if a bit soft. Good producer of runners. Resists viruses and red stele. Susceptible to botrytis. Favored in the Pacific Northwest but widely adapted. Annual in Alaska.

'Seascape'. Day-neutral. Large berries are very good fresh, for jam, and for freezing. Excellent virus resistance. For California, the Pacific Northwest, Hawaii. Good choice for annual production in colder climates.

'Tribute'. Day-neutral. Medium-size berries with excellent flavor. Resists red stele and verticillium wilt. Prone to viruses in Pacific Northwest. Widely adapted.

'Tristar'. Day-neutral. Small to medium-size berries with excellent flavor. Bears well the first year. Resists red stele and mildew but is moderately susceptible to viruses. Widely adapted.

HOW TO GROW IT

Soil Well-drained, acidic soil is optimal; most varieties do not tolerate alkalinity.

Planting In mild-winter areas, plant June bearers in late summer or fall for a spring crop; in colder climates, plant in early spring for harvest the following year. Set out other types in spring for summer and fall berries. The crown

'Seascape' strawberries

should be above soil level and roots covered. Plant on flat ground if soil drains well, especially if it's high in salts; plant on a 5-to-6-in. mound if soil drains poorly. If soil is high in salts and drains poorly, grow in containers or raised beds.

Spacing Plant 14–18 in. apart, in rows 2–2½ ft. apart.

Fertilizer Feed June bearers very lightly when growth begins, and again, more heavily, after fruiting. Everbearing and day-neutral types prefer consistent light feedings.

Water Don't let plants dry out. Drip irrigation is ideal to minimize disease.

Care notes In cold climates, mulch with 4–6 in. of organic material in late fall. When temperatures warm in spring, rake mulch between plants.

Easy Cool-Season Crops for Pots

Cool-season veggies thrive in cooler weather than do warm-season crops, so they are the first vegetables to be planted in spring.

All the crops listed here can be planted in spring and then again in late summer or fall for a fall-to-winter harvest. These all-zone annuals tolerate some frost and (except for carrots) a bit more shade than warm-season veggies. But when the weather heats up, many of these go to seed quickly and become bitter. All need regular water, feeding, and sun for most of the day. Most are very easy from seed, but you can save time and work by setting out transplants of all except carrots.

A / Carrot Given deep, rock-free soil, carrots grow straight and long—reason enough to grow them in containers, where those conditions prevail. Choose a pot that's 8–14 in. deep, depending on the mature length of the carrot (the seed packet will tell you); then sow, water, and wait. If your pot is shallower than 6 in., choose a variety that is shorter when it matures—such as a half-long Nantes type, a round type, or a miniature such as 'Short 'n Sweet'.

B / Kale Unusually high in nutritional value, kale's big, beautiful leaves can be smooth or frilled, blue-green to pink. They can be harvested at any stage, though younger ones are better. Flavor becomes bitter with summer heat, sweeter with fall frosts. Plant one transplant in each 10-in.-deep container.

C / Lettuce Lightly sow different kinds of lettuce in three wide, 6-in.-deep containers grouped together. Try 'Bibb' or 'Speckles' butterhead (Boston) lettuce in one container, 'Oakleaf' or 'Red Sails' loose-leaf lettuce in a second, and 'Outredgeous' or 'Winter Density' romaine in a third. Use thinnings in salads as remaining lettuce matures.

D / Swiss chard The most beautiful chards are colored varieties like 'Bright Lights' (yellow, pink, purple, red, orange, white), 'Rainbow' (another mix of many colors), and the red-ribbed 'Rhubarb' ('Ruby Red'). Plant transplants in a 12-to-18-in.-wide, 8-in.-deep container; it looks especially attractive in combination with pansies and nasturtiums.

TIP Though you can grow any cool-season vegetable to maturity in a container, one category works especially well: mixed greens that you harvest after just 3 or 4 weeks. Usually sold as salad blends or mesclun mixes, they're always from seed. Just prepare the prefertilized soil in a wide, shallow container, scratch in enough seed to cover the soil in the container, and water. Seedlings (usually a mix of lettuce, mustard, kale, arugula, and Asian greens) come up quickly. Shear them off with scissors when they're 3–4 in. tall and use them immediately in salads. Then apply liquid fertilizer, and harvest regrowth when it gets big enough a few weeks later.

Easy Warm-Season Crops for Pots

Warm-season vegetables are frost-tender heat lovers planted after danger of frost is past in spring, maturing in summer or fall.

The annual kinds listed here are grown for their fruit. In low-desert Zone 13, most are planted in winter. In mild-summer climates or places with a short growing season, only short-season varieties will mature, and even those may need help from a heat-trapping mulch or an extra-warm, protected place in the garden. All need full sun, soil with good drainage, and regular water and feeding.

A / Cucumber Try a bush cucumber in a wide, 12-in.-deep container, or grow a vining type up a trellis (tendrils cling). Slicers, picklers, and lemon cucumbers are all available, easy to grow from seed or transplants. Just get a self-pollinating variety.

B / Pepper There are sweet peppers (like bell peppers and sweet cherry peppers) and hot ones (like habaneros and 'Anaheim' chiles); both kinds grow well from transplants in containers at least 8 in. deep and 16 in. wide. Give these maximum sun: heat on the leaves translates to heat in the peppers. 'Mariachi' is especially striking in containers; its mildly spicy fruits appear together in various stages of ripeness from yellow and orange to red.

C / Summer squash Best-mannered of the squashes, summer squash comes to harvest early (because you eat them before they mature). Plant a bush variety in a big pot or in the garden, and you can have a bumper crop of scaloppine or zucchini a couple of months later. Start from transplants.

D / Tomato Where there's room for only one vegetable, make it a tomato. Nothing produces more or better fruit. Place a transplant within a wire cage. Use large containers for large-fruited indeterminate tomatoes, and use hanging baskets or 16-in.-wide, 12-in.-deep containers for determinate varieties or cherry tomatoes. 'Sun Gold', a cherry type, is especially productive, even in a container.

TIP Full-size watermelons may not be good bets for containers, but personal-size watermelons (5 pounds or less at maturity) are excellent. They mature early and don't scramble as far as their full-size sisters. Trailing out of a container, their leafy vines give a certain country casual flair to a deck or patio—and the fruit is terrific. Nurseries often carry these, as do seed catalogs.

Chives

ALLIUM SCHOENOPRASUM
Onion family (*Alliaceae*)
DECIDUOUS PERENNIAL FROM BULBS

✂ **ALL ZONES**

☼ ◑ **FULL SUN OR PART SHADE**

💧 **REGULAR WATER DURING GROWTH AND BLOOM**

Chives are so pretty and easy to grow, they would be welcome additions to the garden even without their culinary value. Plants grow in delicate clumps 1½–2 ft. high composed of dark green leaves that look grasslike but are round and hollow. Clusters of rose-purple flowers (like clover blossoms) appear atop thin stems in spring. Use chopped leaves and blossoms for a delicate onion-like flavor in cooked dishes or as a fresh topping or garnish.

Closely related garlic chives (*Allium tuberosum*) are similar, but their footlong leaves are flat and have a mild garlic flavor. White flowers appear in summer and smell like violets. There is also a mauve-colored form.

HOW TO GROW IT

Planting Sow seed ⅛–¼ in. deep, then thin plants to 8–12 in. apart. Or plant seedlings from the garden center.

Spacing Plant at 8-to-12-in. intervals.

In containers A half-dozen plants will grow well in a 12-in.-wide pot that is at least 6 in. deep.

Care notes When harvesting, use scissors to snip entire leaves from the outside of the clump. Pick flowers as soon as they open and use them in salads. Chives and garlic chives will self-sow. Prevent seedlings by removing fading flowers—or just pull and eat unwanted seedlings.

Chives

TIP Chives make an excellent colorful edging for a flower bed or herb garden.

Mint

MENTHA SPECIES
Mint family (*Lamiaceae*)
PERENNIALS

✎ ZONES VARY BY SPECIES

☼ ☽ FULL SUN OR PART SHADE

● REGULAR WATER

These deliciously fragrant Mediterranean natives are so tough and unfussy, they'll grow almost anywhere. In fact, they spread rapidly by underground stems and self-sowing and can be quite invasive. To keep them in bounds, grow them in window boxes or containers set on solid surfaces (to prevent roots from creeping out of drainage holes and into soil). Avoid the temptation to plant more than one kind of mint in the same pot; they'll become hopelessly intertwined. Mints disappear in winter in the colder part of their range.

Apple mint (*Mentha suaveolens, M. rotundifolia*). Zones 3–24. Stiff stems grow 1½–3 ft. high, bearing rounded gray-green leaves with a scent combining fragrances of apple and mint. Purplish white flowers are held on 2-to-3-in. spikes. Makes a nice tea, garnish, or salad ingredient. 'Variegata', pineapple mint, has leaves with white markings and the faint scent of pineapple.

Golden apple mint (*M.* × *gracilis, M.* × *gentilis*). Zones 3–24. To 2 ft. high, with smooth, deep green leaves that have yellow variegation and a spicy apple fragrance and flavor. Foliage is excellent in mixed bouquets.

Peppermint (*M.* × *piperita*). Zones A2, A3; 1–24. To 3 ft. high. Strongly scented, toothed leaves are dark green, often tinged with purple. Small purplish flowers. Leaves are good for flavoring tea. *M.* × *p. citrata*, known as orange mint or bergamot mint, grows to 2 ft. high and is used in potpourris and in flavoring foods. There are also "fruit-flavored" varieties. 'Chocolate' has the slightest hint of chocolate mint flavor.

Spearmint (*M. spicata*). Zones A2, A3; 1–24. To 1–3 ft. high. Foliage is dark green and toothed; leafy spikes of pale blue flowers. Use leaves fresh from the garden or dried, as flavoring for foods, cold drinks, and jelly. 'Kentucky Colonel' has large, flavorful leaves.

'Kentucky Colonel' spearmint

HOW TO GROW IT

Soil Standard commercial potting soil is fine for mint.

Fertilizer Apply complete fertilizer as growth begins each spring.

In containers Grow different mints in their own containers; usually one plant per container is enough, as plants fill in quickly. In large containers, plant at 1-to-2-ft. intervals.

Care notes Snip off fresh new growth as needed. Replant about every 3 years; it is easy to propagate from runners.

Oregano

ORIGANUM VULGARE
Mint family *(Lamiaceae)*
PERENNIAL

ZONES VARY BY TYPE
FULL SUN, EXCEPT AS NOTED
LITTLE TO MODERATE WATER

These popular "pizza herbs" are grown for the spicy scent and flavor of their leaves, which can be used fresh or dried. Most plants grow 1–2½ ft. high, with a spread of up to 3 ft., but dwarf forms are available. Leaves average 1–1½ in. long, and tiny summer flowers are usually pink-tinged white or purple.

Greek oregano *(Origanum vulgare hirtum, O. heracleoticum).* Zones 8, 9, 12–24. Like oregano, but with broader, slightly fuzzy gray-green leaves that have a spicy, pungent flavor.

Oregano, wild marjoram *(O. vulgare).* Zones 1–24. Grows upright to 2½ ft. high, with a spread of 2–3 ft. Oval dark green leaves; white or purplish pink blossoms from midsummer to early fall. Fresh or dried leaves are used in many dishes, especially Spanish and Italian ones. Colored-leaf varieties need a half-day of direct sun for best color but can burn in afternoon sun in hot-summer areas.

Most wild forms of oregano have scentless leaves; be sure to choose a selected form with a good aroma and a flavor that you like. For best flavor, keep this plant trimmed to prevent flowering, but let some clumps bloom for bees and butterflies. 'Aureum' has bright golden foliage in spring (with morning sun), turning to green by late summer and fall; 'Thumble's Variety' is similar. 'Aureum Crispum' has curly golden leaves. 'Compactum' ('Humile') is a wide-spreading plant just a few inches high, suitable for a groundcover or between paving stones; leaves turn purple in winter. 'Country Cream' (with white flowers) and lilac-pink-flowered 'Polyphant' ('White Anniversary') are compact growers to 4–6 in. and have leaves with a distinct creamy white edge; they are often confused in commerce (and both are sometimes sold as 'Variegatum'). 'Roseum' has rose-pink flowers and green leaves.

Oregano

HOW TO GROW IT

Soil Needs well-drained soil.

Fertilizer Feed once with a balanced fertilizer at planting time, and again each spring for established plants.

In containers Choose a compact variety for a pot at least 6 in. tall and wide.

Care notes For best results, cut previous year's stems to ground in winter or early spring to make room for fresh new growth.

Rosemary

ROSMARINUS OFFICINALIS
Mint family *(Lamiaceae)*
EVERGREEN SHRUB

⚡ **ZONES 4–24; H1, H2**

☼ **FULL SUN**

◊ ◐ **LITTLE TO MODERATE WATER**

Fine-leafed, aromatic, and evergreen, this Mediterranean shrub fits well in Western gardens. Narrow, slightly sticky leaves are glossy dark green, with a mildly pungent flavor and a complex aroma with sweet as well as resinous notes. Leaves are widely used as a fresh or dry seasoning. Small clusters of tiny blossoms in various shades of blue appear through winter and spring and occasionally in fall. Rosemary flowers are edible—add them to salads or use as a garnish.

Plants can be stiff and erect, rounded, or prostrate and creeping, depending on variety. Use taller types as clipped or informal hedges or as the backdrop for an herb garden. Lower kinds are good ground or bank covers. These are among the best for culinary use.

'Arp'. Open grower to 4 ft. tall and wide; best with frequent pruning. Bright medium blue flowers. Hardy to –10°F (–23°C).

'Barbecue'. Grows 5 ft. tall, 2–3 ft. wide, has excellent fragrance for cooking; blue flowers.

'Blue Boy'. Young plant makes a dense, symmetrical mound 8–12 in. high and 14–18 in. across. Pleasant fragrance and flavor. Tender.

'Blue Spires'. Strong vertical grower, to 5–6 ft. tall and as wide or wider. Deep blue flowers. Excellent choice for hedging and for seasoning.

'Gorizia'. Vigorous, rigidly upright, to 4–5 ft. tall and wide. Sweet, gingery fragrance.

'Irene'. Vigorous spreader that covers 2–3 ft. or more per year, eventually mounding to 1–1½ ft. high. Deep lavender-blue flowers. One of the most cold-hardy prostrate varieties.

'Prostratus'. To 2 ft. high, with a 4-to-8-ft. spread. Will trail down over a wall or the edge of a raised bed to make a green curtain. Pale lavender-blue flowers from fall into spring. Effective in hanging pots. Tender.

'Spice Islands'. Upright growth reaches 4–5 ft. tall, making this a good screen or background. Large blue flowers, good fragrance.

'Barbecue' rosemary

HOW TO GROW IT

Soil Good drainage is essential.

Fertilizer A sprinkling of aged compost or complete fertilizer around the plant's base in spring is sufficient.

In containers Plant an upright growing rosemary as the focus of a large (at least 18 in.) container, and plant three trailing types around the edges.

Care notes Control growth by frequent tip-pinching when plants are small. Prune older plants frequently but lightly; cut to side branch or shear.

Sage

SALVIA OFFICINALIS
Mint family (*Lamiaceae*)
SHRUBBY PERENNIAL

'Berggarten' sage

✎ **ZONES 2–24; H1, H2**

☀ ☾ **AFTERNOON SHADE IN HOTTEST CLIMATES**

◊ ◖ **LITTLE TO MODERATE WATER**

This Mediterranean native is the traditional culinary and medicinal sage. It grows 1–3 ft. high and 1–2½ ft. wide or wider, as its stems often root where they touch soil. Aromatic, wrinkled, 2-to-3-in. leaves are gray-green above, white and hairy beneath. Branching stems bear loose, spikelike clusters of ½-in. flowers in late spring or summer; the usual color is lavender-blue, but violet, red-violet, pink, and white forms exist. Look for the following named selections.

'Aurea'. GOLDEN SAGE. Creamy gold variegation decorates the green leaves.

'Berggarten' ('Mountain Garden'). Compact grower to just 16 in. high. Denser growth, rounder leaves, fewer flowers than species; may be longer-lived.

'Compacta' ('Nana', 'Minimus'). A half-size (or even smaller) version of the species, with narrower, closer-set leaves.

'Icterina'. Gray-green leaves with golden border. Does not bloom.

'Purpurascens' ('Red Sage'). Leaves are flushed with red-violet when new, slowly mature to gray-green.

'Tricolor'. Gray-green leaves with irregular cream border; new foliage is flushed with purplish pink.

HOW TO GROW IT

Soil Sage requires good drainage, especially in winter; waterlogged plants rarely make it through hard freezes. If soil is heavy, work in plenty of organic matter and apply a thick mulch of well-rotted compost.

Planting Plant sage in an area with good air circulation to help deter mildew and other fungal diseases. Plant from nursery containers, keeping the crown (where the main stem meets the soil) slightly above soil grade.

Fertilizer One application of complete fertilizer or organic compost each spring is sufficient.

Water During the first year, water moderately, then give little to moderate water.

In containers Sage grows well in pots at least 12 in. wide and 8 in. deep.

Care notes Delay pruning until new leaves begin to unfurl, then cut just above fresh growth; cutting into bare wood usually causes dieback. Replace plants when woody or leggy (every 3 or 4 years).

Thyme

THYMUS SPECIES
Mint family (Lamiaceae)
SHRUBBY PERENNIALS

🌿 **ZONES 1–24**

☼ ◐ **LIGHT SHADE IN HOTTEST CLIMATES**

◊ ◖ **LITTLE TO MODERATE WATER**

Thymes are charming little members of the mint family with tiny, heavily scented leaves and miniature flowers. Upright types are well suited to an herb garden, rock garden, or container; prostrate, mat-forming types make good small-space groundcovers. Use leaves fresh or dried for seasoning fish, shellfish, poultry stuffing, soups, or vegetables.

Caraway-scented thyme (*Thymus herba-barona*). Fast growing to 2–4 in. high, 2 ft. wide or more; stems root as they spread. Forms a dense mat of dark green leaves with a caraway fragrance. Clusters of rose-colored flowers bloom in midsummer.

Common thyme (*T. vulgaris*). Variable plant to 1 ft. high, 2 ft. wide, with gray-green leaves. White to lilac flowers appear in late spring, early summer. Nice as a low edging for flower, vegetable, or herb garden. Good container plant. 'Argenteus', called silver thyme, has leaves variegated with silver. 'Hi-Ho' has even more pronounced silver variegation and is more compact. 'Italian Oregano Thyme' has a strong oregano flavor. 'Orange Balsam' has narrow, orange-scented leaves.

Lemon thyme (*T. × citriodorus*). This hybrid grows 6–12 in. high, 2 ft. wide, with lemon-scented leaves and pale lilac summertime flowers. Leaves of 'Argenteus' are splashed with silver, those of 'Aureus' with gold. 'Golden Lemon' is compact and flavorful, with gold-edged leaves. Low-growing 'Goldstream' has yellow-variegated leaves. 'Lemon Frost' has white flowers on a 3-to-6-in.-high plant. 'Lime' has lime green foliage. 'Doone Valley', with yellow-spotted leaves, reaches only 5 in. high.

TIP Thyme is nice as a path edging, where the sprigs are easily harvested—or just pinched for the enjoyment of their refreshing fragrance.

'Golden Lemon' thyme

HOW TO GROW IT

Soil Provide light, well-drained soil.

Water Give moderate water to get new plants through the first year; they'll need little water after that.

In containers Thymes thrive in small pots (6–12 in. tall and wide) on patios or windowsills.

Care notes Snip off branch tips as needed. Shear or cut back established plants to keep them compact. Easy to propagate from cuttings taken in early summer.

Easy Annual Herbs for Containers

Few plants are easier to grow than annual herbs. You can plant them in containers on a balcony or deck, in a window box, or in colorful glazed pots marching up the stairs to the kitchen.

They intensify flavor without adding calories or fat, and their scented foliage tempts you to pinch and sniff every time you pass by. Buy fresh young starts from your local garden center when they become available in spring, and plant them in standard potting mix. Minimum container sizes are given for each herb below. These reliable choices grow in all zones and need regular water for best growth.

A / Basil (*Ocimum basilicum*). The basic species is a bushy plant to 2 ft. high and 1 ft. wide, with shiny green 1-to-2-in.-long leaves, but there are countless variations on the theme. For big leaves that can be used as flavorful wraps, plant 'Napolitano' or 'Mammoth Sweet'. Compact growers include 'Greek' ('Spicy Globe'), 'Magical Michael', and 'Marseillais Dwarf'. Some varieties have added flavors, from 'Cinnamon' to 'Clove' and 'Lemon'. Best for pesto: 'Genovese' or 'Genova'. Purple-leafed types (pretty, but not quite as flavorful) include 'Purple Ruffles', 'Red Lettuce Leaved', and 'Red Osmin' (shown opposite). Thai basils have spicy, aniselike overtones; 'Siam Queen' is one of the best.

The best leaves for flavorings come from younger stems that have not yet borne flowers, so pinch out bloom spikes as they form. Fertilize once during the growing season with a complete fertilizer. Container size: At least 16 in. deep. Full sun.

B / Cilantro (*Coriandrum sativum*). Forms a lush mound of bright green, finely cut leaves topped in summer by pinkish white flowers. Grows quickly to 1–1½ ft. high, 9 in. wide. Start harvesting the outer leaves when plants reach 8 in. high. Flowers are edible too—or you can let them go to seed and harvest them as coriander. To collect seeds, tie small bags over seed heads when seeds begin to turn brown. Wait a week, shake briskly, and remove the bag. Container size: At least 12 in. wide and 8 in. deep. Full sun; light shade in hottest climates.

C / Dill (*Anethum graveolens*). Airy plant to 3–4 ft. tall and 1–2 ft. wide, with feathery, pungently aromatic leaves. Flat clusters of yellow flowers appear in summer (in winter in the desert). Snip off leaves as needed. Collect seeds as for cilantro (see left below). Container size: At least 1 ft. deep. Full sun.

D / Parsley There are basically two choices. Curly-leafed parsley (*Petroselinum crispum*), shown opposite, is a compact plant just 6–18 in. high and wide, with dark green, very curly leaves. Fresh sprigs and minced leaves make an excellent garnish but are also useful as a seasoning, either fresh or dried. 'Moss Curled' and 'Forest Green' are outstanding varieties. Container size: At least 6 in. wide and 8 in. deep. Full sun; afternoon shade in hottest climates. Even grows well indoors in a sunny window.

Flat-leafed Italian parsley (*Petroselinum crispum neapolitanum*) grows 1½–3 ft. high and 2 ft. wide, with flat, deeply divided leaves that make a pretty garnish and are considered more flavorful than those of curly-leafed types. Among the best varieties are 'Dark Green Italian', 'Giant Italian', and 'Single Italian'. Harvest leaves from the outside of the plant so that inner leaves will keep coming. Container size: At least 10–12 in. wide and 10 in. deep. Full sun; afternoon shade in hottest climates.

British Columbia
1A

Vancouver 4 5
1A

2
1A
2

Seattle
1A 4
5 **Tacoma**
4

WASHINGTON **Spokane**
2
90 2
82 **Walla Walla** 2
Portland 3
Columbia River
4 2 3 84 2
6
4 **Eugene** 2 1A
5 **OREGON**
4 1A 2
17 1A 7 **Medford**
7 2
2

4
7 7
4 7
14 4 8
15 7
Sacramento **Reno**
17 14 **Lake Tahoe**
San Francisco 9
15 14
16 **CALIFORNIA** **Fresno**
7 8 1A
7 5 9
17 7 **Bakersfield**
15
16 14 3 2
23 21 18 11
24 15 10
20 **Los Angeles** 10 40 13
22 19 7
23 10
18 11
21 12
24 13
San Diego 13 10 8

Pacific Ocean

ALBERTA **SASKATCHEWAN**
1B
1B

2 15
Great Falls
1B
MONTANA
90 **Billings** 94
15
90

1A **IDAHO**
2 84 **Boise**
3 2 15 **Idaho Falls** 90
2 **WYOMING** 1B
Great Salt Lake 2 **Ogden** 1A **Casper** 25
3 **Salt Lake City** 80
NEVADA 2 15 80
10 **UTAH** 1A **Denver** 76
1A **COLORADO** 2
1A 70 1A 3 **Colorado Springs**
10 2 25
13 3 2 1A
Las Vegas 10 10 3 2
1A 2 9 2 25
11 **Lake Mead** 1A 3 2 **Santa Fe**
10 1A 3 3 1A
2 **Flagstaff** 1A 3 40
11 40 1A 1A **Albuquerque** 25
12 17 1A 1A 2
10 2 1A 10
13 **Phoenix** 1A **NEW MEXICO**
8 1A 25 2
12 **ARIZONA** 3 10
Tucson 2 10
2

| 0 | 100 | 200 | 300 miles |

| Climate Zones | ✎ | 1A | 1B | 2 | 3 | 4 | 5 | 6 | 7 | 8 | 9 | 10 | 11 | 12 | 13 | 14 | 15 | 16 | 17 | 18 | 19 | 20 | 21 | 22 | 23 | 24 | 25 |

The West's Climate Zones

Each plant entry in the "Easy-Care Plants" chapter has numbered climate zones representing regions where it grows best. The maps here show where the zones are, and on the following pages are descriptions of the individual zones. If you garden near an intersection of zones, pick the one whose description most closely matches the conditions in your garden. (Zone information is also available online at *sunset.com* under Garden.)

ZONE CONSIDERATIONS

The following factors make each zone unique.

Latitude Generally, the farther north an area is, the longer and colder its winters are and the longer its summer days and winter nights.

Elevation Gardens high above sea level get longer and colder winters, often with intense sunlight, and lower nighttime temperatures all year.

Ocean influence Weather that blows inland off the Pacific Ocean tends to be mild all year and laden with moisture in the cool season.

Continental air influence The North American continent generates its own weather. Compared with coastal climates, inland areas are colder in winter, hotter in summer, and more likely to get precipitation and (in open areas) incessant wind anytime of year. The farther inland you live, the stronger this continental influence.

Mountains, hills, and valleys These determine whether areas beyond them will be influenced most by marine, continental, or arctic air. The Coast Ranges take some marine influence out of the air that passes eastward over them. The Sierra-Cascades and Southern California's interior mountains further weaken marine influence. East of the Rocky Mountains, continental and arctic air dominate.

Microclimates Terrain sharply modifies the climate within any zone and any garden. South-facing slopes get hotter than flat land and north-facing slopes. Slopes also direct airflow, as warm air rises and cold air sinks. Because hillsides are never as cold in winter as the hilltops above them or the ground below them, they're called thermal belts. Lowlands into which cold air flows are called cold-air basins.

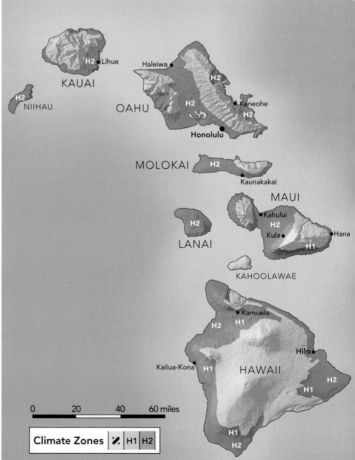

ZONES AND GROWING SEASONS

The following descriptions identify local conditions that make each area hospitable to some plants, trouble for others. A zone's growing season also affects which plants will grow there. The main factor determining growing season is the interval between the last frost in spring and the first frost in fall. Other factors are location, temperature, hours of sunlight, and rainfall. The growing season for each zone is shown as a green band in a bar indicating months from January to December. The yellow color at each end of the band represents shoulder seasons, when light frosts are possible but not likely to bother cool-season crops.

Zone A1

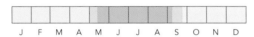

ALASKA'S INTERIOR During summer, plants benefit from long days in the 70s F (low to mid-20s C), with rare spikes to 90°F/32°C. In winter, gardeners can usually depend on snow to insulate plants from winter minimums of –20°F/ –29°C, with occasional dips to –60°F/–51°C. And in permafrost areas, the ground usually thaws to below root level during the warm months.

Zone A2

ANCHORAGE AND COOK INLET Though mountain ranges protect much of this region, plant success depends largely on each area's microclimate. Winter lows average 6° to 0°F/–14° to –18°C, with drops to –40°F/–40°C every 10 years or so. Summer days are usually cloudy and in the mid-60s F (high teens C), with occasional jumps into the high 70s F (mid-20s C).

Zone A3

ALASKA'S SOUTHERN MARITIME CLIMATE Cloudy summers stay mostly in the 60s F (16° to 21°C), with occasional jumps to 80°F/27°C, while winter lows are 25° to 16°F/–4° to –9°C, with extreme lows of –20°F/–29°C. Annual precipitation averages 50 to 75 in.—but Homer gets only 25 in. per year, while Pelican gets 150 in. Cool-weather crops thrive here, but warm-season vegetables mature slowly.

Zone 1a

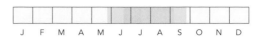

COLDEST ZONE WEST OF THE ROCKIES A short growing season has mild summer days and cold nights that extend the bloom of summer perennials. Winter snow usually insulates plants against lows from 11° to 0°F/–12° to –18°C (with extremes to –50°F/–46°C). If snow comes late or leaves early, protect plants with a 6-in. layer of organic mulch.

Zone 1b

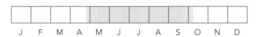

COLDEST ZONE EAST OF THE ROCKIES This zone sees January temperatures from 13° to –4°F/–11° to –20°C, with extremes to –50°F/–46°C. Arctic cold fronts sweep through 6 to 12 times a year, sometimes dropping temperatures by 35°F/19°C in 24 hours. The growing season tends to be warm, relentlessly windy, and sometimes subject to hail storms.

Zone 2a

COLD MOUNTAIN AND INTERMOUNTAIN REGIONS Another snowy winter climate, Zone 2a is considered mild compared with surrounding regions. It is the coldest zone in which sweet cherries and many apples grow. Precipitation averages just 16 in. per year, so irrigation is essential. Winter nights usually hover between 20° and 10°F/–7° and –12°C, with drops to –30°F/–34°C every few years.

Zone 2b

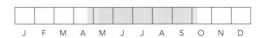

WARMER-SUMMER INTERMOUNTAIN CLIMATE This zone has a good balance of long, warm summers and chilly winters. That's why commercial orchards locate here. Precipitation averages 16 in. per year, but it's much higher in the west and north ends of the zone. Winter minimums are 22° to 12°F/–6° to –11°C, with extremes in the –10° to –20°F/–23° to –29°C range.

Zone 3a

J F M A M J J A S O N D

MILD MOUNTAIN AND INTERMOUNTAIN CLIMATES
East of the Sierra and Cascade ranges, this is the premier gardening climate for deciduous fruit trees and such long-season vegetables as melons, gourds, and corn; just keep them watered, since precipitation here averages only 14 in. per year. Winter minimum temperatures run from 25° to 15°F/–4° to –9°C, with extremes down to –18°F/–28°C.

Zone 3b

J F M A M J J A S O N D

MILDEST MOUNTAIN AND INTERMOUNTAIN CLIMATES
Chilly winters, summers in the 90s F (low 30s C), and a 6- to 7-month growing season make this zone perfect for grapes, watermelons, late apples—anything that needs plenty of time to mature. Winter temperatures range from 29° to 19°F/–2° to –7°C, with extremes as low as –15°F/–26°C. Precipitation averages 11 in. per year.

Zone 4

J F M A M J J A S O N D

COOLEST MARITIME AREAS FROM CALIFORNIA TO SOUTHEAST ALASKA As in neighboring Zone 5, wet winters and mild summers prevail here, but Zone 4 is a bit warmer in summer and colder in winter. You can grow most things if you choose early-maturing varieties. Winter lows range from 34° to 28°F/1° to –2°C, with extreme lows reaching 0°F/–18°C.

Zone 5

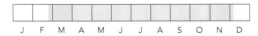

J F M A M J J A S O N D

NORTHWEST COAST AND PUGET SOUND Wet, breezy winters and mild summers favor leaf vegetables, root crops, and berries here. Low heat accumulation slows development of warm-season vegetables and fruits that ripen in fall, but even these prosper if you choose varieties carefully. January minimum temperatures range from 41° to 33°F/5° to 1°C, with 10-year extremes down to 6°F/–14°C.

Zone 6

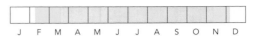

J F M A M J J A S O N D

WILLAMETTE AND COLUMBIA RIVER VALLEYS Warm summers, a long growing season, and cool, wet winters make this maritime climate perfect for growing everything from berries and hazelnuts to apples and Pinot Noir grapes. Winter minimums usually hover just above freezing, but chilly interior air occasionally pushes west through the Columbia Gorge, layering trees with ice. Extreme lows may reach 0°F/–18°C.

Zone 7

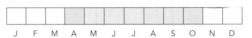

J F M A M J J A S O N D

OREGON'S ROGUE RIVER VALLEY, THE CALIFORNIA GRAY PINE BELT, AND SOUTHERN CALIFORNIA MOUNTAINS Hot summers and mild but pronounced winters give Zone 7 sharply defined seasons without severe winter cold or enervating humidity. Tree fruits thrive here. Typical winter lows range from 35° to 26°F/2° to –3°C, with record lows down to 0°F/–18°C. Rainfall averages 34 in. per year.

Zones 8 and 9

J F M A M J J A S O N D

CALIFORNIA CENTRAL VALLEY Zone 9 is the thermal belt that edges California's Central Valley, while Zone 8 is the colder valley floor. The difference is crucial: citrus that flourishes in Zone 9 cannot be grown commercially in Zone 8. Lows in both zones are 38° to 34°F/3° to 1°C, with extremes as low as 16°F/–9°C. Zone 9 gets 20 in. of rain, 5 in. more than Zone 8.

Zone 10

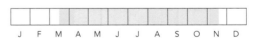

J F M A M J J A S O N D

ARIZONA–NEW MEXICO HIGH DESERT This zone lies mostly in the high elevations of the Southwest. Summer highs are in the 90s F (30s C), while average winter temperatures range from 33° to 22°F/1° to –6°C, with drops to around 0°F/–18°C every few years. More rain falls in the east than in the west, and the Pecos River drainage receives more precipitation in summer than in winter.

Zone 11

CALIFORNIA–SOUTHERN NEVADA MEDIUM TO HIGH DESERT In winter, Zone 11 has mild days, nights that hover around freezing, and occasional drops to 10°F/−12°C; but in summer, many days cross 100°F/38°C, with the highest temperatures recorded at 117°F/47°C. Zone 11 has less rain (about 7 in.) and more wind than adjacent parts of Zone 10.

Zone 12

ARIZONA'S INTERMEDIATE DESERT Zone 12 has harder frosts spread over a longer season than Zone 13, with average minimums around freezing and extreme lows to 10°F/−12°C. Still, it doesn't provide enough chill for some deciduous fruits. As in Zone 13, cool-season planting starts in early fall, while warm-season crops go in during late winter. Protect them against strong spring winds.

Zone 13

LOW OR SUBTROPICAL DESERT Whether gardening below sea level in the Imperial Valley or at 1,100 feet in Phoenix, Zone 13 gardeners plant most vegetables in fall and heat lovers like corn and melons in late winter, all to avoid average summer highs of 107°F/42°C, with spikes to 120°F/49°C. Winter lows average 40°F/4°C, with rare extreme drops to 15°F/−9°C.

Zone 14

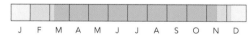

NORTHERN CALIFORNIA AREAS WITH SOME OCEAN INFLUENCE Marine air that moderates Zone 14 pushes clear to Sacramento, Modesto, and even down the Salinas Valley, prospering fruits that need summer heat and winter chill. Winter minimums average 40° to 35°F/4° to 2°C, with extreme lows from 27° to 17°F/−3° to −8°C. Precipitation averages 25 in. over most of the zone.

Zone 15

CHILLY-WINTER CALIFORNIA COAST RANGE Zone 15 comprises cold-air basins, hilltops, and areas far enough north to affect plant performance. The region is influenced by marine air 85 percent of the time and by inland air 15 percent, and most of the zone gets a nagging afternoon summer wind. Average January minimum is 39°F/4°C, with record lows to 16°F/−9°C.

Zone 16

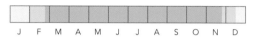

CENTRAL AND NORTHERN CALIFORNIA COASTAL THERMAL BELTS This is one of Northern California's finest horticultural climates. Its hillside slopes are dominated by ocean weather 85 percent of the time. Average winter lows are about 40°F/4°C, with extreme lows around 20°F/−7°C. This zone gets more heat in summer than Zone 17 and has warmer winters than Zone 15. That's a happy combination for gardening.

Zone 17

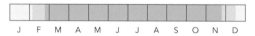

OREGON AND NORTHERN AND CENTRAL CALIFORNIA COASTAL STRIPS Mild, wet, almost frostless winters and cool summers mark this climate. Summer fog comes in high and fast, cooling, shading, and humidifying the land. Winter minimums are in the low 40s F (7° to 4°C), with rare extreme lows in the mid-20s F (about −4°C). Precipitation averages 38 in., but is much higher in the north than the south.

Zone 18

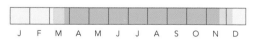

SOUTHERN CALIFORNIA INTERIOR VALLEY COLD ZONES An interior climate, this zone is influenced by ocean air only about 15 percent of the time. Many of Zone 18's chilly valley floors held commercial apricot, peach, apple, and walnut orchards before homes were built there. Average winter lows are 40° to 34°F/4° to 1°C. Over a 20-year period, winter lows bottomed out at 17°F/−8°C.

Zone 19

J F M A M J J A S O N D

SOUTHERN CALIFORNIA INTERIOR VALLEY THERMAL BELTS Interior air dominates the climate of this mostly sloping land 85 percent of the time, keeping it warmer than adjacent Zone 18's valleys and hilltops. Navel oranges, macadamias, and most avocados thrive here. Average January minimums are 43° to 37°F/6° to 3°C, with drops every few years to 25°F/–4°C.

Zone 20

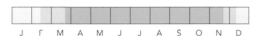

J F M A M J J A S O N D

SOUTHERN CALIFORNIA COLD-AIR BASINS, HILLTOPS As interior and maritime air masses shift across this zone, climate boundaries often move 20 miles in 24 hours. In winter, Zone 20's chilly hilltops and cold-air basins get considerably colder than the thermal belts that connect them. Winter lows are 43° to 37°F/6° to 3°C; 20-year lows average 25° to 22°F/–4° to –6°C.

Zone 21

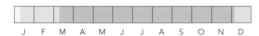

J F M A M J J A S O N D

SOUTHERN CALIFORNIA THERMAL BELTS Gardens here can be bathed in ocean air or sulking under high fog one day and dried out by interior air (perhaps a Santa Ana wind) the next day. This is fine citrus-growing country, with average winter lows around 40°F/4°C and summer highs of 90° to 94°F/32° to 34°C. Ten-year lows have reached 25°F/–4°C.

Zone 22

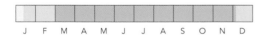

J F M A M J J A S O N D

COLD ZONES ALONG THE SOUTHERN CALIFORNIA COAST Zone 22 consists of cold-air basins and hilltops influenced by the ocean approximately 85 percent of the time and inland air 15 percent. They get more winter chill than the slopes of neighboring Zone 23. Winter lows average 45° to 40°F/7° to 4°C, with 10-year drops to 25°F/–4°C.

Zone 23

J F M A M J J A S O N D

THERMAL BELTS ALONG THE SOUTHERN CALIFORNIA COAST This is the best zone for avocados and is also excellent for cherimoyas, 'Valencia' oranges, guavas, mangoes, and papayas. But mild winters allow only low-chill pears, apples, and peaches. Winter lows average about 45°F/7°C, and summer highs reach 78° to 89°F/26° to 32°C. Frosts are rare, but Santa Ana winds dry plants and break branches every fall.

Zone 24

J F M A M J J A S O N D

SOUTHERN CALIFORNIA COASTAL STRIP Dominated by marine air, winters here rarely dip below 45°F/7°C, and frosts can be years apart. In late spring, morning overcast is the rule. July highs are in the mid-70s F (about 24°C). Where the beach parallels high cliffs or palisades, Zone 24 extends only to that barrier; but where hills are low or absent, it runs inland several miles.

Zone H1

J F M A M J J A S O N D

HAWAII'S MILD VOLCANIC SLOPES Cooler air makes high volcanic slopes good for growing everything from sweet bulbing onions to low-chill varieties of apples, peaches, and plums. Some gardeners in regions high on the dry sides can even succeed with Mediterranean herbs. Warm-season highs range from 65° to 80°F/18° to 27°C; cool-season lows can dip into the 40s F (9° to 4°C), with extreme lows around 35°F/2°C.

Zone H2

J F M A M J J A S O N D

HAWAII'S COCONUT PALM BELT Most lowland lees here get heavy rains from November through March, while May through September is relatively dry. On the windward sides, rain comes year-round from passing storms and tradewind showers. The Kona Coast, however, gets most of its rain in the warm season. Highs hover in the mid-80s F (around 30°C); lows can dip to the mid-60s F (around 18°C).

Regional Gardening Calendars

What to do in your garden throughout the year. Find your region, and then tackle the chores listed, month by month.

PACIFIC NORTHWEST

March

PLANT

Cool-season vegetables. Sow beets, carrots, lettuce, peas, radishes, and spinach, or set out nursery seedlings. Plant seed potatoes.
Lawn grass. Amend and level the top 8 inches of soil, then lay sod or sow seed. Keep the soil moist.
Ornamentals. Shop nurseries for early-blooming trees, shrubs, and perennials.

FEED

Fruiting plants. Give blueberries and cane berries a complete fertilizer before new growth starts.
Lawns. Give lawns the first feeding of the year, early this month. Use a fertilizer blend formulated for turf.
Roses. Fertilize established roses with high-phosphorus fertilizer such as 9-18-9.

TEND

Perennials. Dig, divide, and replant clumps of summer- and fall-blooming perennials such as aster, chrysanthemum, and coral bells.
Lawns. Repair lawns.

April

PLANT

Bedding plants. Choices (among many) include calibrachoa, geranium, impatiens, lobelia, marigold, petunia, and sweet alyssum.
Berries. Set out cane berries and strawberries.
Bulbs. Plant calla, canna, dahlia, fairy wand, galtonia, gladiolus, and montbretia.

Flowering shrubs. Shop for azalea, camellia, rhododendron, and viburnum.
Vegetables. Sow beets, carrots, lettuce, peas, radishes, and spinach.

FEED

Shrubs. After bloom, apply high-nitrogen fertilizer to spring-flowering shrubs.

May

PLANT

Annuals. Shop for bachelor's button, begonia, cosmos, geranium, impatiens, lobelia, marigold, nasturtium, nicotiana, petunia, salvia, snapdragon, sunflower, sweet alyssum, and zinnia.
Edibles. Plant basil, beans, corn, cucumbers, eggplant, melons, peppers, pumpkins, squash, and tomatoes.

Perennials. Set out bleeding heart, columbine, dahlias, geum, iris, lupine, and sweet woodruff.

FEED
Garden plants. Fertilize almost everything, especially fuchsia and annuals that have a long season of bloom.

TEND
Rhododendron and azalea. Pinch off faded flower trusses. See details on page 118.

June

PLANT
Annuals. Plant begonia, calibrachoa (best in pots), coleus *(Solenostemon)*, cosmos, impatiens, marigold, petunia, sweet potato vine, and zinnia.
Edibles. Plant herbs, plus fast-maturing warm-season crops like beans, cucumbers, and summer squash.

FEED
Annuals. Fertilize all long-flowering summer annuals every month with a complete fertilizer such as 6-10-4.
Spring-flowering perennials and shrubs. After bloom is finished, apply a complete fertilizer such as 10-5-4.
Outdoor container plants. Feed container plants with a complete liquid fertilizer such as 20-20-20.

TEND
Fruit trees. Thin apple and other tree fruits after June drop, as described on page 118.

PRUNE
Spring-flowering shrubs. Before they set buds for next year's bloom, prune spring-flowering shrubs using sharp bypass pruners.

July

PLANT
Ornamentals. Set out aster, chrysanthemum, dahlia, and helenium for the fall garden.
Vegetables. Sow beets, broccoli, bush beans, cabbage, carrots, cauliflower, kohlrabi, lettuce, peas, scallions, spinach,

Swiss chard, and turnips for fall and winter harvest.

FEED
Annuals, fuchsia, container plants. Fertilize at two-week intervals with half-strength liquid fertilizer.

TEND
Raspberries. After the June crop is finished, remove canes that bore fruit. On everbearing raspberries, remove only the part of each cane that bore fruit; the lower half will bear next season.
Roses. Feed, water, weed, and mulch; remove faded blooms.

MAINTAIN
Compost. Mix garden waste with grass clippings and mature compost or compost starter to activate a new pile.

August

PLANT
Ornamentals. Shop for seasonal specialties like vine maples, which are coloring up already; plants with berries, such as cotoneaster, crabapple, and pyracantha; and flowering trees and shrubs, such as sterile butterfly bush, mimosa, and tree mallow.
Vegetables. Plant seedlings of broccoli, cabbage, and cauliflower; sow beets, Chinese cabbage, mustard, onions, radishes, and spinach.

FEED
Summer flowers. Feed long-blooming perennials and container plants with full-strength high-nitrogen fertilizer every month.

TEND
Flowering annuals. Pick off all spent blooms from marigold, pelargonium, and petunia to keep more flowers coming.
Perennials. Dig, divide, and replant spring-blooming perennials such as bearded iris and Oriental poppy.
Herbs. For most intense flavor, harvest herbs in the morning just after dew dries.

MAINTAIN
Make compost. Recycle garden waste into compost (see page 107).

September

PLANT
Lawns. Use seed or sod to repair or start new lawns this month.
Perennials. Plant aster, chrysanthemum, hardy fuchsia, and *Sedum* 'Autumn Joy'.
Vegetables. Set out transplants of arugula, leaf lettuce, mustard greens, Oriental leaf crops, and spinach; sow radishes.
Spring-blooming bulbs. Plant bulbs such as crocus, daffodil, grape hyacinth, hyacinth, and tulip..

FEED
Lawns. Apply ½–1 pound of actual nitrogen per 1,000 square feet of turf at midmonth.
Roses. Fertilize lightly with a balanced liquid fertilizer like 10-10-10 after the fall bloom flush.

MAINTAIN
Mulch. In cold-winter areas, layer bark mulch around permanent plants to insulate roots against frost.
Compost. Feed the compost pile with leaves, grass clippings, and spent summer flowers and vegetables.

October

PLANT
Spring-flowering bulbs. Plant all kinds.
Groundcovers. Plant or transplant Carmel creeper, cotoneaster, kinnikinnick, pachysandra, wild ginger, or woolly thyme.
Deciduous trees. Shop for ones with colorful fall foliage, such as maples, Persian parrotia, and sour gum.

FEED
Lawns. Apply 1 pound of actual nitrogen per 1,000 square feet, using a broadcast (rotary) spreader.

TEND
Bulbs. Dig and dry frost-tender bulbs, corms, and tubers. Store them in a cool, frost-free place for winter.
Perennials. Dig and divide crowded perennials such as daylily, peony, Shasta daisy, and Siberian iris. ❯❯

November

PLANT

Garlic, berries. Set out garlic for harvest next summer. Also plant blueberries (their leaves in fall color now) and strawberries for bigger, earlier crops next spring.

Evergreen trees, shrubs. Now is the best time to plant conifers and broad-leafed evergreens such as camellia, cork oak, eucalyptus, rhododendron, and strawberry tree.

MAINTAIN

Watering systems. Drain irrigation systems, disconnect and drain hoses, and insulate exposed outdoor hose bibs.

December

PLANT

Landscape plants. Shop for winter-flowering heath (*Erica*), hellebore, *Mahonia* 'Charity', sasanqua camellia, strawberry tree, wintersweet, and witch hazel.

January

PLAN

Seeds. Catalogs usually show up right around the holidays. Order seeds this month so that you won't be stuck with substitutions later in the season.

PLANT

Bare-root plants. Buy and plant bare-root fruit and ornamental trees, roses, vines, and perennial vegetables.

Winter-flowering plants. Perennials sold as annuals include English daisy, pansy, primrose, and viola. The best conventional winter perennial is hellebore. And among shrubs, try cornelian cherry, heaths (*Erica*), *Mahonia* 'Charity', *Sarcococca*, sasanqua camellias, wintersweet, and witch hazel.

AUTUMN LEAVES Left on lawns, fallen leaves get wet, mat, and smother the grass. But you can put them to work mulching winter flower beds just by shredding them with a bagging mower. Spread them as mulch, and by spring they'll be rotted and almost completely gone.

TEND

Perennial vegetables. Top-dress perennial vegetables such as artichoke, asparagus, and rhubarb with well-rotted manure or compost.

Trees and shrubs. Remove dead, diseased, crossing, and closely parallel branches from fruit trees; then prune trees for shape.

MAINTAIN

Prevent plant disease. On a mild, dry day, spray peach trees with fixed copper or lime sulfur to control peach leaf curl.

February

PLANT

Bare-root plants. Plant cane berries, fruit trees, roses, shrubs, strawberries, and perennial vegetables such as asparagus and rhubarb.

Bedding plants. For instant winter color, buy calendula, English daisy, Iceland poppy, pansy, primrose, snapdragon, sweet alyssum, and viola.

FEED

Perennial vegetables. Spread compost or well-rotted manure over the root zones of artichokes, asparagus, and rhubarb.

TEND

Roses. West of the Cascades, prune hybrid teas back by about a third, saving three to five strong canes. East of the Cascades, you can cut them back further. Everywhere, prune landscape roses for shape.

Fruit trees and grapevines. Prune both. See individual plant entries for more information.

Winter-bloomers. Flowering apricot and plum, forsythia, ornamental quince, and pussy willow are among the plants whose pruned branches can be brought indoors to force early flowering.

MAINTAIN

Spray. Apply dormant spray to deciduous trees and shrubs to help control overwintering insects.

Control pests. Bait for slugs and snails.

NORTHERN CALIFORNIA

March

PLANT

Bedding plants. Set out nursery plants of celosia, globe amaranth, impatiens, marigold, nicotiana, petunia, portulaca, and salvia. Or try cosmos, nasturtium, and zinnia from seed.

Bulbs. Plant calla, canna, dahlia, gladiolus, Mexican shell flower (*Tigridia*), tuberose, and tuberous begonia.

Citrus. Set out plants from 5-gallon cans.

Cool-season crops. Along the coast, set out seedlings of cole crops such as broccoli and cabbage. Also plant carrots, green onions, potatoes, and radishes.

Perennials. Plant all kinds now.

Trees and shrubs. Shop for the earliest-flowering types, including *Acacia baileyana*, azalea, camellia, *Prunus × blireana*, and rhododendron.

FEED

Edibles. Apply a high-nitrogen fertilizer to artichokes, asparagus, berries, and fruit trees of all kinds.

Ornamentals. Plants that are starting to grow actively now benefit from high-nitrogen fertilizer.

TEND

Perennials. Dig, divide, and replant summer- and fall-blooming perennials. For details, see page 120.

Shrubs. To keep them shapely, pinch or lightly prune spring-flowering shrubs such as azalea, forsythia, and flowering quince immediately after they bloom.

Weed. Scratch corn gluten into garden beds and cover with mulch to keep weed seeds from germinating.

April

PLANT

Bedding plants. In cool areas, plant calendula, dianthus, forget-me-not, pansy, and other cool-weather flowers. Elsewhere, plant heat lovers such as cosmos, impatiens, marigold, petunia, sunflower, and zinnia.

Edibles. Plant herbs, beans, corn, cucumbers, eggplant, peppers, squash, and tomatoes.
Lawns. Sow seeds or lay sod to grow or repair lawns.

FEED
Ornamentals. Apply acid fertilizer to citrus, lawns, roses, fall-planted ornamentals, and (after blooms fade) spring-blooming shrubs.
Potted plants. Every two to three weeks, give them a dose of a half-strength liquid fertilizer. Or apply a granular, controlled-release fertilizer.

TEND
Chlorotic plants. Apply iron chelate to plants with chlorotic leaves (yellow mottling between green veins).

MAINTAIN
Mulch. To save water and smother weeds, spread a 2-inch layer of bark chips or other organic mulch under (but not touching) ornamentals and around vegetables.

May

PLANT
Spring-flowering shrubs. Plant azalea, *Brunfelsia*, camellia, lilac, and rhododendron.
Summer annuals. Plant cosmos, impatiens, marigold, phlox, sunflower, and zinnia.
Vegetables. Plant basil, beans, corn, cucumbers, eggplant, melons, peppers, pumpkins, summer squash, and tomatoes.

FEED
Garden plants. Fertilize annuals, fruit trees, perennials, and shrubs. Feed roses after each bloom cycle.

TEND
Chlorotic plants. Apply iron chelate to plants with chlorotic leaves (yellow mottling between green veins).
Fruit trees. Thin fruits from heavy-bearing apple trees late in the month, as described on page 118.

MAINTAIN
Mulch. Spread organic mulch around (but not touching) plants to conserve water and discourage weeds.
Prune. Give spring-flowering shrubs and vines their yearly pruning after bloom.

June

PLANT
Bedding plants. Set out seedlings of impatiens, Madagascar periwinkle *(Vinca rosea)*, marigold, nasturtium, petunia, salvia, verbena, and zinnia.
Edibles. Sow seeds of beans and corn and set out young plants of cucumbers, eggplant, peppers, squash, tomatoes, and herbs.
Lawns. Plant or repair heat-loving lawns such as hybrid Bermuda.
Shrubs. For high appeal and low water need, try blue hibiscus, cape mallow, ceanothus, plumbago, rockrose, and tree mallow.

FEED
Summer flowers and vegetables. Apply a controlled-release fertilizer once this month, or continue monthly light feedings.

TEND
Floppy flowers. Stake tall growers such as aster, bachelor's button, carnation, *Crocosmia* 'Lucifer', *Echinacea*, Shasta daisy, and yarrow.
Roses. Remove faded flowers, apply complete fertilizer, water, and mulch.
Trees and shrubs. Soak deeply at least twice a month. ➤➤

MAINTAIN
Mulch. Spread organic mulch such as ground bark, pine needles, or straw around plants to conserve moisture and reduce weeds.

July

PLANT
Annuals. Plant ageratum, celosia, marigold, petunia, portulaca, salvia, sweet alyssum, and zinnia. For light shade, select begonia, coleus, impatiens, and lobelia.
Perennials. Set out aster, chrysanthemum, dahlia, helenium, and schizostylis for fall bloom.

FEED
Annuals and vegetables. Give leaf vegetables high-nitrogen fertilizer such as 7-1-2, and fruiting vegetables a higher-phosphorus fertilizer like 5-10-10.
Container plants. Feed twice a month with half-strength liquid fertilizer.

TEND
Cane berries. Cut canes of June-bearing kinds to the ground after harvest. Leave new green canes untouched. On everbearing raspberries, cut out the part of each cane that fruited this season; the lower half will bear in fall.

August

PLANT
Cool-season flowers. Sow calendula, English daisy, forget-me-not, Iceland poppy, pansy, snapdragon, stock, and viola for fall-winter color.

CAMELLIAS FOR SUN Sometimes called sun camellias, *Camellia sasanqua* varieties can take full sun in mild climates and no more than light shade (for heaviest flowering) everywhere they grow. They bloom autumn through winter, and they don't have the terrible camellia petal blight problems of their *C. japonica* cousins. Most also take well to pruning, so you can grow them flat against a wall. Nurseries feature these all winter long.

Vegetables. Fall vegetables go in now. Plant seedlings of broccoli, brussels sprouts, cabbage, cauliflower, and Swiss chard; and sow beets, carrots, lettuce, parsley, and radishes directly in garden beds.

FEED
Lawns. Hybrid Bermuda, St. Augustine, and zoysia lawns are growing fast now, so feed lightly with high-nitrogen lawn fertilizer.
Roses. Use a complete fertilizer such as a 9-18-9 formulation to get good fall bloom.

TEND
Bulbs. Dig, divide, and replant bearded iris rhizomes and Oriental poppy.
Edibles. Harvest fruit and vegetables regularly.

September

PLANT
Annuals. Set out transplants of calendula, Iceland poppy, larkspur, nemesia (near the coast), pansy, snapdragon, stock, and viola.
Cool-season vegetables. In the fog belt, plant broccoli and cabbage.
Spring-flowering bulbs. Set out anemone, crimson flag, crocus, daffodil, Dutch iris, freesia, homeria *(Moraea collina)*, hyacinth, ixia, leucojum, lycoris, oxalis, ranunculus, scilla, sparaxis, tritonia, and watsonia.
Perennials. Plant campanula, candytuft, coreopsis, delphinium, dianthus, foxglove, gaillardia, geum, Mexican evening primrose, penstemon, phlox, salvia, and yarrow.

FEED
Flowers, vegetables. Apply complete fertilizer to annuals, perennials, roses, and fall-planted vegetables.

TEND
Citrus. Prevent maturing citrus fruits from drying and splitting with deep watering.
Perennials. Dig, divide, and replant overcrowded perennials that have finished blooming.

October

PLANT
Bulbs. Continue to plant all kinds of spring-flowering types (for suggestions, see September at left).
Cool-season annuals. Set out transplants of calendula, Iceland poppy, pansy, primrose, snapdragon, stock, and viola. Sow seeds of baby blue eyes, forget-me-not, sweet alyssum, sweet peas, and spring wildflowers. In coastal areas, try cineraria, nemesia, and schizanthus as well.
Cool-season vegetables. Early in the month, sow fava beans, onions, and radishes; set out transplants of broccoli, brussels sprouts, cabbage, chives, and parsley. Plant garlic cloves.
Shrubs, groundcovers. Consider natives such as ceanothus, flannel bush, kinnikinnick, red-flowering currant, *Sedum spathulifolium*, and wild ginger.
Lawns. Start or repair cool-season lawns, install new sod, or overseed warm-season lawns with cool-season grass.

FEED
Lawns. Fertilize cool-season types such as rye, fescue, and bent grass with high-nitrogen fertilizer.

TEND
Summer bulbs. After dahlia and tuberous begonia die back, dig and clean tubers, dry them in shade, and overwinter in a cool, frost-free place.
Perennials. Divide and replant crowded perennials such as alstroemeria, daylily, lamb's ears, Michaelmas and Shasta daisies, and yarrow.

MAINTAIN
Slugs and snails. Put out bait, or hand-pick them on cool evenings.

November

PLANT
Spring-flowering bulbs. Continue to plant bulbs like grape hyacinth, sand daffodil, and *Tulipa clusiana*.
Cool-season bedding plants. Set out calendula, English and fairy primroses, Iceland poppy, pansy, snapdragon, and stock; sow bachelor's button, clarkia,

English daisy, forget-me-not, linaria, sweet alyssum, and viola.

Permanent winter color. Plant helle-bore and ericasfor evergreen foliage and color all winter.

Vegetables. Plant garlic cloves now.

Deciduous trees. For fall color, plant Chinese pistache, crape myrtle, liquid-ambar, maple, persimmon, Raywood ash, redbud, and sour gum.

Evergreens. Plant or transplant ground-covers, shrubs, and trees.

FEED

Annuals, edibles. Apply high-nitrogen liquid fertilizer to fall-planted annuals and vegetables.

TEND

Perennials. Lift, divide, and replant crowded or overgrown perennials.

MAINTAIN

Compost. Throw leaves, weeds, and played-out annuals and vegetables into the compost pile.

December

PLANT

Winter color. Plant calendula, Iceland poppy, pansy, primrose, snapdragon, and viola now.

TEND

Trees and shrubs. Use prunings of ever-green magnolia, juniper, pine, fir, cedar, and redwood for wreaths and swags.

January

PLAN

Buy seeds. As soon as catalogs arrive this month, make your selections and order seeds for planting from February through spring.

PLANT

Annuals. For midwinter bloom, buy calendula, candytuft, cineraria, English daisy, English and fairy primrose, Iceland poppy, pansy, snapdragon, stock, and viola.

Bare-root vegetables. Plant artichoke, asparagus, horseradish, and rhubarb.

Bare-root fruits. Apples, apricots, blueberries, cane berries, grapes, pears, plums, and strawberries are available now.

Bare-root ornamentals. Choices include roses, shade trees, deciduous shrubs, and vines.

Evergreen shrubs. Shop for azalea, camellia, lily-of-the-valley shrub, and early rhododendron.

FEED

Perennial edibles. Top-dress artichokes, asparagus beds, and rhubarb with well-rotted manure.

TEND

Deciduous fruit trees. Prune apple, apricot, peach, pear, and plum, removing dead, diseased, crossing, and closely parallel branches, then pruning for shape. Japanese plums usually need consider-able pruning, cutting back vertical shoots to outside branches; European plums and cherries need little work.

Roses. Cut back hybrid tea roses by about a third, leaving the most vigorous three to five canes, forming a vase shape, removing diseased and injured canes along the way. Prune landscape roses to shape.

Shrubs. Prune deciduous types such as butterfly bush, fairy duster, hydrangea, and rose of Sharon.

MAINTAIN

Control pests. Apply dormant spray to deciduous plants to control harmful overwintering insects. Control slugs and snails with bait or by handpicking.

Prevent plant disease. Spray peach trees with lime sulfur or fixed copper to control peach leaf curl.

February

PLANT

Bare-root. Plant roses, trees, other deciduous shrubs and vines, and peren-nial vegetables such as artichokes, aspar-agus, and rhubarb.

Spring-blooming annuals. In low elevations, plant calendula, candytuft, cineraria, dianthus, English daisy, English and fairy primroses, forget-me-not, Iceland poppy, pansy, *Primula obconica*, snapdragon, stock, sweet William, and viola.

Vegetables. In low elevations, set out seedlings of broccoli, cabbage, cauli-flower, green onions, and lettuce. Sow beets, carrots, lettuce, peas, spinach, and Swiss chard.

Early spring-blooming shrubs and vines. Shop for azalea, camellia, Carolina jessamine, daphne, and rhododendron.

FEED

Ornamentals. Fertilize spring-blooming flowers and fall-planted annuals and perennials (but feed azalea, camellia, and rhododendron after bloom).

Deciduous fruit trees. Two to three weeks before they bloom, apply a complete fertilizer such as a controlled-release 14-14-14. Feed other mature trees and shrubs as new growth starts.

TEND

Deciduous plants. Prune spring-flowering deciduous ornamentals such as forsythia and quince after they bloom.

Spray. Control overwintering insects in ornamental and fruiting deciduous trees and shrubs by applying horticultural oil.

MAINTAIN

Control pests. Handpick or bait for slugs and snails.

Prevent plant disease. Apply dormant oil or spray to deciduous plants whose buds are still closed. Horticultural oil kills overwintering insects; lime sulfur or fixed-copper spray controls many diseases. »

CHILL BULBS Crocus, hyacinth, and tulip need six weeks of temperatures below 45°F (7°C) to initiate flower formation. In the mildest parts of California and in low or intermediate Southwestern deserts, where it never stays cold enough, prechill bulbs in the refrigerator crisper for six weeks before planting. Don't put pome or stone fruits in the same crisper, since they emit ethylene gas, which kills the flower buds you're trying to stimulate. Plant after Thanksgiving.

SOUTHERN CALIFORNIA

March

PLANT
Edibles. Along the coast, start cool-season vegetables like carrots, lettuce, and peas. Everywhere, set out chives, green onions, and herbs.
Ornamentals. Plant annuals, plus hardy trees, shrubs, perennials, and vines, and summer-flowering bulbs.

FEED
Lawns. Feed with a high-nitrogen fertilizer such as 32-4-7.
Ornamentals. Fertilize bedding plants and woody ornamentals with an all-purpose fertilizer such as 10-10-10.

PRUNE
Ornamentals. After flowers fade, prune to shape flowering fruit trees and shrubs. Prune most evergreens before spring growth.

MAINTAIN
Apply mulch. Spread a 3-inch layer of bark chips or compost around permanent plants to conserve soil moisture and smother weeds.

April

PLANT
Subtropicals. Try angel's trumpet, bougainvillea, citrus, gardenia, ginger, heliotrope, hibiscus, macadamia, passion vine, or princess flower.
Annuals. Choices include calibrachoa, coleus, cosmos, impatiens, lobelia, marigold, nasturtium, petunia, sweet alyssum, and zinnia.
Bulbs. Try calla, canna, dahlia, gladiolus, montbretia, and Mexican shell flower (*Tigridia*).
Vegetables. Plant cucumbers, eggplant, melons, peppers, squash, and tomatoes.

FEED
Lawns. Give turf grasses a high-nitrogen fertilizer.

Roses. Give roses a high-phosphorus fertilizer to boost flowering.
Vegetables. Mix controlled-release fertilizer into the soil at planting.

TEND
Chlorotic plants. Apply iron chelate to plants with chlorosis (leaves show yellow mottling between green veins).
Lawns. Grass needs 1 inch of water per week to look its best.

May

PLANT
Bedding plants. Try ageratum, bedding begonias, calibrachoa, celosia, gazania, impatiens, lobelia, marigold, nicotiana, osteospermum, petunia, portulaca, Shasta daisy, sweet alyssum, verbena, and zinnia.
Lawns. Lay sod (or plant plugs) of hybrid Bermuda, St. Augustine, or zoysia grass.
Tropicals and subtropicals. Plant bananas, cherimoyas, citrus, jujubes, macadamias, mangoes, and pineapple and strawberry guavas.
Vegetables. Direct-sow seeds of beans, corn, cucumbers, melons, and pumpkins. Set out plants of cucumbers, eggplant, peppers, squash, and tomatoes.

FEED
Subtropicals. Near the coast, apply high-nitrogen plant food to subtropicals showing new growth.
Roses. Apply rose fertilizer such as 9-18-9 after each flush of bloom.

TEND
Fruit trees. Thin apple and other tree fruits as described on page 118.
Tomatoes and peppers. In hottest areas, cover plants with shade cloth to prevent sunburn.

MAINTAIN
Mulch. To conserve water, keep roots cool, and smother weeds, spread a 2-to-3-inch layer of organic mulch around all plants.

June

PLANT
Annuals. Plant seedlings of cosmos, marigold, petunia, verbena, and zinnia.
Perennials. Set out coreopsis, gaillardia, gazania, osteospermum, *Ptilotus*, sea lavender, and yarrow.
Subtropicals. Set out angel's trumpet, bird of paradise *(Strelitzia)*, bougainvillea, citrus, gardenia, hibiscus, and plumeria.
Vegetables. Plant beans, corn, cucumbers, melons, peppers, squash, and tomatoes.

FEED
Citrus. Apply high-nitrogen fertilizer, watering thoroughly after feeding.
Lawns. Use a broadcast spreader to apply a 21-0-0 or 32-4-7 fertilizer to Bermuda, St. Augustine, and zoysia grasses.
Roses. A formulation like 9-18-9 promotes flower formation, while one like 12-6-10 accelerates foliage growth (best for landscape roses).

TEND
Chlorotic plants. When leaves turn yellow while veins remain green, apply iron chelate.
Lawns. Give cool-season grasses such as tall fescue 1 inch of water per week. Warm-season types need ½ to ¾ inch per week.

MAINTAIN
Mulch. Apply a 3-inch organic mulch to suppress weeds and conserve moisture around permanent plants.
Stop watering established native plants. Many are prone to disease when soil around them is kept wet during summer.

July

PLANT
Annuals. Set out cosmos, Madagascar periwinkle, marigold, petunia, portulaca, salvia, verbena, and zinnia.
Perennials. Set out coreopsis, gazania, gloriosa daisy, and sea lavender.

FEED
Blooming plants. Fertilize long-blooming annuals and container plants monthly to keep them producing.
Lawns. Feed Bermuda, St. Augustine, and zoysia grasses with a high-nitrogen fertilizer.
Roses. Fertilize after each bloom cycle; in sandy soil, use 9-18-9; where soil is better, use 12-6-10.

TEND
Iris. Dig and divide overcrowded clumps of bearded iris; amend soil with well-aged compost before you replant.
Lawns. Mow hybrid Bermuda grass at ½ to ¾ inch, standard Bermuda at 1 inch, St. Augustine and zoysia at 1½ to 2 inches.
Summer flowers. To encourage more blooms, cut off developing seed heads of coreopsis, cosmos, dahlia, marigold, rudbeckia, and zinnia.

MAINTAIN
Mulch. Spread a 3-inch layer of organic mulch such as ground bark around landscape plants to conserve moisture and keep down weeds.

August

PLANT
Bearded iris. Buy rhizomes and plant them 1 to 2 feet apart in a sunny, prepared garden bed. Water immediately.
Bulbs. Plant fall-blooming crocus and spider lily for flowers by next month.
Vegetables. Plant beans, beets, broccoli, cabbage, chives, kale, and lettuce this month for fall harvest.

FEED
Lawns. Lightly feed Bermuda, St. Augustine, and zoysia with high-nitrogen fertilizer such as a 32-4-7 blend.

September

PLANT
Autumn crocus. Plant now for quick late summer or fall color.
Bulbs. Set out spring-flowering bulbs like daffodil, Dutch iris, freesia, sparaxis, and watsonia. Prechill crocus, hyacinth, and tulip bulbs (see "Chill Bulbs," on page 273).
Cool-season flowers. Set out transplants of calendula, Iceland poppy, larkspur, pansy, snapdragon, stock, and viola.
Cool-season vegetables. Plant beets, broccoli, brussels sprouts, cabbage, cauliflower, chives, collards, kale, kohlrabi, onions, parsley, parsnips, peas, radishes, spinach, Swiss chard, and turnips.

FEED
Established woody plants. Feed established groundcovers, shrubs (including roses), and trees with a complete fertilizer like 5-10-10.

TEND
Flowers. Remove spent flowers from perennials and roses to encourage another round of bloom. Mulch around plants; water well.
Chlorotic plants. Apply iron chelate to correct chlorosis in plants whose yellowing leaves have dark green veins.

MAINTAIN
Protect plants from wind. When the Santa Ana winds come, put hanging plants, which dry out fastest, on the ground or take them inside. Mist big-leafed plants like banana, bird of paradise, and canna, and have an arborist thin tree canopies to let wind through. ❯❯

BULBS THAT COME BACK Hyacinths and tulips tend to die out in most regions after a few years. But many bulb types keep on coming. The best ones for naturalizing (in the zones for which they're recommended) include allium, crocus, ipheon, leucojum, lilies, muscari, narcissus, scilla, watsonia, and some species tulips *(T. chrysantha, T. clusiana)*.

October

PLANT

Spring-flowering bulbs. Continue to plant all types; but prechill crocus, hyacinth, and tulip first (see "Chill Bulbs," page 273). Bulbs such as homeria (*Moraea collina*), narcissus, scilla, sparaxis, and *Tulipa clusiana* will naturalize.

Annuals. Set out transplants of cool-season annuals such as calendula, dianthus, English daisy, Iceland poppy, lobelia, nemesia, primrose, schizanthus, snapdragon, stock, and viola. Sow baby blue eyes, candytuft, linaria, Shirley poppy, sweet alyssum, and sweet pea.

Perennials. Plant low-maintenance, vigorous ones such as coreopsis, kangaroo paw, lavender, Mexican evening primrose, *Ptilotus*, rosemary, rudbeckia, *Salvia greggii*, santolina, *Verbena peruviana*, and yarrow. For instant color, buy chrysanthemums.

Permanent plants. Plant groundcovers, shrubs, trees, and vines. Try colorful, water-thrifty blue hibiscus, ceanothus, feathery cassia, flannel bush, plumbago, and rockrose.

Lawns. Overseed warm-season lawns with cool-season grasses.

FEED

Seedlings. Apply half-strength liquid fertilizer two weeks after setting out new seedlings.

Ornamentals. Feed established ornamentals with complete fertilizer.

Lawns. Apply 1 pound actual nitrogen per 1,000 square feet.

STRAWBERRY BASKETS If you just want a few fresh strawberries to nibble on through the season (and not a big crop for preserves), buy everbearing or day-neutral plants such as 'Seascape' and plant them in the widest hanging basket you can find. Suspended aboveground, they will be out of reach of snails, slugs, and most of the bugs that chew up strawberries in garden beds.

TEND

Perennials. Divide crowded asters, bellflowers, callas, daisies, daylilies, helianthus, heliopsis, rudbeckias, and yarrows.

MAINTAIN

Mulch. Spread a 2-to-3-inch layer of organic mulch such as compost or rotted manure around permanent plants.

November

PLANT

Bulbs. Plant spring-flowering bulbs now and do so immediately. Exceptions: crocus, hyacinth, and tulip; prechill them first (see "Chill Bulbs," page 273).

Annuals. Set out transplants of calendula, English daisy, Iceland poppy, pansy, primrose, and viola.

Perennials. Plant carnation, columbine, delphinium, gaillardia, gloriosa daisy, penstemon, and yarrow.

Vegetables. Sow beets, carrots, lettuce, mustard, peas, radishes, and spinach. Set out transplants of broccoli, cabbage, cauliflower, kale, lettuce, and parsley. Start garlic from cloves and onions from sets or seeds.

Natives. Plant shrubs such as California fuchsia (*Ceanothus*), California wild lilac, manzanita, red-flowering currant, and toyon.

FEED

Lawns. Feed bent, blue, fescue, and rye 1 pound actual nitrogen per 1,000 square feet of turf.

TEND

Asparagus. Cut asparagus to the ground after tops turn brown.

Tuberous begonias. Dig the tubers, trim dried leaves and stalks, brush off soil, and store tubers in a box of dry, shredded leaves.

MAINTAIN

Water. After each rain, thrust a shovel into the soil and see how deep the moisture goes. If it's dry a couple of inches down, turn on the sprinklers and finish the job.

Weeds. Discourage winter weeds by cultivating and mulching around bedding plants, shrubs, and trees.

December

PLANT

Bedding plants. For immediate winter color, set out calendula, candytuft, cyclamen, dianthus, Iceland poppy, pansy, primrose, snapdragon, and viola. For later color, set out columbine, English daisy, lobelia, nemesia, phlox, and sweet alyssum.

Sasanqua camellias. Buy them now, while they're in full flower.

TEND

Evergreens. Cut branches of holly, juniper, nandina, pine, pittosporum, podocarpus, pyracantha, and toyon for holiday decorations.

MAINTAIN

Control pests. Apply dormant oil to deciduous plants to control harmful overwintering insects. Spray peach trees with lime sulfur or fixed copper to control peach leaf curl. Spray nectarine and peach trees just before buds open.

January

PLANT

Cool-season flowers. Choose from calendula, cineraria, dianthus, English daisy, Iceland poppy, lobelia, pansy, primrose, snapdragon, stock, sweet pea, and viola.

Cool-season vegetables. Set out small plants of broccoli, cabbage, chives, endive, kale, lettuce, mustard, onion, parsley, spinach, and Swiss chard. Also sow seeds of arugula, Asian greens, carrots, peas, and radishes.

Bare-root perennial vegetables. Choices include artichoke, asparagus, horseradish, and rhubarb.

Bare-root fruits. Options include blueberries, cane berries, tree fruits, grapes, and strawberries.

Bare-root ornamentals. Set out ornamental trees and shrubs, roses, and wisteria vines.

TEND

Deciduous plants. Prune dormant fruit and shade trees, grapes, roses, and vines. Wait to prune spring-flowering shrubs and vines until after bloom.

Natives. Water native plants heavily if rainfall is light.

MAINTAIN
Spray dormant fruit trees and roses. Dormant spray kills overwintering insects. Use horticultural oil alone, or mix it with lime sulfur or fixed copper to control peach leaf curl.
Slugs and snails. Handpick them or bait for them.

February

PLANT
Flowering bedding plants. Set out calendula, cineraria, dianthus, Iceland poppy, lobelia, primrose, snapdragon, stock, and sweet alyssum.
Bare-root plants. Plant cane berries, fruit and shade trees, grapes, perennials, roses, shrubs, strawberries, and vines.
Blooming shrubs. Buy and plant azalea, camellia, and tropical hibiscus now.
Vegetables. Plant artichoke, asparagus, and rhubarb from bare-root stock. Put in potato tubers, and start seeds of arugula, Asian greens, beets, carrots, mesclun mix, peas, and radishes. Set out seedlings of broccoli, brussels sprouts, cabbage, onions, and Swiss chard. Lettuce and mustard are easy from seeds or seedlings.

FEED
Flower and vegetable beds. Before planting flower and vegetable beds, work in compost and a complete high-nitrogen fertilizer.
Spring-blooming ornamentals. Fertilize annuals, perennials, and shrubs, but wait until after bloom before feeding azaleas and camellias.
Deciduous fruit trees. Fertilize two or three weeks before bloom.

MAINTAIN
Deciduous fruit trees, grapes. Prune before spring growth (see individual plant entries for a bit more detail).
Apply dormant sprays. They control aphids, black spot, mildew, peach leaf curl, scab, and scale. Use horticultural oil with lime sulfur or fixed copper.

SOUTHWEST

March

PLANT
Annuals. In low and intermediate deserts, plant celosia, globe amaranth, marigold, portulaca, and salvia. In high desert, plant calendula, primrose, snapdragon, and viola.
Bulbs. In low and intermediate deserts, plant caladium and Texas tuberose in light shade, cannas and dahlias in sunny spots.
Edibles. In high desert, plant apricots, cane berries, grapes, peaches, pecans, plums, and pomegranates.
Ornamentals. Set out groundcovers, ornamental trees, perennials, shrubs, and vines.

Vegetables. In low desert, sow bush beans, corn, cucumbers, eggplant, melons, peppers, and tomatoes. In high desert, sow cole crops, lettuce, and onion sets.
Vines. In intermediate and high deserts, plant Carolina jessamine, Lady Banks' rose, silver lace vine, trumpet creeper, and Virginia creeper. In low desert, add bougainvillea and coral vine.

FEED
Feed shrubs, trees, vegetables, and vines with a high-nitrogen fertilizer such as 20-10-5.

TEND
Perennials. Dig, divide, and replant overgrown clumpers such as aster. See page 120. ➤➤

Fruit trees. In the low desert, thin apricot and peach trees: leave only the two largest fruits per foot of stem.

April

PLANT

Annuals. In the low and intermediate deserts, plant heat-loving kinds such as cosmos, marigold, and zinnia.

Citrus. In low and intermediate deserts, plant in full sun, protecting exposed trunks from sunburn with shade cloth or white latex paint.

Lawn grasses. In low and intermediate deserts, plant hybrid Bermuda lawns. In high desert, sow blue grama, bluegrass, buffalo grass, or tall fescue.

Perennials. Plant columbine, coreopsis, gaillardia, gazania, geranium, gerbera, hollyhock, and Shasta daisy.

Trees and shrubs. Plant bottlebrush, cassia, desert willow, eucalyptus, mesquite, and palo verde.

Vegetables. In low desert, set out eggplant, okra, peanut, and squash transplants, plus sweet potato tubers. In intermediate desert, sow beans, cucumbers, melons, okra, soybeans, and squash; set out seedlings of cucumbers, eggplant, peppers, squash, and tomatoes; plant sweet potato tubers.

FEED

Edibles, ornamentals. Feed everything with a complete fertilizer.

TEND

Chlorotic plants. Apply iron chelate to plants with chlorosis (yellow mottling between green leaf veins).

MAINTAIN

Give drip-irrigated plants at least one deep watering to leach accumulated salts from root zones.

May

PLANT

Bedding plants. In high desert, plant summer annuals such as marigold and zinnia.

Subtropicals. Plant heat lovers such as bougainvillea, hibiscus, lantana, Natal plum, and thevetia.

Vegetables. In low and intermediate deserts, plant hot-weather crops such as okra and sweet potatoes. In high desert, plant all warm-season crops.

FEED

Citrus. Use a complete fertilizer such as ammonium sulfate (21-0-0); mulch and water well.

Lawns. Apply a high-nitrogen turf fertilizer (such as 32-4-7).

TEND

Vegetables. In low and intermediate deserts, protect eggplant, peppers, and tomatoes from sunburn by covering with shade cloth.

MAINTAIN

Mulch. Spread organic material such as compost or straw around plants to control weeds, minimize water evaporation, and keep soil cool.

Water. Deep-water permanent non-native plants every 7 to 10 days. Water established natives every two to four weeks.

MINT CONTROL To keep mint from taking over, grow it in containers—one variety per pot. Try peppermint, spearmint, apple mint, and orange mint. You can sink containers into the ground if you like, but you'll still have to control seedlings that sprout around the container.

June

PLANT

Summer flowers. In low desert, plant globe amaranth *(Gomphrena),* Madagascar periwinkle, and salvia. In intermediate and high deserts, plant ageratum, aster, phlox, and sunflower. Plant in evening; shelter seedlings with shade cloth.

Vegetables. In intermediate desert, plant muskmelons, okra, pumpkins, and sweet potatoes.

FEED

Roses. Use a complete fertilizer now and then again after the next bloom flush.

TEND

Lawns. Cut zoysia and St. Augustine at 1½ to 2 inches, regular Bermuda at 1 inch, and hybrid Bermuda at ½ to ¾ inch high.

MAINTAIN

Irrigation. To minimize water loss, irrigate plants deeply in early morning. Build watering basins around roses. Spread a 3-to-4-inch organic mulch around plants.

July

PLANT

Annuals. In high desert, plant celosia, cosmos, globe amaranth, gloriosa daisy, Madagascar periwinkle, marigold, portulaca, purslane, and zinnia.

Heat-loving ornamentals. In low and intermediate deserts, plant hibiscus, palms, and succulents, including agave, aloe, and cactus. Provide shade to reduce transplanting stress.

Trees and shrubs. Set out drought-tolerant ornamentals like blue palo verde, cassia, desert willow, fairy duster, mesquite, and sweet acacia.

Vegetables. In intermediate desert, plant pumpkins and winter squash. In high-desert gardens, sow Asian greens, beans, beets, broccoli, cabbage, carrots, kale, and kohlrabi. In both, sow corn, cucumbers, and summer squash.

TEND

Trees, shrubs. Treat chlorosis (yellowing leaves with green veins) with iron chelate.

MAINTAIN

Mulch. Apply a 3-inch layer of organic matter such as compost or straw around (but not touching) any plants you have to water.

August

PLANT

Vegetables. In low desert, plant corn, snap beans, and summer squash for fall harvest. In intermediate desert, sow cucumbers, snap beans, and short-season corn varieties in the garden.

FEED

Annuals. Feed flowering annuals such as coreopsis, Madagascar periwinkle, osteospermum, and petunia to prolong bloom.
Lawns. Fertilize Bermuda grass lawns with high-nitrogen fertilizer such as ammonium sulfate (21-0-0).

TEND

Chlorotic plants. Treat plants with iron chelate.
Ornamentals. Deep-water trees and shrubs; shallow-rooted plants and those growing in sandy soil need lighter, more frequent watering.
Vegetables. Lightly prune spring-planted peppers and cut back indeterminate (vining type) tomatoes around midmonth to encourage a fall crop.

September

PLANT

Bulbs. In high desert, plant right away. In low and intermediate deserts, prechill crocus, hyacinth, and tulip bulbs before planting (see "Chill Bulbs," page 273).
Perennials. In low and intermediate deserts, sow carnation, columbine, coneflower, coreopsis, feverfew, gaillardia, penstemon, statice, and yarrow.
Vegetables. In low and intermediate deserts, plant artichokes, arugula, broccoli, cabbage, carrots, cauliflower, kale, kohlrabi, radish, and Swiss chard. In high desert, plant leeks, lettuce, mâche, and salad blends.
Winter-spring flowers. In low and intermediate deserts, plant bedding

begonias, bells-of-Ireland, calendula, candytuft, forget-me-not, pansy, petunia, phlox, snapdragon, stock, sweet alyssum, and viola.

FEED

Lawns. In low and intermediate deserts, feed all lawns except Bermuda if you plan to overseed it with a cool-season grass.
Ornamentals. Apply a high-nitrogen fertilizer such as 24-8-16 to the garden's permanent plants.

October

PLANT

Bulbs. In low and intermediate deserts, plant bulbs of Dutch iris, freesia, and sparaxis before midmonth. Prechill crocus, hyacinth, and tulip bulbs before planting (see "Chill Bulbs," page 273).
Annuals. In low and intermediate deserts, plant calendula, dianthus, English daisy, forget-me-not, Iceland and Shirley poppies, larkspur, pansy, phlox, primrose, snapdragon, statice, stock, sweet alyssum, sweet pea, and viola.
Perennials. Throughout most of the Southwest, this is the best month to plant perennials like candytuft, columbine, coreopsis, gaillardia, and penstemon.
Vegetables. In low and intermediate deserts, sow arugula, asparagus, beets, carrots, lettuce, radish, salad blends, spinach, and Swiss chard. Set out seedlings of broccoli, brussels sprouts, cabbage, cauliflower, and kale.
Landscape plants. In the low and intermediate deserts, plant permanent groundcovers, trees, and shrubs.

TEND

Lawns. Overseed Bermuda grass with perennial ryegrass. Fertilize, mulch lightly, and keep moist.

CHECK TRANSPLANTS' ROOTS
Transplants often come with fine netting around the rootball. Roots will grow through to a degree, but the netting will still be there at season's end. To give roots complete freedom to grow out into surrounding soil, peel off the netting before planting.

November

PLANT

Annuals. In low and intermediate deserts, plant bells-of-Ireland, calendula, clarkia, cornflower, larkspur, lobelia, painted daisy, snapdragon, stock, sweet alyssum, and sweet pea. In light shade, try English daisy, pansy, primrose, and viola.
Wildflowers. In low and intermediate deserts, sow Blackfoot daisy, desert bluebell, desert globe mallow, firewheel, Mexican hat, Mexican tulip poppy, and owl's clover. Keep soil moist until plants are 2 inches tall.
Vegetables. In low and intermediate deserts, plant beets, cabbage, carrots, celery, endive, garlic, kale, leeks, lettuce, mustard, onions, parsley, radishes, spinach, and Swiss chard.
Hardy trees and shrubs. Plant acacia, cassia, *Cordia boissieri*, desert spoon, fairy duster, mesquite, oleander, palo verde, *Salvia greggii*, and Texas ranger.

FEED

Roses. In the low desert, deadhead roses and feed with a complete fertilizer to encourage repeat bloom.

TEND

Citrus. Water citrus trees just once every three to four weeks in clay soils, once a week in sandy soil.

December

PLANT

Annuals. In the low and intermediate deserts, plant annuals from nursery packs for winter and spring color.
Living Christmas trees. Choose types suited to the desert, such as Afghan pine. Indoors, place the tree in a bright, cool spot away from heating vents, and water to keep soil moist. Limit the tree's indoor stay to two weeks.

FEED

Lawns, ornamentals. Apply high-nitrogen fertilizer to lawns or ornamentals whose leaves look yellowish green. If trees or shrubs have yellowish leaves with dark green veins, the problem is chlorosis; treat with iron chelate. ❯❯

TEND

Trees. In high desert, protect young, thin-barked trees from sunscald by painting trunks with white latex or covering them with tree wrap.

MAINTAIN

Control plant disease. As soon as leaves fall, spray deciduous fruit and ornamental trees and roses with dormant oil to control overwintering insects.

January

PLANT

Bulbs. In low desert, plant summer-flowering types such as amaryllis, canna, and gladiolus.

Bedding plants. Set out ageratum, aster, calendula, chrysanthemum, cineraria, coreopsis, hollyhock, pansy, petunia, snapdragon, sweet alyssum, and verbena.

Vegetables. In low desert, plant bare-root asparagus and onion sets, and sow seeds of arugula, beets, carrots, chives, cucumbers, melons, radishes, salad blends, spinach, and summer squash. In intermediate and high deserts, sow arugula and plant onion sets.

Bare-root. In low and intermediate deserts, buy bare-root roses, strawberries, ornamental and fruit trees, and grapes.

FEED

Annuals, vegetables. Apply complete fertilizer to flowers and vegetables you've recently planted.

Citrus. Feed mature citrus trees now, just before flowering, with an ammonium sulfate fertilizer. (Wait until next month to feed younger trees.) Water first; a day later, sprinkle fertilizer evenly out to the drip line. Use these guidelines for trees more than 4 years old: 2½ pounds for grapefruit, 4 pounds for oranges and tangerines, and 5 pounds for large lemon trees. Water again after application.

TEND

Prune. In low and intermediate deserts, prune deciduous trees and roses.

Water. Between rains, water trees and shrubs deeply every three weeks, more often if the temperature is above 70° F.

February

PLANT

Perennial wildflowers. In low and intermediate deserts, plant African daisy, coreopsis, desert marigold, evening primrose, penstemon, and salvia.

Warm-season crops. In low desert, sow beans and corn.

Cool-season vegetables. Plant chives and potatoes, and sow arugula, lettuce, peas, radishes, and salad blends. In intermediate and high deserts, plant beets, carrots, cole crops, rhubarb, spinach, and Swiss chard.

Bare-root plants. In high desert, plant cane berries, roses, shrubs, trees, and vines.

Groundcovers. In low and intermediate deserts, plant Baja evening primrose, dwarf periwinkle, Hall's honeysuckle, perennial verbena, prostrate myoporum, star jasmine, and trailing indigo bush.

FEED

Bulbs. In low desert, feed bearded iris, daffodils, and other spring-flowering bulbs in late February with a low-nitrogen fertilizer such as 5-10-10.

Lawns. Give cool-season grasses 1 pound of ammonium sulfate per 1,000 square feet; water thoroughly.

Ornamentals. Fertilize non-native trees and shrubs.

MAINTAIN

Prune. In mild parts of the high desert, prune deciduous fruit and shade trees, grapes, and roses.

BEST GARLIC Garlic is roughly divided into two classes: the soft-necks and the hardnecks. Softnecks like 'Silver Skin' grow best in milder climates and are the ones most commonly sold by green grocers. Hardnecks like 'Korean Red' and 'Spanish Roja' excel in colder climates ('Music' is a great choice in Alaska) and are favored by chefs for intensity of flavor without as much bite as softnecks.

MOUNTAIN

March

PLANT

Bare-root roses. Plant after soaking rose roots in a bucket of water overnight.

Cool-season vegetables. Sow beets, carrots, peas, and radishes. Set out transplants of lettuce, spinach, and Swiss chard, and plant onion sets or green onion starts.

Bare-root strawberries. Try everbearing 'Fort Laramie' and 'Ogallala', and June-bearing 'Guardian' and 'Honeoye'.

April

PLANT

Annuals. Plant calendula, English daisy, pansy, snapdragon, sweet alyssum, and viola.

Bare-root plants. Set out berries, fruit trees, grapes, nut trees, roses, asparagus, and rhubarb.

Ornamentals. Trees, shrubs, and groundcovers can go in now.

Vegetables. Direct-sow beets, carrots, lettuce, onions, parsley, peas, radishes, spinach, and Swiss chard. Set out seedlings of broccoli, cabbage, cauliflower, and onions. Plant seed potatoes.

FEED

Fertilize asparagus and ornamentals with a complete fertilizer like 16-16-16.

TEND

Lawns. To control weeds, apply a corn gluten–based preemergent herbicide.

Deciduous plants. Prune winter-dormant trees, grapes, roses, and vines.

May

PLANT

Annuals. At lower elevations, plant ageratum, amaranth, browallia, cleome, cosmos, gazania, gomphrena, heliotrope, lantana, marigold, nicotiana, osteospermum, petunia, portulaca, sanvitalia, scabiosa, statice, verbena, vinca, zinnia, and zonal geraniums. At higher elevations, stick with cool-season annuals such

as calendula, pansy, snapdragon, stock, sweet alyssum, and viola.

Lawns. Plant a new lawn from seed or sod, or overseed an old one.

Perennials. Plant bleeding heart, columbine, coral bells, delphinium, lupine, Maltese cross, penstemon, phlox, Shasta daisy, veronica, and yarrow.

Summer bulbs. When the soil warms up, plant acidanthera, calla, canna, crocosmia, dahlia, freesia, gladiolus, ixia, and lily.

FEED

Fertilize perennial vegetables and flowers, roses, and shrubs. In sandy or mineral soils, use a complete fertilizer, like 14-14-14; in loam or clay, use a higher-nitrogen organic like 7-1-2.

MAINTAIN

Prune. Remove dead, diseased, or injured branches from spring-flowering shrubs after bloom.

June

PLANT

Landscape plants. Set out ornamental shrubs, trees, groundcovers, and vines.

Baskets and window boxes. Good plant choices include bacopa, calibrachoa, ivy geranium, lantana, *Nolana*, osteospermum, trailing lobelia, trailing petunia, and verbena.

Perennials. Set out aster, blanket flower, coreopsis, helenium, penstemon, rudbeckia, salvia, and Shasta daisy.

Vegetables. Sow beets, bush beans, carrots, lettuce, onions, peas, and summer squash, and plant seedlings of eggplant, peppers, pumpkins, tomatoes, and watermelons.

FEED

Lawns. Use a high-nitrogen fertilizer.

MAINTAIN

Prune spring-flowering shrubs. Shape forsythia and lilac after bloom.

Thin apples. In all but the coldest areas, thin apples after June drop, as described on page 118

July

PLANT

Bearded iris. See page 192 for planting instructions.

Heat-loving flowers. Replace spent clarkia, Iceland poppy, lobelia, pansy, and stock with heat-loving annuals such as blanket flower, gazania, globe amaranth, gloriosa daisy, Madagascar periwinkle, marigold, Mexican sunflower, petunia, portulaca, sunflower, and zinnia.

Summer-blooming shrubs. Colorful choices include bluebeard, butterfly bush, rose of Sharon, and spiraea.

Vegetables. For fall harvest, plant beets, broccoli, bush beans, cabbage, carrots, cauliflower, green onions, peas, radishes, and spinach.

TEND

Lawns. Mow bluegrass lawns 3 to 3½ inches high so that blades will shade roots and help retain soil moisture.

Raspberries. For summer-bearing raspberries, cut canes that have borne fruit down to the ground. Let new green canes grow; they'll bear next season's crop. For everbearing raspberries, prune out the section of each cane that fruited; the remainder will fruit next season.

MAINTAIN

Deep-water trees. Attach your garden hose to a T-shaped root irrigator, push the probe deep into the soil around trees and shrubs, and deliver water right to the root zones. ❯❯

August

PLANT

Spring flowers. For early-spring bloom in prepared, weeded beds, sow seeds of delphinium, foxglove, pansy, snapdragon, viola, and wildflowers. In coldest areas, wait until September to sow wildflowers. Set out perennials from nursery containers.

Vegetables. In areas where frosts aren't expected until late October, sow seeds of beets, carrots, radishes, and spinach for fall harvest.

FEED

Lawns. Apply a high-nitrogen turf blend such as 32-4-7.

TEND

Woody plants. Around midmonth, reduce water to fruit trees and other woody plants to help coax them into fall dormancy. Don't feed again until next year.

September

PLANT

Bulbs. Plant spring-flowering types such as crocus, daffodil, hyacinth, and tulip.
Lawns. Sow seeds or lay sod for a new lawn early in the month.
Perennials. Set out campanula, delphinium, dianthus, penstemon, phlox, salvia, and yarrow.

HOW TO MEASURE SPRINKLER OUTPUT At about 1½ inches high, a tuna can is perfect for measuring sprinkler output. Just put an empty one inside the sprinkler's watering radius and turn on the water. Check back at 20-minute intervals until you have an inch of water in the can; that's how long the sprinkler must be on to give lawn 1 inch of water.

TEND

Bulbs. Dig and store dahlias, gladiolus, and other tender summer bulbs after their foliage dies back.
Perennials. Lift and divide clumps of crowded perennials such as daylily, hosta, peony, and Siberian iris, except in highest elevations.

MAINTAIN

Remove mulch. As soil temperatures drop, pull mulches off the root zones of warm-season vegetables so that the sun can heat the soil.
Compost. As annuals and vegetables die back, sheet-compost them (chop them up and bury them where they grow) or put them in a traditional compost pile.

October

PLANT

Permanent plants. Set out groundcovers, trees, shrubs, and perennials no later than six weeks before the ground normally freezes in your area.

TEND

Mulch. After the first hard freeze, cut back perennials and mulch beds of bulbs, strawberries, perennial flowers, and vegetables.

November

PLANT

Garlic. Plant cloves of garlic before ground freezes.

TEND

Roses. After temperatures drop below freezing for a few nights, mound soil over the plant base, being sure the soil covers the bud union (the enlarged knob from which canes emerge). After the soil surface freezes, set a cylinder of chicken wire around each plant and fill with shredded autumn leaves or straw.

MAINTAIN

Tools. Clean and sharpen tools before storing them for the winter; rub steel blades with oil to protect against rust.

December

PLANT

Living Christmas trees. Choose types that thrive in your area and will do well in the landscape. Good choices include alpine fir, white fir, Engelmann spruce, and Douglas fir.

TEND

Trees, shrubs. Knock snow off the branches of shrubs and trees before it breaks or disfigures them.

January

PLAN

Order seeds now. Order from seed catalogs now, so you won't face substitutions later as many varieties go out of stock.

TEND

Trees, shrubs. To keep branches from breaking, knock snow off trees and shrubs; cut off any broken branches.

February

TEND

Trees and shrubs. In the garden, knock snow off evergreen shrubs and small trees, where it can break or deform branches.

BARE-ROOT STRATEGY Bare-root plants are inexpensive and easy to handle, and they quickly adapt to native garden soil. Ironically, their weakness is that if they dry, they die. For success, dig the planting hole before you buy the plant. Have the nursery wrap the roots in damp sawdust or moss for the trip home; then plant immediately. Bare-root roses benefit from a 24-hour soak (roots only) in a bucket of water before planting.

An easy-care garden
uses tough plants and
permeable paving. Leaf
textures and colors
keep it interesting.

Credits

PHOTOGRAPHY

courtesy of Ames True Temper: 18 top left, 18 top middle, 18 bottom left; Annie's Annuals & Perennials: 149, 177 middle right, 221, 229, 258; Maryellen Baker/Getty Images: 215 right; Debra Lee Baldwin: front cover left (design: Linda Sowers); Ball Horticultural Company: 141, 161, 206 top right; Leigh Beisch: 82 top right, 82 bottom left, 83 (design: Hank Jenkins, Lushland Design; styling: Philippine Scali; container from Pottery and Beyond; outdoor pillows by Hable Construction); Richard Bloom/Getty Images: 155; Mark Bolton/Getty Images: 197; Markus Botzek/Corbis/Bridge/Alamy: 115; Marion Brenner: 4 (Patricia Wagner Garden Design), 27, 50, 51 both, 116 (Laura White and Jude Hellewell, Outer Space Landscape Architecture; bistro table and chairs in Carrot by Fermob from Flora Grubb Gardens [floragrubb.com]); Rob D. Brodman: front cover right, 20, 21 top right, 21 bottom left, 22 bottom left, 26 bottom, 31 top left, 92, 106, 107 all, 110 left, 117 left, 117 middle, 142, 208, 237 middle right, 253 top right, 256; Deni Brown/Getty Images: 234; Gene Burch: 246; Burke/Triolo Productions/Botanica/Getty Images: 111; Burpee Seed Company: 132, 190 bottom, 193, 196 bottom; Chris Burrows/Getty Images: 148, 177 top middle, 186 bottom left, 211 left; Rosemary Calvert/Getty Images: 135; David Cavagnaro/Getty Images: 241; Jennifer Cheung: 24 (design: Jason Isenberg), 38 bottom, 41 bottom (design: Steve Siegrist Design), 60 right (Gabriela Yariv Landscape Design), 63 top (design: Heather Lenkin), 63 bottom, (Jared Vermeil, VermeilDesign), 75 (design: Brooke Dietrich), 91 (Gabriela Yariv Landscape Design), 93 (Elizabeth Przygoda, Boxhill Landscape Design), 277 (Elizabeth A. Przygoda, Boxhill Landscape Design), back cover bottom left (design: Heather Lenkin); Jeffery Cross: 28 bottom left, 28 bottom middle, 30 top right, 30 bottom left, 30 bottom middle, 30 bottom right; DEA/G. Cigolini/Getty Images: 225 middle right; Christine M. Douglas/Getty Images: 185; Carole Drake/Getty Images: 222; Laura Dunkin-Hubby: 183; Ron Evans/Getty Images: 133; David Fenton: 12 (design: James Pettigrew and Sean Stout, Organic Mechanics), 17 top right; fourwindsgrowers.com: 245; Brandon Goldman/Getty Images: 114; John Granen: 58 (design: Jill Goodsell), 268; Art Gray: 17 bottom left, 62 (Greg Sanchez, GDS Designs); Anne Green-Armytage/Getty Images: 177 bottom right; Bret Gum: 10 top (design: André Price Jackson), 34 (design: Di Zock Gardens), 35 (design: Di Zock Gardens), 41 top (Molly Wood Garden Design), 64 (design: André Price Jackson), 283 (design: André Price Jackson), 288 (design: Joe Stead); Steven A. Gunther: 37 left (Anthony Exter, Anthony Exter Landscape Design), 37 right (design: Judy Kameon, Elysian Landscapes), 60 left (design: R. Michael Schneider), 61 (design: R. Michael Schneider); D. A. Horchner/Design Workshop: 25 top, 281, back cover middle; Martin Hughes-Jones/Alamy: 130; Anne Hyde/Getty Images: 186 top left; Sandra Ivany/Getty Images: 122 bottom left; G.P. Kidd/Getty Images: 173; Ernst Kucklich: 67 top right, 118 bottom right, 172; Holly Lepere: 274 (landscape design: Grace Design Associates; house design: Michelle Kaufmann); Chris Leschinsky: 59 bottom (design: Jeffery Gordon Smith); Janet Loughrey: 181; Jennifer Martiné: 80, 81; Jim McCausland: 88 (design: Rebecca Sams and Buell Steelman, Mosaic Gardens), 118 top left, 137, 178, 180, 192 bottom, 214; J. R. McCausland: 96 (design: Rebecca Sams and Buell Steelman, Mosaic Gardens), 244; Ericka McConnell: 10 bottom (Alexandra Angle Interior Design; styling: Miranda Jones); Joshua McCullough/PhytoPhoto: 6–7 (Laura M. Crockett, Garden Diva Designs), 174, 237 top middle; Monrovia: 179, 188, 198, 199, 206 top left, 206 bottom left, 227 middle right; Maria Mosolova/Getty Images: 196 top; Terry Moyemont: 89 (design: Carol Johanson); Kimberley Navabpour: 67 top left, 71 top right, 76 all, 77, 146, 151, 160, 168, 169, 177 top left, 195, 201, 213, 218, 220 bottom, 237 bottom middle, 239 right, 240, 253 bottom left, 259, 261 top left, 261 bottom left; George Olson: 117 right; Martin Page/Getty Images: 189, 190 top; Jerry Pavia: 225 center; Linda Lamb Peters: 67 middle right, 67 bottom right, 68 bottom right, 85, 101 (design: Gay Bonorden Gray), 124, 126, 129, 136, 138, 139, 144, 147, 152, 158, 159, 162, 170, 182, 202, 203, 204, 207, 209 left, 210, 211 right, 212, 216, 217, 223, 225 top middle, 225 bottom left, 225 bottom middle, 227 top left, 227 middle right, 227 top right, 227 bottom right, 230, 231, 237 middle right, 237 center, 242, 257, 261 top right, 261 bottom right; Photos Lamontagne/Getty Images: 82 bottom right, 186 top right, 200, 225 middle left; www.plantdelights.com: 156; Norm Plate: 59 top, 98 (Randy Allworth, Allworth Design), 140; Norman A. Plate: 22 bottom right, 131, 187, 225 top left, 249; Proven Winners: 68 top right, 145, 153, 165, 177 top right, 232; Howard Rice/Getty Images: 227 center; Lisa Romerein: 5 (Deborah Richmond and Olivier Touraine, Touraine Richmond Architects), 74; Andrea Gómez Romero: 29, 84, 163, 177 middle left; Ellen Rooney/Getty Images: 237 top left; Prue Roscoe/ACP/trunkarchive.com: back cover top right; San Marcos Growers: 225 top right, 237 top right; Harley Seaway/Getty Images: 205; Susan Seubert: 36 (design: Ketzel Levine); Tara Sgroi: 16; Skagit Gardens: 154; Inga Spence/Getty Images: 248; Eric Staudenmaier: 38 top (landscape design: Russ Cletta); Thomas J. Story: front cover middle, 8, 13 (design: Kathleen Shaeffer), 14, 17 bottom right, 18 top right, 18 bottom middle, 18 bottom right, 19 top middle left, 19 top middle right, 19 top right, 19 bottom right, 21 bottom right, 22 top left, 22 bottom middle, 23 only, 26 top, 28 top left, 31 bottom left, 31 right, 32 (styling by Miranda Jones), 39 (design: Nancy Goslee Power), 40 (landscape design: Rob Pressman, TGP Landscape Architecture; architecture: Jeffrey Michael Tohl, The Architecture Studio), 42 (design: Brooke Dietrich), 43, 44 both (design: Baylor Chapman and Lila B. Design), 45 (design: Baylor Chapman), 46–49 all (design: Antonio Martins), 52–53 both (design: Judy Kameon, Elysian Landscapes), 54 (design: Davis Dalbok), 55 (design: Jared Vermeil, Vermeil Design), 56–57 (design: Caitlin Atkinson), 70, 71 top left, 71 middle left, 71 bottom left, 72–73, 78, 79, 86 all, 87, 95 right, 97 top (Brent Green, GreenArt Landscape Design), 97 bottom (design: Jeni Webber and Associates), 99 (Jay Thayer Landscape Architects), 100 all, 108, 109 right, 112, 120 both, 121, 164, 166, 167, 175, 177 center, 177 bottom middle, 192 top, 194 top, 209 right, 219, 220 top, 227 top middle, 227 bottom left, 227 bottom middle, 233, 237 bottom left, 237 bottom right, 251 top left, 251 all, 253 top left, 255, 271, back cover top left; Sue Stubbs/ACP/trunkarchive.com: 122 top left, 122 top right, 122 bottom right, 123; courtesy of Sunset Western Garden Collection: 215 left; Marcia Tatroe: 9; Terra Nova Nurseries, Inc.: 127, 134, 143, 150, 157, 171; E. Spencer Toy: 19 top left, 19 bottom left, 19 bottom middle, 28 bottom right, 30 top left, 66, 68 top left, 68 middle left, 68 middle right, 68 bottom left, 69 (design: Tanya Eggers), 94 both, 95 left, 102, 104, 119, 194 bottom, 228, 235, 247, back cover bottom right; Trish Treherne/Bliss Garden Design: 90; Tracy Tucker/iStock.com: 105; Mark Turner: 67 bottom left, 238, 239 left, 254; Mark Turner/Getty Images: 128, 253 bottom right; Visions BV, Netherlands: 191; Coral Von Zumwalt: 1, 11 (design: Judy Kameon, Michael Kirchmann Jr., and Ivette Soler, Elysian Landscapes); Bjorn Wallander: 82 top left; Rachel Weill: 2–3; Jo Whitworth/Getty Images: 184, 177 bottom left, 225 bottom right; Bob Wigand: 243; Doreen L. Wynja: 67 middle left, 71 bottom right; Ebbe Roe Yovino-Smith: 25 bottom

ILLUSTRATION

Jane McCreary: 107 bottom left; Damien Scogin: 109 left, 110 middle, 110 right, 118 middle left, 118 bottom left, 262 all, 263 all

Index